SOCIAL HILL

Jason Hill

ISBN: 1539160572
ISBN 13: 9781539160571

To my children, Jah and Robbie
This is for you.

ACKNOWLEDGMENTS

First and foremost, I want to thank my mother. In spite all of our ups and downs, she has always been there for me, and without her not only would I not have life, but this book would not be possible. Mom, I love you.

Although God can still part the seas, I find he most often chooses to bless us through other people. There are many who are part of the pain, and later the glory, of my story. Among those I must thank are those who know my lifelong dream of being a published novelist, and there is one person whose encouragement over the years stands out more than all others.

Shelby Wiezycki Woods.

Thank you, Shelby, for all of your support. You always knew I could do it. And now I have.

Clara Guerrero, one of my dearest friends, knows what it took for me to get here. Thank you. Debbie Hoos, you know, too. I didn't break the baby.

For always offering a word of support when I needed it, and plain old moral support, I thank my dear friend, Paulette Price.

Time would fail me if I went on to thank everyone to whom I feel grateful. However, I would be remiss if I didn't mention at least a few of the names of people who are special to me, and to whom this book is dedicated, like Ronald Smith, Ruben Quintero, Feleshia West, Dessa Trujillo, Oscar Guardiola, Desiree Crain, Gracie Parra, Jean Kallisto Price, Ronald Fuller, Christina Martin, Rene Melendez, Lori Belknap, Jessica Hernandez, Krishna, Norma Windhorst, Timothy Engelbrecht, TK Khan, Rachel Holden, Mary-Jo Foley, Hannah Westall, Patricia Acheampong, Clifton A. Kotara, Abby Lopez, Ernie Sanchez, Darren Jackson, Kimberly Marsh, and Uta.

And a special shout out to my good friend, Deborah Wynne.

BOOK I

Bound Aries

1

I AM A GOOD MAN. That's how most people look at me. But I am in no sense of the word an easy person. And I guess it must be true. Why else would I endure three months of living in my car with my kids rather than break my word to someone I owed, turning my life, and theirs, upside down? Or, why else would a recent ex, other than my wife, tell me, "You're not a bad person, I don't hate you," and then proceed to take an AR-15 and blow my heart to smithereens? I hope it's true what my ancestors, the slaves, used to say, "trouble, don't last always," cause I'm in fairly good health, and I have likely another forty years left. And I hope I don't have to spend the rest of them here, in this halfway house of the body and spirit, of veterans and ex-cons of every race and strata, facsimiles of men but men all the same. Me, I clean up well, but don't let the smooth taste fool you, I am afflicted with an invisible sickness most people could not guess at.

Come to think of it, I am the one who cannot guess at it most of the time.

On the very first day of the year—after the close of a bad previous one—I was leaning against the counter in my mother's kitchen, salivating for the black-eyed peas and cornbread she had specifically prepared for this occasion. My mother's house was where I, along with my wife and two children, were living temporarily. We'd moved out of the townhouse in December, our home for eight and a half years, right before being evicted. I'll tell you more about that later.

Ordinarily, I'm not a big believer in superstitions, especially those native to Texas where we lived then. I'm a Chicago kid, after all. I was weaned on Polish sausages and bratwurst, but I'd heard recently that it is a well-known custom in the South which said if you eat like a poor man on the first day of the year you'll eat like a rich one every day thereafter. And what screams poor more than black-eyed peas and cornbread? Although it wasn't exactly the stuff of life, I didn't exactly hate the aroma that the combination was filling my mom's kitchen with. *How did these wacky traditions first start anyway?* I thought to myself as I debated whether I was going to go with Tabasco or hot sauce. Growing up on Chicago's South Side during teendom, I'd cut my teeth working as a busboy in a decades-old soul food restaurant owned by my mother's side of the family. Just as my mother and her cousins had done coming up in the Civil Rights Era. I always ate for free, roast turkey legs smothered in gravy, collard greens, succulent candied yams slow-baked in cinnamon and maple brown sugar and orange juice, cornbread stuffing, ham, and sometimes, black-eyed peas, with an endless catalog of blues songs—B.B. King and Bobby "Blue" Bland, mostly—playing on the Wurlitzer jukebox in the background. If I close my eyes, I can still hear the deafening rumble of the elevated trains—the El, we called it—so close overhead right outside on 63rd and King Drive that had it ever decided capriciously to tip over above our heads, the restaurant and everything in it—workers and patrons alike— would've been goners for sure. I emerged from those years, unscathed, however.

That is, on the outside.

Besides, after the way the second half of the preceding year had just gone, I could've used a little good luck, and I wasn't leaving anything to chance. Anyway, once those familiar smells were loosed, there was no Armor against them.

"We are probably the only family in America eating black-eyed peas in the middle of the night," my daughter said, gazing around the table.

"Oh, surely that can't be true," Mama said. "Lord, this is a tradition that's even older than I am! We just haven't observed it since we've been down here because it's more of a Southern *thang*, but your father reminded me of it."

I didn't know it then, but this was going to be as good as it got for the whole year. The first day of the year was also the happiest. It was me, my mother, my brother Philip and his eight-year-old son, Quentin, and my two kids, Jacob, and Danielle, and my wife. So, where I want to start telling is right here... This was the weekend we left the Hotel Atwater. Or rather, stormed out. And it wasn't *we*, either.

Stay tuned, and don't change the channel.

It was months ago now, but the Hotel Atwater was a funny name at the time. I used to call my mother's house in Alamo City by that name, a private joke between me and my wife that grew legs. I'm not going to start by telling you the hospital I was born at in Chicago or anything. Besides, if I can't tell you what you're about to hear without having to dredge up my entire life history, the terrorists have already won. Let's not do their job for them.

Hell, this story practically tells itself. I'll just start with all the drama that transpired that weekend, around New Year's, before I got my fingers burnt and had to come out here and take a poor man's sabbatical. Here I sat, in this sort of purgatory, convalescing from the blows rained upon me. Alone, like Moses on the backside of the Arabian desert, chunkin' snakes and killin' lizards, while He That Keepeth Israel waited ever so patiently to scare the living bejeezus out of him forty years hence at that Bush, the Universe having hung him—and me—out to dry.

You can decide for yourself later when I'm done telling you all this *All My Children* shit just how powerful those damn black-eyed peas were.

Anyway, we had just come in from outside, from looking up at the night sky as fireworks cascaded around us on the residential street while Mama's neighbors shot their wads, our senses pummeled by the deafening booms and cracks as the firecrackers ruptured in our ears one after another for several minutes. Some of those bad boys actually seemed so close above us that it really did seem for a moment like those fiery, scalding sparks would descend upon us and charbroil us to a crisp, burning us in effigy. My autistic son nearly pissed his pants and fled inside.

How come I always got the feeling somebody was missing from our family gatherings? I had thought so for a while, looking around. It was such a pitiable display. We didn't play enough board games; we didn't seem involved enough, or Cosby Show-like I guess. In the old days, I had thought we needed more crumb snatchers. Three was a pretty lame amount if you asked me. Maybe Darlene and I should've had another. Darlene's my wife. But shoulda woulda coulda is always the lowest form of conversation if you want to know the truth.

Years ago, when I got married, I figured Darlene would liven things up a smidge—I mean, at holiday get-togethers and all. No such luck. For one thing, she was always the only Caucasian around. Not that there was anything wrong with that. Just too sheltered, too different. Ten years my junior, too. Also, we were never really compatible from the start. Married nine days before our daughter's birth, if that tells you anything. As for my in-laws, the less said about them, the better. It's not that I had anything against them, and Mama tried her best, but I had come to realize we would never be the kind of family I had envisioned.

Not by a long shot.

"Trump is like that guy that'll say anything to get laid," my brother was saying. "Fo' real."

"Except this time he's trying to fuck the country," my stepfather said, eliciting laughter from the kids.

"Howard!"

"Sorry, honey."

"Oh, well," my mother said. "The important thing is, we're all together. That's what the holidays are all about! Everyone gathered together. Wouldn't you agree, Tony?"

I said, "Eh? Ah. Yes, very much," and poured myself more wine. I tended to black out when Mama got all sentimental and stuff at times like these.

"And we've got our health and strength, thank you, Jesus. Darlene has a good job making good money again now; Danielle's birthday is in a few days. Philip is going to be getting a job soon, knock on wood. Quentin is doing well in school, and he's growing up to be so smart! Grandpa got lucky playing his numbers the other day..."

Evidently Mama was going in order around the table. I could never tell who, exactly, Mama was transmitting this information to. I mean we all already knew the score, and who owed who and who owed what. But we all indulged her since she was underwriting most of those debts at the time. I still rolled my eyes, though.

"I told you, I don't know if they're going to call me back yet for a second interview!" Philip said.

Philip was seven years older than me and something of a ne'er do well; that's why he was annoyed. I take that back. He was *always* annoyed about something. His dark features were deformed into a permanent scowl around his eyebrows and forehead. I'm not kidding. Also, his paper was never straight. He was in the weed game, but with that as with everything else he did it all back asswards so he was always the lowest on the totem pole. Bumper to bumper in drug traffic.

My mother and Howard lived on Atwater Creek (hence the nickname) in a newly-built Roosevelt-style home, one story, chock full of all the most up-to-date accouterments, down to the faux-marble granite countertops and the rear-covered patio. Double-pane windows. You've probably seen the kind. Very upscale, very Texas. The home for their *On Golden Pond* years I guess. And yet she still always found something to complain about. In spite of her many promises to the contrary in the days and months before she moved in, back when an upgrade from their previous residence of twenty years, which was quickly falling apart, seemed like a pipe dream (because of their shaky credit). But she did it. She got the house, against all odds. Didn't stop her from being forever bent out of shape about something, though, as I'd desperately hoped.

Philip, he's a halfway decent father now. He didn't use to be. He used to be a crummy father. He has a grown daughter somewhere. We don't know where she is. I wouldn't know her if I bumped into her on the street. Maybe I already had, hell, it's a small world. Anyway, she was the collateral damage of Philip's much longer-than-normal arc to what passes for maturity these days. Now he has a terrific son, my nephew Quentin, half-black, half-Cambodian. I think his mother's Cambodian anyway; don't quote me on that. All I know is her people come from one of the Pacific Rim countries, and her last name is Vann if that tells you anything. Her name comes up in my brother's phone under "Minivan," and it's not too far from the truth. He likes to complain now, but I tell him no one put a gun to his head when he bedded her.

Now they're divorced even though they were never actually married. Sort of like what happened to Michael McDonald and Patti Labelle in the studio during the Reagan administration. They had shacked up during Quentin's first few years, but my brother's so insufferable most of the time. Predictably, she left.

The fact that my story just happens to start at the beginning of a new year is just a coincidence, a cosmic accident. In case you were wondering. It seems fitting in hindsight, though, since what happened seems almost biblical.

If a meal is mainly black-eyed peas and cornbread, it's hard to know when it's over. Darlene got up to clear the table, finally, but she refused all offers of help in her typical stuttering voice, and so the rest of us adjourned to the living room. The channel on the idiot box was turned to politics, and the candidates were pandering to a more perfect Idiocracy. The start of the year was also the kickoff to the presidential primary season. Yippee. I saw my reserve of self-medication rapidly dwindling. In fact, I suspected Philip was getting antsy. "Where da herb at?" he said at one point, in his typical, Napoleon-complex voice. "Who's hogging the joint?" I thought when he disappeared into the kitchen, he was going to motion me over and pull one out, but he was just going to get some coleslaw. Or *cold slaw*, was what he called it. But all that was interrupted when suddenly Mama said to Howard, "Don't you dare! Don't you dare sit on my *table!*"

My heart stopped. When she said the last word, she was almost in tears.

"I was j-just," Howard stuttered.

"No!"

"I've never broken a table."

I couldn't help but chuckle when he said that. I've never broken a table. Just how many glass coffee living room tables had he made a practice of sitting on in his life? "Anything is possible," I said, laughing.

"Always strive for higher heights," Philip said from the kitchen. "For real."

Mama was still fussing at her husband. I can't remember everything she said, but it ended with, "...and then I have to take you to the hospital."

Of course, I lost it when she said that. I started laughing like a madman. I placed my right hand over my stomach, and my head arched back.

"I done seen it happen," Philip said, "I done seen that shit happen!"

"I know it!" my mother said. "Everybody thinks that it can't happen to them!"

In my best Fred Sanford imitating a 1940s Bing Crosby-type, I crooned, " *'It Had To Be You.'* "

(who are you, the black Andy Williams)

Now it was Philip's turn to laugh hysterically. And he did. He really did. Mama wasn't laughing. You have to admit I got off a good one there, though.

I laid down the remote and started to follow Philip into the kitchen, but Mama put a hand on my arm, "Tony," she said.

"Yes, ma'am," I said.

"I want to talk to you about something in my room, but I don't want to embarrass you in front of everybody."

Dunh-dint-dunnnnn. I followed obediently—I wasn't sure if she knew that using the word embarrass in front of everybody had already accomplished the very thing she was trying to avoid. When my mother was calling herself not trying to hurt my feelings she could be like she was drinking and driving in an 18-wheeler, I swear she could. She was shorter than me, but stronger by far, even in her bathrobe—had an uprightness in her gait that spoke of defiance in the face of adversity. You see a woman who's reinvented herself, who's shown a kind of genius for turning life's lemons into lemonade, alive and kicking at seventy-one.

"Go like this," she said when we were behind her closed door.

"Huh?"

"Just do it." Then she parted her lips and exposed her gums like she was Mr. Ed or something.

Oh, Lord. "Mama…"

"Your teeth look terrible."

"My teeth are fine."

She was always fixated on this kind of stuff with me. It got on my nerves sometimes. Check that, all the time. The minute I went in I was sort of sorry I had. She had the Bible opened on the bed, and there were pills and roaches everywhere, and everything smelled like bad ganja. Then she began making a chewing motion with her mouth closed only she looked like she was trying to demonstrate how to chew gum on the outside of your teeth. "That's how you chew," she said, finally. "It's very unappealing."

"Um…"

"Oh well, I guess it don't matter cause you already married so it ain't like you tryin' to impress nobody!" She tickled herself pink with that one. She erupted in a hoarse laughter.

I drew in my lips and sighed audibly.

"You don't have to get an attitude!" she said.

"I'm not."

"You are."

"Well, for one thing, next time you call me out of the room because you don't want to embarrass me, it might be a good idea if you don't actually use the word 'embarrass' while you're doing it."

"I didn't."

"You did. But you don't remember, as per usual."

She raised her eyebrows, and the corners of her mouth turned down in a frowning disapproving way. For a moment I got the feeling she was about to launch into one of her famous tirades. Then all of a sudden Mama looked like she had something of great import, something right on the money to say to me. She sat up more in her bed and sort of moved around. It was a false flag, though. All she did was grab an errant roach off the comforter and try to chuck it into the ashtray next to her. She missed. It was only three inches away, but she missed anyway.

I walked over and picked it up, flicked it into the tray. All of a sudden, I wanted to get the hell out of that room. I could feel a terrific lecture coming on about something. I didn't mind it so much, but I didn't feel just then like talking about my disability benefits or Darlene's paycheck or if there would be enough left over to get dental work done and smell stale weed and look at her in her bathrobe and frazzled hair and pajamas at the same time. But you can't stop a mother when she wants to say something. They just do it.

"I'm old, what do you expect? I have a condition."

I rolled my eyes. "Oh, you have a condition all right. It's called convenient amnesia."

"Why are you so self-righteous all the time?" She lifted her arms in a huff only to bring them crashing back down on her lap. The ultimate exercise in futility. She looked like she was going to cry. "No one understands what *I* go through."

Here we go. I stared straight ahead. She couldn't tell what I was thinking. I wore, and still do, these dark tinted Ray Bans and so no one was able to make out my eyes. They weren't for show, though, they were actually prescription no-line bifocals. In addition to having awful teeth, I have astigmatism to boot. But who am I to complain? There are children starving in Africa right now.

"Would you do something for me?" I said, staring at the wavering tip of her joint. "Would you do me a favor."

"What?" Her voice was dull and monotone. I looked at her.

"Let's talk about it a week from today. If you still want to."

Now she looked at me, her fingertips seared by years of smoke burns, her blackhead-freckled face befuddled and confused. "Tony, promises don't work with you. You just go right on with—"

"Stop it!"

She stopped, looking at me, fascinated, suddenly uncertain.

"In a week," I said. "In a week." My voice had lost all its authority and dropped to a whisper. "Please. I'm not promising anything. A week. If you still want to. We can talk about Dusty or the refund or anything you want."

We looked across the cluttered bedroom at each other for a long time, and when she lifted the spliff to her mouth to take a drag without saying anything more, I began to feel small. God, I needed a beer. Just a cold one to put things in their proper perspective—

"I caught Danielle looking at pornography the other night on the computer," she said abruptly. Danielle, if I haven't already told you, is my daughter and the youngest of the two, and the apple of my eye. "It was after everyone was asleep, or so she thought."

Wonderful. Another country heard from. At least she had moved on to a different subject. Cops are killing people with they arms up, and her main focus was my grill?

"I'll deal with it."

"Tony! What are you going to do! She's going to end up dancing on a pole!"

"She's not going to end up dancing on a pole."

"*Hmmph!*"

"I'll talk to her about it. And keep your voice down you don't want the whole world to hear you."

"Those images are burned into my brain forever. Lawd today," she said, shaking her head. "She's lost her innocence, and you don't seem to care."

"Of course, I care."

Like it was my fault that the culture was steeped in sex—and I never use the word *steeped* lightly—and my daughter was just like any other red-blooded American girl. I didn't like at all what my mother had just told me about my adorable little girl—that's not what I'm saying—it's just that my mother's hands weren't exactly clean in this department either.

All of a sudden, I thought of something I hadn't thought of in years. I suddenly remembered this time around when I was twelve, maybe a year younger, I found a large hardcover book under her bed with lots of these sepia-colored photos of men and women in various, ahem, positions. All tastefully done, mind you. My mother never knew that I'd found them or that those images had a quite formative impact on my ideas about one of life's most important drives.

For better or worse. I reminded her of this.

"I can't keep up with all the things you say did or didn't happen. I don't keep a journal like you," she said.

"I think you're just tired, and tense, and understandably upset, and that's why you're thinking the worst. But everything's going to be okay. The solution is to have an honest and frank talk with her and that's exactly what I intend to do. As soon as the sun comes up."

She didn't say anything. And then, "I just know I want my house back is all."

She said it like she was talking to herself, but I knew it was meant for me. I clamped up. I really should get an award for all the stuff I *don't* say. I really should. After a few moments

I turned to Howard, who had just come into the room, and said, "So, are y'all gonna have any more children?"

"What?" he said.

Howard, who was slow on the uptake due to a military accident involving gaseous fumes years ago and so got a nice deposit from Uncle Sam every month, was the kind of guy you had to say everything twice to. "Are y'all gonna have any more children?" I repeated.

"Huh?"

"Are y'all gonna have any more—

"—children!" He broke out into loud laughter. "That's what I thought you said, boy! What are you, crazy! We ain't tryin' to have any more children, boy!"

I was laughing, too. People said I was corny sometimes, but I didn't care.

Anyway, I suddenly remembered this time, in October I think it was, that Jimmy English and Steven Tichener and I were flipping through the book, which was called *Making Love* by the way, behind the old academic building. They were nice guys, especially Tichener. It was just before dinner, and it was getting pretty dark out, but we kept our eyes glued to those pages anyway.

It kept getting darker and darker, and we couldn't see the women in their birthday suits any longer, but we didn't want to stop doing what we were doing. Finally, we had to. This biology teacher, Mr. Blankenship, stuck his head out of the window and told us to skedaddle basically. If I get a chance to reminisce about something like that every once in a while, I could almost stand a few more weeks of living under my mother's roof.

Almost.

We went back into the living room. On the TV, Trump's slogan, 'Make America Great Again,' was emblazoned on a goofy hat atop his orange head. That guy wouldn't know greatness if it bit him in the ass, I thought of saying, but instead said, "America's greatness will not be defined by that charlatan, that demagogue."

It bothered me more than I liked to let on that my mother had made fun of my discolored teeth and chewing.

I walked over to Darlene and pulled her gently off to the side.

"Sweetie?"

"What?"

I hesitated, looking at my wife's distracted face.

"One of my aunts in Chicago sent me a Facebook message asking if I knew an Elizabeth Kazak here in S.A. She said she'd sent her a private chat about you and wanted to know if my aunt was related. Isn't that weird?"

"Um-hm."

But it was no good. Her mind was somewhere else, not with me. Thinking about something else.

(*she said she had proof that you are cheating on me, Darlene*)

"What else did she say, honey?"

"Nothing," I said as we rejoined the others.

2

STAND AND DELIVER is what I always say. Stand and deliver. For twelve years and counting, I had been doing just that. If I had wanted to turn the world upside down, I sure as hell should've done it while I was still single. Once I bought the cow, I couldn't even turn the TV channel.

At 3 p.m. on New Year's Day, Danielle had a talent audition. This meant I had to get out of the house and face people. Oh happy day. Mama phoned and said she'd see us there. "Don't be late," she warned me. "If you're late, she can't be in it, and I don't get my money back."

"Or here's an idea," I said. "Why don't the kids go with you and Darlene and I will meet you there."

"*What*...I have to go downtown, I ain't just goin' to the audition!" she railed. She paused, and then: "I have things to do! Do I have to give you my whole..." She mangled the last word, and I couldn't quite make out if she was trying to say 'agenda' or 'itinerary.' I don't think she even knew. I don't know why, but it was little stuff like that which really irritated me.

"Oh, I didn't..."

"I'm just sayin'," she said, exasperated. "Please…please don't let me down. Or your daughter."

Which is when I could have told her, "The truth is I don't really feel like going," so she could come back with, "As long as you are staying under my roof I think the least you could do is support what I do for your children." For once, though, I kept quiet. I thought about the tax refund coming in February, and I kept quiet. This seemed to throw Mama off her stride. I held the phone to my ear as I waited for her next words, and then she cleared her throat and said, "I'll swing by the house and pick them up in about an hour."

"Well. Okay," I said.

"Don't make me have to come in the house when I get there. Have them ready to come out. Promise?"

"Promise."

I tried to look on the bright side after I hung up. At least now Darlene and I would get to spend a rare moment in the house alone. We hardly ever got to, and I was way past the point of requiring from her marital due. Though whether she was up for it, I had my doubts.

Saturday morning turned out so clear that I drank my coffee on the porch, but the chilly air chased me back inside. I'd left my favorite sweater in the house. It was this men's Apt. 9 marbled chunky cardigan, size large, black with flecks of gray throughout. I saw it in a store window when we were beating the constable to the punch of moving our things out of the townhouse. Just after I'd found out, we were no longer covered by the damned Chapter 11 bankruptcy filing. It only cost me sixteen bucks. No, really.

Sixteen.

Anyway, the way I wore it, I only zipped it up about a third of the way. Very corny, I admit, but I liked it that way. I looked good that way. The fabric had seen better days cause everyone kept borrowing it. Jacob wore it to school on cold mornings. Darlene took it to work with her some days.

After I had my breakfast, it was only around eleven, and we weren't heading to the audition till around two. Darlene was on the couch catching up on her sleep, and Jacob was playing his NBA game on the X-box. I figured now would be as good a time as any to have a talk with my daughter.

Then I was walking to the room the kids were staying in. Danielle was finishing getting dressed and I approached her, and we embraced. We were always happy to see each other. Her resemblance to me went much deeper than her physical features. I hugged her tight, tight, tight. She squeezed back, saying, "Good morning, Daddy."

"Morning, sweetheart," I said. "You sleep okay?"

"Yeah. I did."

I was glad. Everything was all right. Jacob was happily occupied. Mommy wasn't working overtime for a change. Danielle was loving me. There were no bad things. And not everything people said on Facebook could always be believed.

But shit ain't always what it seams. When it's sewn together.

For now, though, I felt copasetic. For the most part. Danielle ducked off to the restroom to brush her teeth. I went around the room very quiet and all, looking at stuff for a while. I just felt good for a change. I didn't even feel the effects of not taking my VA-prescribed antidepressants and mood stabilizers in over a year of Sundays.

Danielle's clothes were on this chair right next to the bed. She's very neat for a child. I mean, she doesn't just throw her stuff around like some kid. She's no slob. She had the jacket to this blue outfit my mother bought for her in Chicago hung up on the back of the chair, then her blouse and glasses and stuff were on the seat. Her shoes and socks were on the floor right underneath the chair, right next to each other. My mother shops nice for her. She really does. My mother has terrific tastes in some things. She's no good at buying toys or anything like that, but clothes she's perfect. I mean, Danielle always had some outfit on that would knock your socks off. You take most girls her age, I mean, even if their parents are middle class and all, they usually have some terrible getup on. Not Danielle. Her shoe and dress combinations ate other girls' shoe and dress combinations for breakfast. And then you had the high school boys walking around with their pants all low and shit. The black ones, anyway. I never saw a white kid yet who felt the need to wear his belt around his ass instead of around his waist like the Creator ordained.

I was privately confident that Jacob, what with his Asperger's and all, would never go through that phase.

I sat down on the bed and looked at the books on the shelf. It was mostly Mama's stuff, collected over decades, mostly books. Not all, though. Sticking out from the rest was Danielle's journal, the one she'd been chronicling her childhood in about six times a month for the last year or so. It'd been my idea for her to start keeping one. I always lamented how much stuff from my childhood that I didn't recall. The small things. I wished someone had told me to keep a journal when I was her age. I always told her she didn't understand now, but that she'd thank me later. As in adulthood later, when her unassisted memory of being a kid seems like a giant blur. Like mine does.

I sort of opened it to the middle and took a look at it. The entry at the top was dated "October 5" and it was from the previous year. This is what ol' Danielle had in it:

> *Human relationships is the topic today, and why people want what they can't have. I think that people want what isn't available to them because they like those things but can't get them. Like how Mommy and Daddy are. Mommy doesn't really know how to pay the taxes and the bills, or remember things, but we still love her. And how Daddy manages everything and remembers a lot...*

I sat there on the edge of the bed and read the entire entry. Funny, I didn't remember this one. It didn't take me that long, and I can read that kind of thing, kids' notebooks, my daughter's or anybody's, all day and all night long. Danielle knew I read her journals from time to time before you get the idea that I was violating her privacy or something. She was way too young to have deep secrets anyway. In fact, I would often tell her when to write in it and what to write about. But whatever she put down was always in her own words.

Sometimes I wondered if I was doing it as much for me as I was for her.

She came back into the room. "Hey."

"Hey. We need to talk, sweetheart."

She didn't say anything.

"Grandma told me what she caught you doing the other night. On the computer. What you were looking at. Now, before you think—"

Just then, all of a sudden she burst out into tears. Her frame collapsed from one of preteen confidence to shame in an instant.

I wrapped my arms around her. "It's okay, honey," I said. "Why didn't you say anything? You and I are usually so close."

"I know," she said, sniffling. She couldn't bring herself to make eye contact.

All this came out of left field, to tell you the truth. It shouldn't have, though. The damn culture was so inundated with the fruits of the sexual revolution that now the present-day kids of the children of that generation—the ones that gave us the revolution in the first place—were now the victims of their own grandparents and their unabashed disco 'n' coke-influenced hedonism. Follow that? Neither did I. That's how jacked up it was. Hannah Montana twerking on live TV against Robin Thicke's genitalia in front of millions of impressionable youth at the MTV Video Awards. And that was just one of a myriad of examples. I hated it. I really hated it.

Caligula would be proud, if he were watching from the cheap seats.

That was one thing that worried me about this country. Like I said, *steeped*. Much as I loved it being a veteran of the Navy and all, it was the saturation of sex in the media that I hated the most. Much as I was addicted to it myself, I was really kind of a prude when it came to my own kids.

This time, though, I decided to go for the jugular. I wasn't going to paint the Mona Lisa with a crayon.

Holding Danielle in my arms, I said under my breath, "Atta girl…Atta girl…"

We'd created a character by that name a few months before—Atta girl. She was a superhero whose primary superpower was the power of encouragement. Kind of like what Reagan or Truman had said about being able to get great stuff done if you didn't mind who got the credit. We'd come up with some original names for members of a team: Johnny Depth, Ann Nonimus, Papa Razzi, Phil Harmonic, and several others. My personal favorite: Roger That. (He had the cheekbones of a model and the chin of anchorman.) Only thing was, Darlene's father was named Roger and that was the reason that, while he had been my favorite, I also hated him. That had been when I'd been going to art school, but Danielle knew Daddy couldn't afford to go there now. She also knew her mother and father worried about bills most of her young life, and that Daddy had been a stay-at-home father raising her and her older brother for most of their young lives. From kindergarten through the end of grammar school, after he'd been fired from a good job as a travel agent when they were still toddlers. He was at home when they got on the bus in the morning, and he'd still be there when the bus driver dropped them off in front of the townhouse in the afternoon. She was old enough now to understand that he drew an income, not from any disability rating he'd received from being a veteran, but from what he told her was called Social Security, and that it was because of something he had called bipolar something.

She understood a great many things about her parents, and not all of them were good. She knew Mommy worried about Daddy's mood swings and his overall mental health. Some of the things she worried about were too grown-up for her to understand—vague things that had to do with security, Daddy's *self-image*, feelings of anger and resentment and the fear of what was to become of them—but the two most important things on her mind right now were probably that Daddy was going to light up that behind for looking at porn, or that Daddy had gone off to do the 'bad thing.' Danielle knew perfectly well what the bad thing was since Mommy, who had a simple way of viewing the world, had given it that nomenclature before Danielle could even talk. She knew because her grandma and grandpa did the bad thing, too. Once, Mommy told her, Daddy had what was called a panic attack after not doing the bad thing for a long time and then suddenly doing it again. Over time, though, Mommy had come to accept the bad thing as a part of his life—even sometimes copping it for him—and she could even begin to see how it was a benefit and not a detriment.

Yes, Danielle understood a great many things about her parents.

"Daddy," she said. "Can I ask you a question?"

"Anything."

"Tell me the truth. How far can I go with boys and still be okay and have God like me?"

I sensed the chance to teach an important lesson. So, in my best *Father Knows Best* voice I replied, "Well," I said, sighing, "there are two important forces that govern the Universe—centrifugal forces and centripetal forces. The term centrifugal force comes from Latin roots. It means *fleeing from the center*. Centripetal force is *a force toward the center*."

"Daddy, you're making it complicated!"

"I'm sorry. What was your question again?"

"The question, Dad, was 'how far can I go with a boy and still be proper?'"

"If I answer you," I said, "can we then talk about why you did what you did the other night?"

"Yes."

"Well, sweetie, it all depends on how far you want to go," I told her, gently leading her by the hand to Grandma's nearby quilting project. "Take this little tuft of cotton here." I picked up the cotton and molded it into a tight little ball. Then I blew dust off the record player over in the corner of the room. I placed the cotton ball on the very edge of the turntable and said, "Now turn it on."

She did so, and after three or four revolutions the little cotton ball went flying out into the room.

"Turn it off," I said, "and now put the cotton in the center of the record. Now, turn it on again."

Again she was obedient, and round and round the turntable went. But this time, the tuft of cotton didn't budge.

"That is what I mean by centrifugal and centripetal forces. You get it now? One force causes an object to flee from the center, and the other directs an object toward the center."

I smiled as my mind drifted back to one of her favorite amusement park rides as a child. "Remember how much time you used to spend on that big ol' spinning wheel in the fun house? You and all the other kids...scrambling toward the middle and trying to hold your places as the huge wheel spun round and round?"

Danielle's eyes gleamed as she remembered how she'd slip and slide on the big wheel. "Yeah," she said, "I would try to move from the edge to the middle and get traction and use my hands to pull myself up. But it was hard! All these other kids would be trying to pull me back down!"

I thought about how what she'd just said reminded me of what high school had been like. "In a way, life is like that," I told her. "Life is struggle. Pain, plus work. Sometimes...sometimes it's like, you know, crabs in a barrel. People going downward, sometimes tend to drag those nearby down with them. We, on the other hand, are trying to climb against those forces that are pulling us down.

"Now, back to your original question. How far can you go as you enjoy the companionship of a young man all depends on where you want to go. If you want to go up, and onward, you have to learn to live within a certain set of boundaries. And love living in them. If you want to go down and out, you can choose a life without boundaries."

"I want to go up, Daddy," she said without hesitation. "I want to reach my goals."

I felt a wave of pride surge through me as I looked in the eyes of the only part of me that was still innocent, uncorrupted. I said, "You know one of the reasons why the world is so messed up today?"

"Huh?"

"Let me put it this way. If two cars are going to the same place, and one is going sixty miles an hour, and one is doing ninety, which one does it seem like will get there faster?"

"You're being Captain Obvious now, Daddy."

Captain Obvious was a fictional TV character from commercials, sort of like Flo from Progressive, or Burger King. We'd spent several hundred hours watching TV together over the years, along with her brother, and we both thought they were often funnier than the programs they were sponsoring. I feigned a comical salute, bringing my hand up to my forehead like I was reporting for duty. "All right, Miss Thang, fair enough," I said. "But what happens if the guy doing ninety gets pulled over by the police cause he's going way past the speed limit?"

She thought about it for a moment, but it didn't take her long to formulate an answer. "He goes to jail."

"That's right. They go to jail. Now, tell me again who got to their destination faster."

"The one doing sixty."

"Exactly. The bottom line is this—you'll get to where you want to go faster, and be happier, if you learn to love living within the right boundaries, rather than outside of them."

I smiled wryly to myself as I contemplated the irony. The young girl standing before me, this beautiful amalgamation of chromosome and bone and blood, culled from the DNA of two parents whose worlds could not have been further apart, would not even be breathing right now if I had, years ago, followed the sage advice I had just given her. Yet it made me sad to think of her and Jacob as mere accidents. That what held their parents together had more to do with economic necessity than with love, more with *com*passion than actual passion, more with the forfeiture of personal fulfillment—borne of carelessness—rather than the finding of it, and more with libido than with storybook romance.

"My Daddy's smart."

"Don't tell anyone," I said with a wink.

Then she started looking at me funny. "Dad," she said, "how come you and Mommy haven't told me yet when my birthday party's going to be?"

"I already told you, we're going to—"

"You're lying! I'm not gonna have one or else you would've shown me the invitations by now!" Then she hit me on the arm with her fist. She got very physical when she felt like it.

"I'm not having a party! I knew it!"

She broke away from me and started walking around back and forth in a small circle. She got very emotional when she wanted to.

"Who said you're not having one? Nobody said—"

"School starts back on Monday, and I'm not gonna have any invitations to hand out!" Then she smacked me again with her closed hand. If you don't think that hurts, you're crazy.

"You broke your promise!" she said. Then she flopped on her stomach on the bed and put her pillow over her head. She flops better than Manu Ginobli, I swear. She does that quite often. She's a twelve-year-old Erica Kane sometimes.

"Cut it out now," I said. "You've always had a shindig every year you've been on this Earth, and this January 6'll be no different. Come on, Danielle, take that thing off your head."

She wouldn't take it off, though. You can't make her do anything she doesn't want to. She strong like bull. We were Tonto and the Lone Ranger, the episode where Tonto keeps a pillow over his head unless he can get more screen time. But all she kept saying was, "You broke your promise, Daddy." You could hardly understand what she was saying with that damn pillow over her head.

"Come on, take that off your head. Come on. Hey Danielle, please, please, will ya…"

She wouldn't take it off, though. I tried pulling it off, but she's strong as a bull. You get tired of fighting with her. Boy, if our national security depended on her keeping a pillow over her head, we'd never again have to lose sleep over a foreign threat.

"Danielle, please, come on outta there," I kept saying. "Hey, hey, Danielle Willow Hill, *olly olly oxen free!*" She wouldn't come out, though. A hostage negotiator couldn't get her out.

Finally, I got up and invaded my mother's room and got some half-smoked joints out of the green metal box they kept on the bed. I stuck some in my pocket.

I was all out.

3

AS A HARBINGER in my marriage of things to come, sex—or the lack thereof—was always a lagging indicator. Right up there with the unemployment rate or the Dow Jones Average. Sometimes I liked to imagine we had our own stock ticker in damned Times Square or something. My own personal Nasdaq for gettin' some. A labia majora sighting meant stocks would close higher. It used to happen all the time.

But during that holiday season?

A bear market. Think Lehman Brothers, or worse.

Think Enron.

Anyway, it had become so infrequent at the time this story begins that I'd ditched the Fox Business metaphors and just referred to the act by the name that suited it best: The Darlene Prerogative. And in that respect she was very much like the good Lord: she may not always come when you call, but she was always on time.

A R&B song played in my head. It was low and raunchy, and in the silence of my cranium it played naughtily, as if issued from one of those old-fashioned jukeboxes that used to play in the soul food restaurant I'd worked in as a teen—the one I told you about. That Wurlitzer.

Love was over, and my wife was in the shower.

My wife.

Now, sprawled out on the chaise lounge in the other guest room, I wondered how many so-called beds I had made love on with this woman as my partner. We had met fifteen years ago back when I was new in town and had first done it in my black Dodge Neon with the standard transmission. I was head over heels at first, those first couple of days.

It wore off quickly.

That had been less than ten months after Uncle Sam kicked me out of his Navy, told me I was *Other Than Honorable*, that if I wanted to get high I could go to my brother since he was the one who'd passed me the joint that caused me to fall from grace in the first place. But not before I had snagged the Most Valuable Recruit Award coming out of Basic just a few months prior. That had been in 2000. So long ago? A few months after meeting we had moved in together, had landed jobs at the same telemarketing company, and had held on to the apartment through the spring before 9/11 happened. I remember that bed, vaguely, a queen-size from Rent-a-Center that I had for a good hot minute before they repoed it. When we made love on it, the unoiled frame doubled as a metronome. That spring, she had finally managed to emancipate herself from her parents. I had rescued her from a truly piss-poor existence. They want you to depend on them, I had said. The longer you live in that filthy place, the longer you sleep on that top bunk upstairs in the same room as your younger brother, the longer they can keep you under their thumb. It's good for them, Darlene, because they can go on making the State of Texas believe that they did indeed homeschool you after they yanked you out of junior high. But it's not good for *you*. We had wept and talked about it over and over again in that bed, that year. Back when Jay-Z dropped that H to the Izzo song that you couldn't take a shit without hearing for about fifty million consecutive weeks.

(Mama sitting up with the covers pulled around her waist, a joint burning between her fingers, looking me in the eye— in that snide, domineering way of hers—telling me: *It's not too late, you know. Why can't you find yourself a nice black woman instead of this fluffy butt white girl? I swear your children never get with the one you want them to get with! I really wish she was like Madison. She's not as pretty as she was, but I guess she'll have to do. A little makeup wouldn't hurt, I'm just sayin'.* But at last, she had come around.)

She hadn't been completely off-base.

I knew that I shouldn't think this, but my wife wasn't exactly the type that drove you wild with desire. She had all her life been slightly overweight, with an innocent, apple-shaped face and blonde hair that she would later always dye red or auburn, and a soft, pink, half-open mouth, the top lip short enough to reveal her top front teeth. (I used to call her 'Applehead' till she asked me to stop recently.) It didn't help matters that she was pale as hell. Whenever Darlene attempted to tan, I was quickly disabused of the notion that my wife had anything other than two skin settings: tomato, and al*bino*. But who was I to nitpick? It wasn't like chicks had been lining up around the block in those days to get my number.

Self-burn.

It had been my idea for her to move back in with her folks—we're too different, I had said. When I had unloaded the last of her things on her parent's front lawn and watched her re-enter their dilapidated and smelly abode, where her wild and white-haired old mother practiced a form of white witchcraft—Wiccan, I think she called it—and her empty-eyed father, a German-American man who, though he wore pants around his own house, was as henpecked as they come. No, it was clear who really wore the pants in that dark and foul-stenched...place. For all of Darlene's life.

A witch

In spite of myself, I drove away sobbing violently. She had attached herself to me during one of those woe-is-me epochs in my life, and I had sort of gotten used to her. That was back before my first diagnosis, in the days before I knew there was a name for what I had, what I was.

And while I was grateful, I could see that it just wasn't going to work. She had offered her body in those early days, among other things, as a balm against life's vicissitudes. And while the sex had been a good thing, it wasn't the best thing. The *only* thing. I was just at that point in my life learning that.

Now, I'm not saying Darlene Ann Neumann had the personality of the block of ice Pauly Shore dug up in *Encino Man* or anything, but let's just say that whatever virtues Darlene might have otherwise possessed—and she did have some, don't get me wrong—titillating conversation definitely wasn't one of them. And so we spent that summer living apart and I began to slowly believe I'd disentangled myself from something far worse than sleeping alone. Later on, I found out it wasn't so. I got a call from her around the time the Twin Towers got knocked down, and she said she had news.

I'm pregnant.

How do you know it's mine?

You're the only person I've been with.

And my damn bleeding heart, which had always made me an easy mark for a certain type of female, though never the kind I wanted—too nice for the cheerleaders, too *white* to be down with the fine-ass sistuhs.

For now, you can move back in with me.

For what?

I guess…to see if this baby is mine after all.

The birth. The baby had been very light-skinned the day he was born, almost white, but he was mine all right. You could tell by the mouth. And to tell the truth, I didn't mind. We found out about his Asperger's Syndrome a couple years later. You can't tell right there at the hospital, you know. Anyway, I'd been about to say Hi to thirty, and I had always wanted a family. Especially since the Navy thing hadn't worked out so well. You know, for whatchamacallit. Structure.

Then Danielle came the next year—albeit unexpectedly—my beautiful daughter. Her mother and I made it official nine days before she was born.

That had been the best year, the worst year. After Danielle had come into the world, I took a paternity leave from a damn good job. I had been working in the collections litigation department of a large bank. Fortune 500, large. I worked with a good friend there named Paula. Anyway, one day shortly after my paternity leave time expired, after I'd been back on the job a couple days, I walked away from my desk in a huff over something—job abandonment, was what they called it—a decision which, as it turned out, led to me finding out the name for what I was. What made me crazy. They foot the bill for my initial diagnosis and treatment, allowing me to stay home all that year with our newborn while I got back on my feet using the cocktail of doctor-prescribed medications they put me on. Like I said, it was a decent job. We had our first car, a pre-owned Toyota technically old enough to vote with windows powered by the strength of my left arm. Bright, downwardly mobile young marrieds united in the unholiest of matrimonies.

The babies forced a reconciliation between me and my mom, a reconciliation that held, for the most part. That is, until the next falling out, of which there were several. When Darlene and I fell on hard times, as was often the case as I struggled to keep a job more than a few months at a time, she was our safety net. And she wasn't shy about voicing her opinions when it came to where we lived, rules for the kids, how we allocated what little money we had left after the rent and utilities were paid. She never said anything overtly, but the message came through loud and clear anyway: this was the price Darlene and I had to pay (and maybe always would) in exchange for her help, being made to feel guilty because she was always behind on her own bills. It was my mother's way of keeping the thumbscrews handy.

Anyway, after Danielle was born, Darlene went back to work as a cashier for San Antonio's biggest employer, a large chain of grocery stores peppered throughout the city. During the days I would stay home and peck away at a novel I'd had in mind, a story that never got published. I'd feed the kids their bottles in the sun dappled kitchen of our two-room third-floor apartment, following my favorite hometown team—the

Chicago White Sox—from afar, and my newly adopted team—
the San Antonio Spurs—on the virus-infested desktop I had
managed to hold on to from my bachelor days. Darlene would
walk in the door around six (or seven if the rush hour crowd
came in before she could clock out), and while the kids slept
I would serve her dinner, after which we would retire to the
bedroom and watch reruns on TBS of *Everybody Loves Raymond*
and *Seinfeld*.

In those days, my drinking and smoking were still in
check. On some nights Philip, who had also recently relocated
down here after he could no longer hack it in the Windy City,
would drop over and there would be a case of beer and some
bud—what Darlene had called the bad thing, at least in those
days. Arguments in which she seldom participated because
her knowledge of anything outside of the latest goings-on
with Victor and Nikki Newman on *The Young & The Restless*
was severely limited. Disputes over whether the Cubs were really going to break the curse this year and win the pennant,
debates about who was the hottest rapper in the game, Fitty or
Eminem; sometimes listening to mixtape rap battles on boot-
leg CDs. Those and a dozen others. No, a hundred.

Some things are hard to remember. I'm thinking now of
when Darlene emerged from the shower. I mean I can't remember exactly what I was doing when I heard her stupid
footsteps coming down the hallway. We were the only ones
in the house cause Mama and everyone else were on their
way to Danielle's audition like I told you. I probably was still
looking out the window with a silly look on my face basking

in the damn afterglow or something. I was worried, though, thinking of a way to broach the subject of her strange behavior recently. When I really worry about something I get all OCD with my fingernails, and it's hard for me to stop doing it until I get them just right. So that's probably what I had been sitting there doing, transfixed, when she showed her face again.

If you knew my wife, you'd have been worried, too. We'd observed our twelve-year anniversary just a few days before the New Year, and I know what I'm talking about. She could be a pathological liar when she wanted to be, she really could. I wanted the truth.

Just don't piss on my foot and tell me that it's warm rain. That cherubic, innocent-looking face was all show, like those perforated lines on ketchup packets.

Anyway, the hallway was all carpeted, and I couldn't hear her footfalls coming toward the guest room where I was. I don't even remember where I was sitting when she came in, at the window or on the chaise or whatever, I really can't remember. I know she came in dripping wet all over the place from her hair and all. She looked at me and then looked away. As if I didn't exist.

"Darlene, I want to discuss something," I blurted. I had surprised myself because I'd planned to wait until she'd dried herself and gotten dressed and wasn't dripping like a leaky faucet all over the place.

Darlene, with a shade of irritation, said, "Can it wait at least until I get dressed?"

I didn't answer.

She disappeared again, out of my sight, but very much in my thoughts. And not in a good way. Time poured through the hourglass for a few moments. These were the days of our lives. Where was Macdonald Carey when you needed him?

She came back in. She didn't say one word like she usually did about how she had enjoyed our coitus. Not one. Neither did I. I just watched her. All she did was thank me for letting her wear my favorite sweater again. She hung it up on a hanger and put it in the closet. Then when she was putting on her pants, she asked if I knew where her cell phone was. I told her it was in the hallway over by the computer.

She walked over and retrieved it while she was buttoning her blouse. She stood there examining it, sort of checking it out with this very stupid expression on her face. She always had her damn head in that phone when she wasn't working or watching TV. The kids and I often had to compete for her attention when we were supposed to be having family time over the years. She had insisted on a new one even when our finances were unraveling, and I had obliged, of course. Darlene was mad about that thing.

All of a sudden, she said, "You were snooping around in my phone?"

"You've been acting so strange lately, I took it upon myself to see what's going on with you."

"Why did you need to do that? You could've asked me! You know I don't like it when you go through my things!"

"Why are you shouting at me?"

She was mad as hell. She was really furious. "You're always doing that—going through my phone when my back is turned." The tenor of her voice took on a vibration that I'm sure only the next door neighbor's dogs, and I, could hear.

"All right, give it back to me then," I said. I went over and snatched it right out of her hand. Then I tossed it into the living room. It landed softly on the pullout sofa where I'd been sleeping solo for the last few nights, undamaged.

"What the hell you do that for!"

I didn't even answer her. I just stood there. Then I sat down at the kitchen table and we both didn't say anything for a long time. She got her phone again, and I pulled out my lighter and lit a roach. You weren't allowed to smoke in the kitchen or living room, usually, but you could do it late at night or when everybody was out, like now. Besides, I did it to annoy Darlene. In all our years together she had never so much as even taken one hit off of a joint. Not one. She knew herself, you had to give her that. It was really kind of amazing when you thought about it actually.

Finally, I said, "I saw what your check is gonna be."

"And?" That was one of her favorite retorts. *And?*

"Your pay increase doesn't look like it's taken effect yet. Your check stub online still said eight-somethin' an hour."

"It probably is," she said. "So what? I told you the first check of the year wouldn't show it. It'll be on the next one, not this one. Stop obsessing over it."

"Darlene, you getting fired from Walmart last Labor Day is why we're in this situation in the first place. That's why we couldn't afford to pay for the bankruptcy plan and had to move out. Wanting to know what your check is going to look like is not obsessing. I have to do our budget."

"Yeah, *I'm* the one who dropped the money order into the washing machine," she said, tilting her head to put on her earrings. "Yeah, that was all me."

I couldn't argue with her. She had a point. It had been ever since last July, when I had bone-headedly left a $500 money order—which was supposed to go toward the rent—not when she later got sacked from her job as a cashier at Walmart, on *Labor Day* of all days (I never got over that) that we had begun to exceed our usual quota for misfortunes for the rest of the year.

We never quite recovered.

"And then there's Dusty," I said, breaking the silence.

Dusty was our housecat. We'd gotten him as a kitten two years before and for the first time, he was separated from us. I was very attached to him. That's something else I forgot to tell you; I've always loved cats for some reason. If that means I have to turn in my Alpha Male card, so be it. Dusty was at a veterinarian about thirty minutes outside of the city, and we were paying a pretty penny for every day he was there. Of course, it was an added expense on top of everything else I had to deal with, but it was worth it because my mother refused to let me keep him at her house during our temporary sojourn there.

It was just as well, because while he'd been there—since we had gotten the hell out of Dodge in mid-December—he'd finally gotten the spay or neutering or whatever you call it that we'd been unable to afford during the years he'd been with us. It was only supposed to be temporary. Darlene Ann Hill and I were expecting a tax refund in early February that would be a minor windfall, allowing us both to be reunited with our beloved feline, and also to get back on our feet. I say *our beloved feline,* but everyone knew he was my pet, more than anyone else's.

All of a sudden, right then and there, my mind drifted back to the time when he and I bonded. When he truly became mine. He was still a kitten, maybe an adolescent teen cat, if there is such a thing. I was sitting in the living room on the beige suede sectional we had for several years. It was old and ratty-looking from years of neglect. Money was always tight, and a new couch was last on our list of priorities.

I don't recall what was on TV or anything like that. All I know is somewhere along the line the gray-and-white animal was slowly making the transition from playful kitten to affectionate companion. I needed one, Lord knows, being a stay-at-home dad like I was, going stir crazy from the monotony of being a domestic god.

I dangled my hand. "Come."

Obedient, the little cat leaped onto the couch and settled in my lap to purr. Later, as I lay still, watching the boob tube, he tucked his paws under him and arched his back in a semicircle and assumed what from then on was my favorite pose. "Special lovin' *kitty*!" I exclaimed like a silly child as I gently stroked his curved back.

I'd never had another cat in all my years who liked to snuggle as much as Dusty. I was dying to get him back. I missed him so much.

I snapped out of my reverie and told Darlene, "The next payment to the vet is tomorrow, so I needed to know what your check was. That's all."

"I know that already, too," she said. "Come on, we're going to be late if we don't leave now."

The audition was at a children's modeling agency over on Dezavala Street. Finding a place to park had been another fine mess—wound up in a space five blocks away. "I told you we were going to be late," Darlene told me. She tossed the words behind her back as I trailed her at a decent clip, her mammoth purse bouncing between her arm and her rib cage. We weren't the only stragglers, it seemed; I saw a few other parents bringing up the rear, with us. It was a small consolation, however; I knew I was going to probably hear a mouthful from Mama later on.

In the agency basement, the other girls were older, and most of them had both parents in tow, also like us. I saw no sign of my mother or Howard, though—not that I tried very hard. The two of us settled in folding chairs in the back of the room, and I turned my program into a makeshift telescope. Then I saw them. They were trying to get through the legs of people in our row with as little fuss as possible. My mother started chattering apologetically in this polite, chirpy tone she puts on whenever she's in public. She was an aspiring singer herself, and I often felt she was living vicariously through her granddaughter, never mind how I felt about it. Me, I was more concerned that Danielle focused on her grades and wasn't too keen on ripping and running to all these different auditions that never panned out into anything profitable. At least not yet. "Oh good, you made it," she said when at last she and Howard had taken seats next to us, "and you didn't miss anything." She was smiling.

"They haven't taken the stage yet?"

"Uh-unh," she said, shaking her head.

"Good. Traffic was bad."

My mother said, "I don't know why you men-folk always leave too late. You know you have to account for traffic."

Normally I'd have taken umbrage at that sexist remark, but I smiled obliviously and gave her the program in my hand.

It was still New Year's, and the sun would be going down soon. Then Darlene leaned forward, wearing a yellow-green blouse that made you want to blow chunks—so pale and vomity-looking. "Hi, Carol," she said. "And Howard," she added.

Howard gave a sincere nod of the head that was almost a bow, and my mother said, "I'm so excited!" She was grinning like a schoolgirl.

When we were alone again, Mama said, "That went very well, don't you think?"

I felt exhausted, all at once. But I had an epiphany. It suddenly struck me that there was nothing she could ever say that wasn't just so fucking predictable. Even the lowering rays of sunlight tilting through the basement windows were expectable, as were the textured indentations on the brown linoleum floor, even down to the played-out bubblegum Top 40 hit *Call Me Maybe* coming over the PA system.

And the audition: well now, it just doesn't get any more tedious than that, does it! You can't get much more boring than a children's singing audition. The younger girls were staggered and obedient, wandering around the stage in poorly-choreographed movements that were supposed to make us parents say "Awww!" in response. The last group—Danielle's group—was a cacophony of off-beat vocals and chanteuses struggling to blend into a halfway coherent whole. I hadn't realized before that Danielle was so tall for her age. She stood head and shoulders above her young peers. They placed her down at the end, where (I supposed) she was meant to stand out less. But when they all did one of their special moves she still stuck out like a sore thumb. It couldn't be helped. I was proud, and feeling a bit superior, since I'd secretly concluded I had given my little girl better, more nutritious meals than the other parents had given their princesses growing up.

But my mother said, "Wasn't that wonderful?" applauding so fast her hands looked like hummingbird's wings.

Between sets, the curtain descended, but you could see it moving all over the place as the children rustled behind it. It made me think of a bun in the oven—Darlene's pregnant stomach, the baby's foot or fist punching against the cotton fabric of her shirt.

Seems like yesterday, amazingly enough.

It felt like an eternity.

The shortest girls came out last and showed the taller girls how to do it, but I was too jaded to watch. I let the sopranos and tenors and altos in front of me dissolve into a visual blur, and when the rest of the audience clapped, I unfolded my arms and hung an artificial smile on the outside of my face.

4

SATURDAY, THE NEXT DAY, I woke up late, because I'd had a bad night. I didn't get much sleep and dreamed hazy dreams I couldn't quite remember. I'd suffered from Grade-A late insomnia for years anyway, so I was used to it. It was afternoon before I really got going.

The second day of the year was gray and wet, cold, with slivers of sleet that lanced my face as soon as I stepped outside. I defrosted the windshield of my car—a new model Mitsubishi Outlander Sport, purchased eleven months prior on my own credit, a first. I let the engine warm up and then drove slowly down the access roads, braking earlier than I really needed to as I approached each intersection. These San Antonio drivers didn't know their ass from their elbows in inclement weather like this, I swear. Almost no other slabs were on the road anyway. The AM news had bad reception, like the satellite was crispy, but I could make out the traffic station saying the sleet would continue throughout the day. Lucky it was a Saturday, the radio announcer said, since most of us could stay home curled up with a good book.

After traffic and weather, the news came on with an update on the primary campaigns. Sound bites of Trump flooded the interior of my ride. He was delivering his anti-immigration, xenophobic gospel in these sort of short, clipped, staccato half-sentences. Kind of like Hemingway on crack. You know, everything's terrific and great, and it was the same adjectives over and over again. No thought was ever really completed, and it was all about him. He was part carnival barker, part motivational speaker. It was working for him to great effect, though. The crowds at his rally were whipped into a frenzy, and their cheers came through loud and clear in my car's speakers.

He'd been running for six months already, and I had seen him on TV several times. What was amazing about Trump was he never really spoke in full sentences. When you were listening to him, it was one thing, but if you saw his words written down and transcribed, it all made very little sense. Sometimes when I had nothing better to do, I would read his tweets, just for fun, imagining them in his voice with his trademark pauses and hubris.

Crooked Hillary called it totally wrong on TPP
She went with – OBAMA – and now she says we
need her to lead
She. would be. a disaster

Clinton is trying to wash away her bad judgment
call on TPP
With big-dollar ads
Disgraceful

And his campaign seemed to be nothing more than his children, some guy, and a Twitter account. But the corporate media ate it up like the lapdogs they were, and he was ahead in all the polls preceding the upcoming New Hampshire primary. Still, the chattering classes had him as a long shot to actually win his party's nomination. I switched to FM after that.

First, I stopped by an ATM and withdrew a significant amount of cash from my debit card, which had received my benefits deposit the night before, just as it had every first of the month for the previous five years, without fail. It was 2:07 by this time, and I still had time for my other errands. I still had to drive out to China Grove, Texas, and pay the veterinarian. The entire round trip would take an hour in itself. I wouldn't be leaving the vet with Dusty in tow, however. I couldn't do that until the whole bill had been paid, and that was going to take another few weeks. Besides, the plan was for him to be reunited with us in early February when we got our own place again. That was the plan, anyway. But you know what they say—you wanna make God laugh?

Tell Her your plans.

By 4:17 I'd finished running around paying bills and whatnot, but I held off on a return to the Hotel Atwater till I'd separated my remaining cash into different compartments. Then I filled up the gas tank with fresh petrol. When the tank was topped off, I went back into the station and got my change, because I'd given the cashier a twenty and it was full on less than that, wouldn't you know. I went over to the newsstand and bought myself the latest copy of the San Antonio Express-News. I had worked for that paper as a carrier for about five months out of the previous year using my new wheels, it just so turned out. The first real job I'd had in a long time. I had loved it. It felt great pulling my own weight again for a change instead of sitting on the couch collecting a check. I tucked the paper under my arm and walked back to the car. Next came a trip to the storage unit where most of our possessions were being kept. And after that came Darlene.

She was bareheaded—her artificially-colored red hair was matted against her skull in the light drizzle that was coming down. She hadn't spotted me yet. I had to take her to pick up her paycheck. She swung her bag to her other shoulder, and she fastened the bottom button on her coat. Then she happened to look in my direction. She came to a stop, and I rolled down the passenger side window as she approached.

"Greetings and salutations," I told her.

"What took so long?" she said, getting in.

"I'm driving careful in this weather."

"Well…we have to hurry because they stop giving out the checks after a certain time."

"All right," I said. "The next one will be direct deposited, though, right?"

"That's what they said."

Her mouth took on an uncertain look as if she didn't want to count her chickens before they hatched, but she stayed quiet. Then she said, "Get off the access road and take the expressway."

"*So I'm cool now?*" I said. It was another private joke between us. It was accompanied by a flick of my wrist, and a motion of my hand as if I was a DJ mixing and scratching vinyl records on a turntable at a basement house party.

She let herself smile then. And I was smiling too. I had my favorite sweater on again. I clutched her left hand as I drove. Her coat sleeve was as supple against my palm as a hamster's belly. It made me feel caring, and sensitive, and heroic. It made me feel like a man.

🦢

Atop the Mount Rushmore of the Great Loves of My Life, and holding the most prominent place, etched in stone, was the Standard and the chief cornerstone—Madison Ford. No one would ever take her place.

I'd first met Madison Ford on a blind date that'd been arranged by my college roommate, Richard, and another neighborhood friend. It was late August, and we were both about to go to our respective institutions of higher learning in a few days—I, to the University of Illinois two hundred miles south of the City of Broad Shoulders; she, Howard University in Washington, D.C. I can't remember everything we did that night—it was about twenty-five years ago, after all—but I do remember we hit up an ice cream parlor pretty hard, the six of us, at the end of the date. It was cool. I was smitten with her immediately.

It was the summer between our senior years in high school and our freshman year in college. We were about to embark on new chapters in our lives.

Madison. Before meeting her, I'd spent the better part of high school getting pushed around and bullied. The joke was my peers didn't go to high school, they went to school *high*. Except me, that is. I eschewed all vices. I was a goody-two-shoes, I admit. Behold—the Incredible Untattooed Man!

Hello, world. Meet the black Napoleon Dynamite.

A fish out of water. During orientation in the summer before my freshman year at Hyde Park High—in the hood, not the rap hood, I mean the real hood—my dear mother, not knowing any better, dressed me up in a three-piece suit and took me to the high school where I was seen by dozens, maybe hundreds, of my future classmates. I was a marked man from that day on. I'd begun to think 'nerd' was my name after a while and on several occasions, I almost answered to it. At junior prom, I wound up having to take the girl nobody wanted.

We were a perfect fit.

Madison. Now that girl. She was the first one. My first love, my first girlfriend. She was the daughter of a Creole father, I remember, and her complexion was the milkiest you've ever seen. She was black, and she wore it proudly, but if we had lived in the Jim Crow Era, she could have easily passed for white. She was very conservative in her beliefs, and she was a staunch Christian. Even her hair was conservative.

A year later, after I'd flunked out of college because of playing hooky during the week of finals at the end of my sophomore year, I relocated to Maryland to be near her, and we began worshipping together. She had been pursuing a degree in microbiology. About once a month I'd accompany her family—Madison, her mom, and her younger brother, Thomas—on a three-hour trek south, into Chesapeake, Virginia, to a small church in the sticks. Father, Son, and Holy Spirit, was what it was called if memory serves.

Small church, to be sure. Hardly bigger than a decent living room.

But it got live up in that piece, I shit you not.

All of a the sudden, as we were driving away from Darlene's job after having picked up her check, I got Madison on the brain again. Once I got her on it was hard to get her off. I thought about her and that church. We were deeply in love.

We said we were engaged to each other. Besides being a strict fundamentalist, she believed in something called 'deliverance,' and after we had gotten even closer, the whole summer long we practiced it—almost exclusively on me—practically every visit, listening to sermons about it on cassette tapes damn near 24/7. What was deliverance? The casting out by force of demons from yourself or another person.

> *From this day on the kingdom of Heaven*
> *suffereth violence,*
> *And the violent take it by force*

Had that been from the Book of Matthew? All I remember from those visits is seeing the pastor in the pulpit briefly and then me lying on my back rootin' the rug. That's what they called it. 'Rootin' the rug' was something I often did, as several church members laid hands on me and shouted for the bad spirits to come out: spirits of the Occult, Mother Mary, Lust, Lasciviousness, and the like. You get the idea.

The drill for getting deliverance was, I'd sit in a pew all calm and tranquil like—not so much as even wanting to swat a fly—a paper towel in one hand, my head bowed over a plastic wastebasket, getting prayed over. The demons were supposed to come up and leave the body through phlegm and spit, for some reason. Nothing fancy. Not at first. No one got their money's worth, however, if you didn't by the time it was all said and done, wind up on your back on the carpet looking up at the ceiling, screaming and hollering like a madman and calling the poor folks layin' hands on you everything but a child of God. This happened exactly once a month for an entire summer. Her mother's idea.

They were all into it. I was putting on an act, I think, looking back; but I had to do it because Madison would accept nothing less than a godly man.

I needed a spiritual enema. A colonoscopy for the Spirit, of the Spirit, and *by* the Spirit.

I often wondered about the weird looks that must've been on passerby's faces as they strolled by, undoubtedly and unexpectedly overhearing the shouts and screams of the nuttiest Christians on the spectrum, Pentecostal exorcisms pealing through the stifling summer night air, while the supplicants inside spoke in tongues and let their backbones slip on the carpet in front of pews as the sun dipped below the horizon on the Chesapeake Bay.

I remember Madison, kneeling over me and kissing my forehead. I had my eyes closed most of the time all this kind of stuff was going on, and I usually had someone's knee on my chest and two people pinning my legs and arms down. Part of the act was making like you were struggling like a madman to get free of their Kung Fu grips and half Nelsons. A couple of times I almost suffocated. That would've been quite a way to go out! *How'd he die, officer? Oh, he got the shit choked outta him by a bunch of Jesus freaks,* as yellow police tape is drawn and flashing lights from the squad cars turn the scene alternating hues of red and blue. Anyway, I couldn't bear to actually be looking them in the eyes while I was delivering these DiCaprio-level performances. "Tony," I would hear Madison say from somewhere above me, "sweetheart, I love you. *And I rebuke that spirit of self-abuse and lust out of you, in Jesus's name!*" It wasn't fair that she led the charge; she had inside information. Then she would pepper my forehead all over with kisses again and again and call for reinforcements—an angelic guns of Navarone—as I gyrated on the floor in orgiastic spasms of a charismatic righteousness.

Or a charismatic hustle. Sidney Poitier would've smiled in admiration.

Shaking the trees, was what they were doing. They didn't know what they were looking for, however, and judging from my life ever since then, I sure as hell don't think they ever found it.

On Saturday evening, I reclined on the crimson suede sofa in the front, doing a piece of art and watching CNN while the kids entertained themselves in their part of the house. Darlene was watching cable in the second guest room in the dark, behaving herself, presumably. Mama and Howard were in their room, which adjoined the front where I was, behind a closed door. I was drawing a picture of a new character I was working on, Bedlam Boy. I was afraid to tell my mother, but the dishwasher was running again, leaking soapy water all over her precious kitchen floor. I was afraid because she could fly off the handle at the word 'Boo'. Abraham Lincoln said no man is so rich as who has a godly mother. And he was right, for the most part, but he'd also never met Carol Clark, the Indomitable One.

The door swung open, and she emerged, crossing from her room to the kitchen. I stopped her before she could make it.

"Listen, Mama, I want to talk to you about the dishwasher..."

"My God, what about it? Is it leaking again!"

Oops. I quickly got up and walked into the kitchen with her to survey the damage.

"It doesn't look so bad," I said.

"It was an accident!"

"Well, now," I replied, "so was the Chicago Fire. And Philip!"

She wasn't laughing. "No, I mean Howard didn't close it all the way when he ran it! I am so tired," she said, placing both hands on the counter and lowering her head.

Philip wasn't here this night. He was at his own place with his son. "Go back in the room," I told her. "I'll fix it. But I really do think you finally need to bite the bullet and get a guy out here to look at it. I told you before, but I didn't want to press the issue."

She lifted up her head. She trusted in that One whom King David said was 'the Lifter up of mine head,' the Ancient of Days. When you walked into her house, the first thing you saw was a large picture—resting in a nook in which they kept their car keys—with all the various names of Christ in the Bible from the Old and New Testaments. There were more than you think: The Bright and Morning Star, the Lamb of God, the Lion of Judah, the Everlasting Father, the Prince of Peace, the Desire of All Nations, the Lily of the Valley, among many, many others. And, of course, the Lord. There had to be at least a hundred of them on there, even ones I didn't know about.

"Hey, Ma, did you take our clothes out of the dryer? I can't find them."

"Yeah, I washed them again. I wanted to get some of the old stains out."

"Yeah, but they were fine when I took them out the first time."

"I saw some stains you didn't see."

"Well," I told her, "maybe that can be one of the things you major in since you wanna go back to school. And while you're there, don't miss the class about moving to Alaska."

I stood there as she walked back into the room after I promised I would take care of it for the two hundred and nineteenth time.

I want to say something about my son, Jacob, for a minute. I know I haven't told you much about him, but he was very special to me as well. He was thirteen, looking more like his mom every day—especially in skin tone—with a stomach to match because of his voracious appetite.

He was a good kid for the most part, although he was known to have meltdowns when he didn't get his way. Like I said, he looked very much like his mom. Even his eyes were very light. I can't describe the color except to say hazel. Beautiful, really. He had fat cheeks, and he peed in the bed six nights out of seven. We nearly went broke going through plastic bed covers and, well, diapers—for lack of a better word—for kids his age. If I had a nickel for every time over the years that Darlene and I had been called to his elementary school in the middle of the day because he smelled like urine and we needed to bring a change of clothes, we'd be able to pull up stakes and move out right now.

That was all on me, though.

In the days when I didn't know any better, in those early days in my new career as a stay-at-home dad (I'm not making excuses), I rose every day before sunup and dressed the kids and got them ready for school. But in those early days, I didn't put him in the shower first before putting him on the bus. I learned, though. I was a very devoted father. If anyone made the trains run on time, it was me. I truly was the straw that stirred the drink in my house. Even though I didn't work, I managed all the finances, got the car fixed when it needed repairing (I'd often been stranded on the side of the road over the years, requiring the help of a Mexican mechanic who I'll probably tell you about later), got all the loans, just about took care of everything important. When the townhouse was empty for hours on end (as it often was, except for Dusty and me), there was nothing to do but watch TV and drink beer and scour the bathroom and kitchen drawers to see if I'd hid any weed from myself without realizing it. Nothing to do but bitch at my wife and yell at the kids and drink some more. It was hard to sleep at night because I had nothing to do all day.

But that was the deal Darlene and I had. The implicit and deliberate juxtaposition of traditional gender roles in postmodern America, standing shakily on the tectonic plates of its ever-shifting economic fault lines.

Not long after that diagnosis and treatment, the one I told you about, I went back to work for a few more years. Or at least tried to. The only thing was, I could never seem to reach the two-year anniversary point with any job. Not one. And it wasn't for lack of trying. I'd worked various jobs over the years since that first one, at the soul food restaurant, when I was pulling down that brown paper bag money, that pay-you-under-the-table money, that IRS-can't-tax money. That you da only one with cash after-school money. *Sure, I'll buy you some chicken wings the number two, please* Walking home with my pay, overshadowed by the El tracks, through neighborhoods that would make you understand why its dark inhabitants easily adapted to crime, keeping one eye open like CBS. In the hood like I was James Evans. My curmudgeonly great Aunt Virgie ran the place—the restaurant—my maternal grandmother's sister. She should've been a travel agent cause she was a trip in her own right, too, but I'm not going to say any more about her.

Well, it's strange I said that, because I actually *was* a travel agent back in the day before I stopped working for good. I was a government travel agent working for a place that booked flight, hotel, and car reservations for high-level government employees. Up until the newspaper delivery job came along, that had been the best gig that I'd ever had. Good benefits. Even better travel benefits, but I never availed myself of them. I'd already traveled to a lot of places, all in the States— Phoenix, Seattle, New York, Miami, and several others—from my days in Maryland in the post-Madison era of my time there, after she dropped me like it's hot. In those days, while I remained in Maryland—in spite of no longer having a reason to be there—I began working for Northwest, the now-defunct airline my mother had worked at to keep food on the table for thirty years.

I forgot to tell you about that, too. My mother was living in Maryland at that time, too. Nowadays she collects a pension from Northwest after three decades of service, but in those days— the mid-90s in my post-Madison years there—her job with Northwest had relocated from Chicago to Baltimore, wouldn't you know, at their reservations office near BWI Airport.

It was like serendipity, in a way.

In fact, she knew Madison's mother and Madison herself, from all of us having lived, also strangely enough during this time, in the same suburban Maryland apartment complex simultaneously for a few months. Another twist of fate. How I used to love walking up the hill to Madison's apartment—just a stone's throw—between the brick buildings, longer than they were high, my feet crunching on the rocks, the yellow sun slanting through the passages, to my fair-skinned sweetheart, just steps from a spacious third floor three-bedroom I had been living in with my mother. It felt cozy. We almost forgot we were from Chicago. Sometimes, in our naughtier moments, Madison and I flipped the script. We'd never had intercourse, but let's just say we had carnal knowledge of one another before she exited, stage left, from my life. I think that's one of the reasons why she left me, in the end. I was the one who'd introduced physical intimacy into the equation, but boy did I push the envelope! She was consenting, of course. Kisses were given, bodily fluids were exchanged. In the end, though, I think she felt I'd spoiled her.

She dumped me unceremoniously on a June 11, 1993, a day which shall live in infamy—at least to me—with a message left on my mother's answering machine. I was standing in the den of that Maryland apartment—the complex was called Crestleigh, and to this day they were the best apartments I've ever lived in—when I pressed play and heard it.

She later got married, in October of that same year, to a much older (and much darker) man that I never met.

Anyway, I was talking about Jacob. He was a good boy, but sometimes he could get on your nerves because he was like that cartoon character Jacob Two-Two: only he didn't say everything twice, you had to *tell* him everything twice. The difference between Jacob and Danielle was, whereas my daughter was unusually intelligent for her age and could see the nuance in things—the gray areas—Jacob, because of his autism, saw things in black and white. Yes, or No. Good, or Bad. He was very concrete in his thinking, and I liked that about him. He was also emotionally intelligent, and hilarious. I loved him.

I remembered the day he was born. We couldn't take him home for a week because he'd been having respiratory problems. Darlene and I, still unmarried, bawled in the car on Houston Street outside the hospital after she'd been discharged.

I got up and walked into the bathroom to take a leak. I was greeted by a pool of yellow liquid and feces in the toilet. I knew who it was immediately. Jacob.

That's when I lost my temper.

5

AMERICA. Not only did we send a man to the moon, but we also gave him a Spacely Sprockets contraption with big ol' knobby tires to ride on that moon. *A damn moon buggy!* And, also only in America, in the age of Obama, was I—a black man—able to get away with running roughshod over a white woman like I did for most all of the years my wife and I were conjoined.

In the South, of all places.

But she was not the object of my wrath now. It was my son.

He had forgotten to flush the toilet again. I had told him… about this goddamn thing over and over again. The last thing you wanted to see when you were going to the head to take a piss was a damn toilet-full of someone else's pee. And shit. Even if it was your firstborn's. I was beside myself.

The smell of cornbread had turned into the smell of terror that I was about to strike my son.

The bathroom was right off the children's room. I yelled his name loudly anyway. He came quickly, all one hundred eighty pounds of him, almost tumbling over himself as he ran, eyes wide shut with fear.

I could overhear a commercial playing on a TV from somewhere. It had this stupid weepy-sounding piano, all sad-sounding and stuff, and the narrator, a woman, saying all plaintively, "*We had moved to this area a year ago...where not everybody embraced cultural differences...*"

Oh God, I thought. I knew where that was going.

My son looked up at me.

"How many times have I told you not to leave the toilet without flushing it!" I yelled at him.

He stuttered something. In that, he was similar to his mother, too. She, at times, exhibited somewhat of a speech impediment. It wasn't all the time when she did. Only when she got really happy about something, like meeting a friendly new person, and her words were coming faster than her brain could keep up. That was another thing about Darlene. She was a very touchy-feely person. She thought everyone was her friend. She mistook their astonished faces in banal conversations, not for their amazement that a grown woman could act so childlike—which it was—but for actual interest in the vapid things that she had to say.

It used to embarrass me when we were out in public in the early years (she might still have marks on her shins from all the times I secretly kicked her under the table at social gatherings), but after a while you get used to it. Eventually. Still, when some of the people we'd met over the years took me to the side in private, they'd each to a man confess to me that it made them feel uncomfortable. They'd never said anything for so long, they explained, not wanting to hurt her feelings. Yeah, it was bad.

That's what I was thinking about when I...when I hit my son. Well, slapped him. Across the left cheek. I didn't know it that night, but that slap—and the reverberations that rippled from it like concentric circles expanding in a pond when one shatters its tranquility with a stone or pebble—was about to alter the course of my whole life. Forever.

And unchangeably.

Anyway, it didn't take long before a bright red mark appeared on his cheek.

Too bad they didn't make Ray Bans for mood swings.

It was just the two of us there in the bathroom. I was breathing all heavy. I don't know why; doesn't take much physical exertion to hit your kid. His eyes were filling with water, and he was looking at me so sad and stuff that I turned away for a moment and aimlessly played with the towel hanging from the shower rod behind me.

I turned back, facing him. I commanded him to return to his room.

I had removed my White Sox cap to wipe my forehead. I was sweating. I put it back on and then straightened the brim in the front, the way I liked it. And then I went over and took a look at my stupid face in the mirror. You never saw so much fury in your life, in the features that looked back at me. It partly scared me, and it somewhat fascinated me. Slapping my son kind of made me feel big. In control. I'd only been in two fights in my life, and I lost both of them. I'm not too tough. I try to be a peacemaker if you want to know the truth.

I had a feeling Mama probably heard all the commotion and was awake, so I walked over to the edge of the hallway to see if she was coming. But it was too late.

She was already standing in the middle of the children's room, her hands on her hips, holding court, and looking astonished with her mouth parted as Jacob and Danielle sat cross-legged on the large queen size bed in the corner, looking scared.

I say 'bed,' but it was really just two queen-size mattresses without a bedframe stacked and sitting on the floor. But you get the idea.

It was pretty dark, and I stepped on someone's shoes on the floor and nearly tripped. A quadrangle of light spilled onto the hallway carpet from the open bathroom door. My mother had a lot of white hair for someone who prided herself on trying to look young. She looked sort of spooky in the dark. Danielle sort of sat up in bed and leaned on her arm.

"What are you doing?" I asked my mother.

"What do you mean what I am I doing," she said. "I was trying to sleep before I heard somebody yelling, it sounded like! Was that you? Where's the light?"

She couldn't find the light.

"What do you want the light for?" It was right next to her hand. She finally found the switch and turned it on. The kids put their hands up so the light wouldn't hurt their eyes.

"Jesus!" my mother said. "What the hell happened to you!" She meant the red welt forming on my son's left cheek and all.

"I had a little situation with Jacob," I said, answering for him. "Just go back to bed, I'll handle it."

"For Chrissake his cheek is swollen!"

"I said just go back to bed, I've got this."

"Go back to bed? You know what time it is, by any chance?"

"It isn't late. It's only around eleven or eleven-thirty."

"Only around?" Mama said. "Look, I got to get up and go to church in the morning! You guys start hollering' and fightin' in the middle of the dam—what in the world was the damn fight about anyway?"

"It's a long story. I don't want to keep you up, Ma. I'm thinking of your welfare."

From somewhere—I knew where now, it was the room Darlene was in—the sounds of another commercial—this time for the McRib sandwich—came into our room, all patriotic-like:

> *Oh beautiful, for tenderloin*
> *From sea to beefy rib*
> *For smoky, saucy barbeque*
> *You're gonna need a bib!*

Glad to see *someone* was staying entertained.

After that, I heard a news clip about Miss Missouri being excited to be the first openly gay Miss America in history. All I could think, though, was: *So she's a muff diver, is what you sayin...*

I was in a strange mood that night, looking back. In hindsight, the situation brewing could have easily been deescalated. If I'd been thinking clearly that night, I would have remembered one of my favorite proverbs and said and repeated to myself, in an undertone, "A soft answer turneth away wrath."

Instead, what was my fool butt doing? Stroking the sides of my temples and badly losing an inner fight to keep my hasty and sarcastic—sometimes hurtful—tongue, that bitter stove—fueled by the imperishable pilot light of my manifold, darkly hopeful intelligence—bit and bridle. It would soon prove a vain effort, though—because, after all, who knows better what psychological buttons to push on you than the one who carried you and gave you life, and brought you into the world?

Mama was going ballistic, exploding. She was on a warpath; and I was the Cherokee nation to her Andrew Jackson. A *battle royale* began to ensue, pitting—in this corner—my inalienable God-given right to discipline my own children the way I deemed fit, no matter the jurisdiction, which, in this case, was the Hotel Atwater, behind enemy lines and bereft of authority—and in the other, my mother's indefatigable maternal sense of her own kind of manifest destiny.

We were going to have a Trail of Tears, too. At least I was.

This was not going to be a teachable moment.

One thing I was happy about, though, was that I, being a veteran, didn't own a gun. A Glock or a .38 Special or something. Or a gat, if you prefer the urban vernacular. Cause if I had, all bets were off. I didn't have PTSD or any shit like that from my brief stint in the military—hell, I never even saw time on a ship—but they said veterans in America were committing suicide at a clip of 22 per day, and they weren't doing it with razor blades and belts or ropes in most cases. I didn't need the added volatility that a deadly weapon would bring to our familial battlefields, where invisible boundaries of respect were drawn and fiercely defended in bright verbal lines, scorching—not the Earth—but rather the already frayed and fragile cords of the ties that bound us in the bundle of life together, all of us, whether we liked it or not. Lines of separateness and autonomy and communication that—especially in matters of corporal punishment—have been erected between parents and their adult children since time immemorial. Or, at least, were supposed to be.

Still, when you're a man financially dependent on your recently remarried mom past the age of twenty-eight—like I had been for so long, until last year when I, like I said, had a run of good luck at the beginning of the year and had, at long last, finally unshackled us from her government-insured, codependent and seemingly inexhaustible purse strings of perpetual debt and obligation.

That had been a happy day.

Usually, in our fights, neither one of us could get a word in edgewise, as we both sought to interrupt and shout over each other, lest the other actually prevail in making a salient and coherent observation. It was a shame the way we carried on at times. Never-ending quests to be the victor in our legendary and familial thrillas in Manila, over the terrain of personal rights and parental authority.

Remembered transgressions were just more matches for the emotional bonfire.

So: no gun. Like I said, it was one silver lining under a purple, cumulus cloud-filled sky of bad blood and gin made from tears, where the level of precipitation and its severity was measured in the number of spiteful comments each one could manage to reel off, comments which concerned perceived slights—often imaginary—borne of simple misunderstandings and the too easily taking of offense. Misunderstandings that could have been cleared up, in many cases, with a simple conversation, spoken at a low volume.

One thing I know, though, if I did have one—a gun—I know what I'd do with it. Take the gat, cock it, aim it at all my baby pictures, I'll tell you what.

Futuristic handgun
If you act foul, you get two shots
And one

That was Lil Wayne, aka Weezy. Now, he definitely—and often quite cleverly (see above)—glorified the gun culture. There was no shame in his game. As it was, America was gun crazy anyway. Fucking NRA. And Texas? Are you kidding? You need all this identification to just take a piss these days, but you're telling me I can, even if I'm crazier than a West Virginia bedbug—in this country, walk into a gun store and walk out with a firearm, a weapon of war that can shoot several dozen rounds per second and obliterate human flesh as those rounds tear through it—without even so much as a background check? Australia'd had a spate of mass shootings many years ago, and you know what those kangaroo-loving, shrimp-on-barbie-eatin' blokes did? They confiscated all the guns. Every last one of them. They haven't had a problem with mass shootings since.

Not in America, though, where—instead of hiding crazy and shoving it away, down at the end of the hall in that crawlspace all the way over by the boiler room—we paraded it on our nation's collective front porch and gave it a mint julep. Garnished with a toothpick umbrella of whatchamacallit.

Hypocrisy.

I had probably avoided incarceration stemming from past domestic squabbles much earlier than recently as a result of not being a gun nut. Being from the Chi, it's a wonder I made it out of those urban, gun-flooded streets without ever so much as seeing one up close. I'm from the city, after all, where they invented the fine art of gunning down teens standing outside at bus stops, just for their Air Jordans—

'scuse me? Do you know how to get to Greenspoint?

Oh, you mean Gunpoint? Break yo'self, nigga, and come up outta them kicks

Where stray bullets had cut down many innocent lives in their prime, and would yet again. Where walking to the mailbox was risky behavior. As was engaging in almost any activity that required you to, at least in our neck of the woods back then, go outside for longer than, say, two minutes. Where the brim of your cap had to be just right, facing dead straight, before going out the house, to indicate you were neutral—non gang-affiliated, like me—depending on which hood you lived in, where powerful local and surprisingly well-organized gangs, like the Blackstone Disciples, waged life and death battles in turf wars over South and West Side neighborhoods that the city of Chicago foolishly thought *it* owned, skirmishes more deadly and more violent than any and even the most hotly disputed congressional gerrymander.

Living for the city—endless hours spent walking long distances home near and under the El tracks—because you didn't have enough change to ride the bus, over the potholes and gravel, hot holes and what-have-you. Where dope fiends tried to gaffle you—along with their drug-dealing apostles—and not only cokeheads but the Feds in the Mercury Topaz.

Most of your friends also come from families where Papa, like yours, was a rolling stone, and wherever he laid his hat was, indeed, his home. Only in *our* case, the father *didn't* die, as the one in the famous song had—and, yeah, he left us all right—but not *alone*, like in the song—but an actual *loan*.

As in debts. *Bills!* Quite a few of them actually, if memory serves.

Looking back, it's amazing I navigated my way out of that labyrinth.

I walked out and went to the kitchen. I snatched a cold Miller High Life from the fridge and eased down the narrow hallway and back to the room. The thought of getting into it with my mother made me thirsty. When I came back, Mama was eyeballing me. She asked me again what the hell the fight with my son was about for about the fiftieth time. I stared back, lifted the can, sucked some excess High Life off the rim of the pop-top.

I thought about not answering, but then I said, "You know, just because I give up my personal space by living here doesn't mean I give up my parental space."

The kids were sitting on the mattress, dead quiet. I could tell they were scared. This was a showdown, and they had seen how scary Daddy could get before. My sheep know Me, and they know My voice. Only I wasn't always the good shepherd.

You know, Mama, Jesus owned a Honda, but he didn't brag about it.

What are you talking about?

He said in John, "I came to Earth, but I do not speak of my own Accord."

Mama laughing. "You have such a dry wit."

Good times, good times

All of a sudden Mama blurted, "You don't love Jacob as much as you love Danielle!"

I froze. I couldn't believe she'd said that. I didn't answer right away, though. I felt a sense of power and righteousness suffuse through me. Of all the things she could fix her mouth to say to me, questioning my love for either of my children was a bridge too far, beyond the pale. Call me anything you want from six ways to Sunday, but I'm sorry, saying, even implying, that I loved my daughter more than my son, just because he had autism—as it seemed she was doing—was the same to me as blasphemy. My love for my kids was sacrosanct. I wasn't just going to stand there and take it.

"What?" I said. "Where were you when Darlene and I were bawling our eyes out in the front of the hospital when we couldn't take him home with us? Where were you when we had to put him in special needs classes because he was in fifth grade doing math a first grader should do!"

I don't remember much after that. I slammed the beer down and started for the door. I didn't want to hang around in that stupid atmosphere anymore.

I stopped in Darlene's room on the way out and picked up her hand as she reclined on the chaise, gave her a big phony handshake. "Thanks for all your help in there!" I said.

"What's the idea?" she said.

"No idea. I just want to thank you for being such a god-damned good wife, that's all," I said. I said it in this very sincere voice.

"You should calm down."

"I'm not even upset about anything!" I said.

She sat up in the chaise and leaned on her arm.

"Come on, get up," I said. "We're about to bounce. I have enough money from your check and mine to get a hotel room for the night. Because some people around here want to control everything!" I said, loud enough, I hoped, for my mother to hear.

"What!" she said. "Are you crazy? We can't just leave."

That was another crap thing, I thought disgustedly: my mom and my wife had a financial relationship, completely independent of me. Last year when I'd been in the middle of working for the Express-News for what turned out to be about one hundred seventy consecutive nights, my mother and Howard had turned over a car they no longer needed to Darlene. Only thing was, she needed to continue making the payments, via my mother. The car was, wouldn't you know it, the same as mine—color and all—only one model year older. I swear. And she needed that car now more than ever to get back and forth to her new job as a charter bus driver with Star Shuttle, where she was making bank. Her checks, which at previous jobs had been chicken feed, now were regularly in excess of a thousand every two weeks. Net, not gross. And every month she forked over hundreds of dollars from her checks to my mother to pay the note. So, like I said, it was complicated. She didn't want to mess that up. That's probably what she thought when I told her to get her ass up, we were going.

Fine, though. If she wanted to stay here, let her then—*I'm Patrick Swayze*. I'd been kicked out of worse places! I wasn't going to stay one moment longer in a place where boundaries weren't respected, where they shouted out your failures and whispered your accomplishments! I'm blowing this popsicle stand! Besides, I didn't feel like standing there in the middle of the room with the TV glowing in the darkness surrounded by piles of junk my mother was hoarding and hovering over Darlene while I waited for her to make up her goddamn mind. She had her own car anyway. Like I said, I had access to a little capital, at least until the next time I was broke, and no one was putting a gun to my head forcing me to stay here, where controlling mothers said things that made you want to bitch slap the shit out of them. Where did she get off anyway—*she couldn't see what was in my heart!*

She had better be damn glad, I thought to myself, that I at least had gotten me *some* deliverance back in the day!

Shit.

Now I was walking in and out of the front door frantically, and her complaining that the door was wide open and critters were going to come in and me putting my stuff in the car and the kids crying and her worrying that the neighbors were going to hear all our dirty laundry. She called it 'putting our business in the street.' She was standing in the foyer with her hands on her hips and sometimes pacing back and forth, pleading with me in varying degrees of importunity. She was crying in parts, as usual, making herself the victim in the situation. That was my mother's unique genius if you could call it that. No matter what it was—your freaking dog could've just died or something—if you were crying about it in front of her, she'd find a way to turn it around and try to get you to see that it was really her that was being put out somehow.

The kids didn't know what to do. Daddy was being irrational, I heard my mother say to them. I was in a mood, all right. I didn't know what I was going to do, where I was going to go. Stay in a hotel in my own town? How many hotels would I get to know? How long was this going to last? Was I going to look stupid later on when I had to come crawling back to her with my goddamn hands out because a fool and his money are soon parted?

I'm sorry, kids. Daddy's got to go. I know, I know. School starts again on Monday, and I'll be here every morning to pick you up, okay? I'll never miss a day. I promise.

Jacob.

Yes, Daddy?

Daddy's sorry he hit you, okay? Please forgive Daddy.

Okay.

Like I said, I didn't know what I was going to do or where the hell I was going. You don't have to go home, but you gotta get the hell outta here! My life up till then had been sort of like a How-Not-To Manual anyway, so why not bitch things up for myself even more? I checked my account and didn't have damn near as much as I'd hoped—or needed.

One thing was for sure, I thought to myself as I drove away in the night, regret is a tough thing to digest. It's a slow process. Now, I ain't got nothin' but time.

6

MOJANUARYFOURTH 11:58pm

*W*hat a difference a few days can make.

I'm sitting on the floor in the bathroom of Room 101 at the Sleep Inn on Richland Hills in San Antonio, TX, with my two children, Danielle & Jacob, asleep on separate queen beds just outside the door. I'm well supplied with herb, thanks to a new connect, Quincy (8250 Timber Grand, also a brotha in an interracial marriage), who I met a year ago around this time. I paid for two grams, but he gave me an eighth. I don't know what that equates to money-wise, but it's a lot more than what I paid for. Therefore, I am happy…

I've eaten more than the usual number of bananas so far this year, and I've resolved to continue doing so. Right now, golden slumbers are filling my children's eyes, as they slip away, drifting on clouds of peace as their loving father watches over them, protecting them, as always. I posted on Facebook that I feel more like a mother than a father sometimes the way I dote on them all the time. And I don't know where the hell their other parent is, or what she's doing.

Or, who.

As you know, we had a good New Year's Eve. The whole kit and caboodle: Mama, Philip, Howard, me and my family, and Quentin. And said ball and chain.

Then all hell broke loose.

On Saturday night, January 2, Mama opened the door to her room at the Hotel Atwater and crossed from her end of the house to the other end, where the kids were just getting ready to call it a night. I can't remember if what I'm about to relate happened before or after she made that trek; nevertheless, it is an important part of the story. Jacob had left a toilet full of feces—I'm still bipolar—behind, and I flew off the handle. He had forgotten to flush the toilet for the umpteenth time. It is a problem we dealt with a lot last year. But I regret what I did to him. I love him so much.

I love them both so much.

I'm listening to "Yesterday" by the Beatles, and it is apt right now, and I'm crying. Mama! Why can't we just get along?!? I do love you, but, in the words of Neil Sedaka, "What is a man, what has he got…" You know the rest.

I was tempted to PMO just now, but I resisted.

Anyway, a ruckus ensued when Mama began to imply that, because I disciplined my son, I didn't love him as much as I should. Things were said, boundaries were crossed, and here I am.

It's my fault. It's my fault because I put myself in the position to need to live with her again (for the first time in 15 years) because of bad financial decisions. Speaking of which, I have an important bankruptcy meeting tomorrow that I must attend. It's actually required that Darlene is there, too, but she cannot, both because of her new job and because she chose to stay with my mother and Howard over me.

I know I have a mental illness. A few close friends have reached out to me: thank God for Facebook. I've been very candid on Facebook about what's happening. That's unusual for me. I usually don't share my trials and tribulations online, but I feel differently about this incident. It may have to do with the fact that it happens at the start of a New Year when everyone is supposed to be happy. But one thing is for sure: I will always watch over my offspring come hell or high water: Jacob Alexander and Danielle Willow, and Dusty—I will yet continue to overcompensate for the absence of my father, wringing every ounce of joy from this life to leave on their childhood as a memory—though it slay me, I will.

So, I dropped the kids off at school this morning. I recorded them walking into Luna Middle School on my iPad (formerly Jacob's). I record many things on the iPad lately. I still haven't completely moved out of #701. I have to get out of there. I'm going to pay a lot for being there so long. I just didn't have enough energy yesterday to do all the things I needed to do on Monday. I came back to the hotel room and just rested. I really didn't rest much. I made a list of things I needed to do, like clean the car's interior (which is a hot mess). I never did that, but I did, unfortunately, spend a whole lot of money. In addition to the $250 that I paid to China Grove Vet Clinic, I had to pay another $88 in late fees. It's just as well, though, because Dusty's welfare is important to me. And I want to be someone who is known for meeting his obligations. I pawned the MacBook Pro at Money Mart off 410, not the usual one, for $300. I may be in danger of hellfire for pushing Howard until he fell down at the front door on my way out (we got into it), but it was only after he had already threatened me.

This is all déjà vu. Not only the beginning of 2009, when my sister repossessed her black Toyota 4x4 from us, leaving us carless, but also last March, when I absconded with the kids and left Mama and Howard stranded in Chicago and went to a downtown hotel before getting on the road and driving 28 hours back to San Antonio all by my fucking self—and now I've done it again, kidnapping my own kids and taking refuge in a hotel.

I told my daughter, in a fit of rage (unfortunately), that one day she's going to look back and thank her lucky stars that she had a father like me. Fathers like me don't come along every day, I knew that much. Staying with their mother all these years, for their sake. They will never be able to appreciate what it has cost me to do that when most men in my situation would have left long ago. I'm trusting in my covenant, with YHWH, to see me through this present trial. I have $90 left. I have a check out there that I submitted to the Chapter 11 trustee to pay the first payment of the second plan. But it's going to bounce higher than a basketball in the next few days because I've been spending like a drunken sailor, not at all sticking to the 'every dollar' budget that I told myself I was going to make last week when Darlene's check came.

I parked the Outlander in front of the CVS Pharmacy in the Colonnade shopping center and switched off the ignition. I was grateful for reliable transportation. Back when we could never afford a new car, we'd had a ten-year-old pre-owned Honda CR-V that was on its last legs in the days before I got this. If I could've kept it running for just a few more months, I thought at the time, it could retire with full honors anyway. And if I could keep on saving the money that went to a car note, I could stand on my paper and head butt Yao Ming.

"Want y'all to stay in the car, ok? I'll bring you some snacks."

"Why we can't we come in?" Danielle said.

"I have to make a phone call. It's private stuff."

"Is that why you didn't make it back to the hotel?"

"Check."

Like I told you, Darlene had insisted on a new phone in spite of our crumbling financial situation. The reason was, she kept dropping her old phones in the toilet or something. Really. It happened at least twice that I can remember. So I had forked over the two hundred dollars for the new device, bad enough, and a ninety-dollar fee for the contract, which really hurt. And so far, at least she had managed to keep this one dry.

"Can I have a Slim Jim, Daddy?" Jacob asked.

"Yes. You can sit in the driver's seat and play with the radio while I'm gone."

"Okay. Yay, Danielle, I get to sit in the driver's seat!"

"Can I sit in the front, too, Daddy?"

"Yes."

"Yay!"

Unlike our previous vehicles, which they were young enough to remember, this one suffered no shortage of modern gadgetry. They were always eager to play with the controls. As I got out, the kids opened the back doors and relocated to the front. I zipped my sweater up halfway to the top. Danielle opened the Outlander's glove box and took out a battered gas station map from Missouri. We had stayed at the Economy Inn in St. James, Missouri, last March, in the wee hours—when I gave up believing I could make the entire twelve-hundred-mile trip from Chicago to S.A. without rest, purely on adrenaline and rage—while I was driving back from our vacation.

(the one where you left your mother and Howard stranded)

I had always loved road trips. I loved driving, if for no other reason than just to bang out and listen to dope music. It was therapeutic. As far as I was concerned, music was the best part about driving.

I went to the drugstore counter, got Jacob's beef jerky, a newspaper, and a copy of *Photoshop Creative*. I gave the boy a five and asked for my change in quarters. With the coins in my hand, I walked outside and lifted my phone to my ear. I dialed the number for Sherry, the landlord from the old townhouse, so I could tell her I needed a little more time to move our things out. I'd sent her an email weeks ago in which I'd told her I'd be out by December 16. Well, obviously that hadn't happened. Plus, I couldn't count on Chacho, the mechanic I told you about, to help me (even though I had called him the day before after I had dropped the kids off at school). As many times as he'd been there for me in the past, he was also notoriously unreliable at times, and so I wasn't surprised.

From here I could see the kids in the car through the slanting rays of sunlight. Their heads were bobbing to some tune on the radio. It sounded like Rihanna. I felt a wave of nearly desperate love for them. The emotion showed on my face like true grit.

I supposed I could have made this obligatory call in the car; I certainly wasn't going to say anything rated R. It was my pride that said no. I didn't like the kids hearing me talk to people I owed money to. These days it was almost always my pride that did the talking, because along with my kids, ninety dollars on a debit card, and one dark gray Mitsubishi nearing its first birthday, my pride was all I had left. The only things that were mine. Even the debit card was a joint account. A year ago, I had been getting approved for loans left and right. There had been money—although you had to pay it back, of course. It had been very easy to get approved for loans online without ever having to leave the house, I found out. Most of them I got approved for in my pajamas. I was playing with toe jam when I got the confirmation emails. Not only did I have the online loans I was juggling, but also local loans at brick-and-mortar shops called finance places. I'd spend literally half a day driving all around San Antonio to pay them, sometimes getting cash back from them unexpectedly, which always felt like pennies from heaven. Things had been great—a year ago. All at once there was enough money left over at the end of Darlene's two-week pay periods to start a modest savings account with an infinitesimally small pittance of an interest rate. Hey, better than nothing, right?

Most times, because of my smoking habits, there had never been a penny left over, even though sometimes Philip would front me a dime bag. Darlene and I had begun to talk cautiously about finding a real house and making a down payment in a year or so. A real house—not a townhouse, where you were connected to everybody and their uncle and you heard their loud ass music on the other side of the goddamn wall, nearly coming to blows when you walked over to confront them about it.

I had to watch my temper.

Chicago.

It was there that Mama and I really had beef. And then I proceeded to cook that beef well-done on the double with cheese.

(*when you stranded her and her husband in Chicago*)

The whole thing had played out like a scene from some Shakespearean play. Or a comedy of errors, rather. The dilapidated motel walls, the soul food restaurant on the first floor—from where I'd gotten the delicious breakfast of eggs, grits, and ham that I was holding in my right hand when I returned to their room from the familiar and bitterly cold Chicago streets.

The fleabag hotel, where my mother had insisted we stay at to save money, against my wishes, had a soul food restaurant on the first floor. The kind that reminded me of my teen years. I didn't know the simple act of buying breakfast down there, just prior to returning to my mother and Howard's room upstairs, was going to set of World War III.

Or, at least, its prelude.

And the whole time Howard was just sitting there, blind deaf and dumb, oblivious, on his side of their temporary bed, playing with gusto the role of Harvey Milquetoast. He was typecast. Mama launched into one of her most epic tirades that morning, all because I'd come up with breakfast for myself, without consulting her, holding it in a white plastic bag for all the world to see, and her saying she had plans for us that morning, which included breakfast at the house of Howard's sister, Hazel.

"How could you get something to eat? We were going to eat at Hazel's house!" she had yelled.

(*you just hate it when I'm not dependent on you, don't you*)

"I was hungry," I had told her.

What had followed that encounter in her and Howard's motel room, which was just steps away from the one I shared with the kids across the hall (Darlene had stayed in Alamo City because she couldn't get the week off—it was the kids' Spring Break week), was one of the angriest, most furious nights of my life. The pacing, the calculating. My hands shook. I couldn't sleep. My temper was like a rabid dog on a frayed leash. I had walked over to her door in the middle of the night, after going to the ATM a few blocks away, fearing all the time that I was leaving my kids in a dangerous situation by leaving them alone in that room, in that fleabag of a motel in a particularly unsavory part of Chicago's South Side. And that was saying something.

Left alone, with the riffraff and winos idling on the glass-riddled streets in the wee hours, here, where my mother had demanded we stay at because it was a lot cheaper than the four-star hotel I'd planned for the kids and me (with my *own* money, before she turned those thumbscrews again). And when she, at last, had opened the door, I flung the goddamn money she said I owed her on the floor at her feet and walked away without saying a word. Had ended up outside a Starbucks downtown, at five in the morning, still dark, kids sleeping peacefully in the back seat, and the only thing that kept me going was the knowledge that I held their lives in my hands. And that I had to do something mammoth, taking them all the way back to the home we still shared as a family with their Mommy in central Texas.

By myself.

Unlike how we'd all gone up there, to Chicago—Mama and Howard sharing the driving duties, with me, back when she and I had been getting along—I was going to have to do this all on my own. Twelve hundred miles. Eighteen hours, if you went by the Google Maps app on my phone, but, who was I kidding? I knew goddamn well it was going to take much longer than that! There was going to be an element of danger on this ride, I had known, trying to do this with no one to share the driving duties with me.

(*I would stay, Mama, but the game isn't worth the candle*)

My pride had been doing the talking back then, too.

Now, I waited as Sherry's number rang in my ear several times with no answer. *Come on, dammit. Answer. Let me get this over with.*

The car walloped the highway as we sped home, charging toward central Texas. With the latest Bluetooth technology at my fingertips on the steering wheel, in that ultra-modern contraption, that blessing from the skies, barely two months old, I banged out to my favorite music—jazz, R & B, gospel, classic rock, and even Radio Disney for the rugrats (when we could get a decent reception, that is).

I felt my anger subside, and give way to transcendence. I was charged up, driven forward by a nastily and profoundly powerful inamorata. I was always taken away by music, an ardent devotee of scream therapy. I sometimes imagined myself, against the panorama of the big expanse of sky outside the windshield, a victor against impossible odds, triumphant, and that, perhaps in my lifetime, I might still achieve a modicum of success in some yet worthy endeavor, before my number was up and it was time to go the way common to all mankind. I thought about what a vehicle like this might help me accomplish, now that I no longer had to worry about our previous hooptie breaking down because of a persistent radiator leak.

We were off, and we had gone too far to reverse course now, even if I had suddenly felt the pangs of remorse.

Which I didn't. At the time, anyway.

My mini SUV went cruising and gliding through the night roads and came out into daylight. Eventually. Tall stacks, an arsenal of filth, discharged silently into the night air as we passed through the industrial towns with beautiful plumes of noxious smoke. *Don't let the smooth taste fool you, remember* And the kids, looking at the map of our progress as we traveled through Arkansas, with Jacob exclaiming, "We only have one more inch to go!" And me thinking, *Well, that's the longest fuckin' inch in the world*, but instead saying, "No, son, that inch represents hundreds of more miles. We have a long way to go. Go back to sleep."

Only hours earlier, I had awoken the children at four in the morning as they slept unawares, and crept out of the motel after silently packing our belongings, sub rosa, lest my parents—amateur night owls—hear me, abandoning them unawares.

"*Shhsh!*" I said to my children.

They were just behind me, closer to me than white on rice—no pun intended—as the door rested on the suitcase Jacob was carrying. Since we'd been staying in the fleabag, which had been for the better part of the week, our motel room door had been known, at least to my ears, to be somewhat loud when closing. I knew it was going to go click when the lock connected with the chamber. It was one of those locks you see in upper-scale hotels. That had struck me as funny. It was the only thing modern about the place. I don't think of myself as a snob. I just knew I had the wherewithal, at least at that time, when Lady Luck was still smiling on me, to do better. And as usual, you could count on my mother to make her unsolicited perspectives of my spending habits known.

Even on vacation, I had to keep my bags packed, since she was good at sending me on guilt trips.

Most of our arguments were about money.

"Jacob, be quiet," Danielle whispered behind her.

It was dark outside, of course. I was wearing my sweater. It was probably much lighter out, but my Ray Bans darkened all I surveyed. But it had worked. We were creepin', like Left Eye from TLC, but without the tender loving care. We loaded our things into the car in the empty parking lot, and we drove away.

That had been hours before. Now, we were speeding into daylight. The acid stench of gas refineries went into our lungs like a barb. The sky released its fury. The cloudbursts were louder than God's revolver. Far out, the shuttered factories had the look of a dystopia-to-be. Through the ashen light of dawn, the farmers entered their barns. Under my foot the carburetor hummed, the Goodyear tires throbbed fast on the slabs of the pavement. The gusts were so robust that even my sturdy Outlander wavered. We plunged over the Mason-Dixon Line while the stripes of crossbeam shadows came at us through the juddering windshield. In the back seat were books, empty bottles, paper bags, and cat litter particles—Tidy Cat, I remember, the one in the yellow bag—and a copy of *Writer's Digest*, March edition. *I'm not going to be able to make it without pulling over somewhere,* I remember thinking. This was real. My life. How could I have fucked it up so badly?

It had been a good vacation. At the start. Mama and I had been on good terms. I had just purchased the new car a few weeks prior. She never said anything overtly, but I knew she had been impressed at my ability to pull such a thing off. Without her. On that last day of January, when I drove away from the dealership—actually night, as the kids and I sat in the stupid office of the salesman at the dealership all freaking day getting the deal done—I sent a text to my mother, to whom I wasn't speaking at the time, wouldn't you know; I raised my smartphone and snapped a picture of the kids standing next to the vehicle, its sleek gray exterior gleaming under the dealership's floodlights.

"*Hallelujah!*" she had texted back. It was the first time we had communicated in weeks.

"Nothing beats a trial but a failure," I texted back. That was one of her favorite sayings. She pulled it out whenever she was going through some kind of trial, which was often.

Raising us in Chicago in the 80s, everyday life had been like a contact sport.

On second thought, scratch the word *like*.

Like I've mentioned, I spent my early and late teen years Chicago's South Side, right over by 62nd & Stony Island. During a time when everyone blew their horn or waved when passing by. The word y'all was a proper noun and ain't was definitely a word. We went outside, we got dirty, drank water straight from the hose, ate whatever our moms or grannies cooked, ate fruit without washing it, played 'Piggy' in the streets and touch football in the alley. We weren't afraid of anything but stray dogs. The streetlights were our reminder that sunset was our curfew. Chicken was always fried, not baked, and Kool-Aid was the house wine. School was mandatory, even if it wasn't your time to go. A change on the birth certificate was a cinch. Shopping carts were 'baskets' and washcloths were 'washrags.' 'Soda' was 'pop.' Oh, and if you disrespected your elders you were going to get hit with whatever was close by.

(*she never forgave you, son*)

Come on. Answer, dammit!

As a shorty, whenever kids were outside, at the basketball court or whatever, and one of the teams was a man short, they couldn't count on me. I was in my room studying the World Book Encyclopedia—the entire 26-volume set—as well as studying dictionaries, thesauruses, understanding words and putting them together inside my head. But I'd come outside sometimes, though. In the hood, you live in dog years. As kids, I remember once this elderly lady told us, "You guys might never live to be twenty-one years old. I seen hoop dreams deflate faster than you can say, Jack Robinson." So, at fourteen or fifteen years old, you were damn near a grown man. In your mind. You know what I mean? You're doing things, you're hanging out all night, you're selling drugs. You might have a car. You might be paying your parents' rent and taking care of the whole household. You know tomorrow ain't a promise so you hustle. To survive. So, those years, living the way you are, turning twenty-five is like turning fifty. You're an old soul.

At least that's how it had been for me.

"God bein' willin' and da creek don't rise," Mama would say in those days. It was usually because Philip was stealing out of her purse back then, and, well, you've seen my mother. We had lived in a complex called Park Shore East at the time, which was located right behind my high school, a long pale gray monstrosity that stretched one and a half blocks, resembling a concrete Titanic.

There was no answer, and I hung up.

I walked back to the car. I handed Jacob the Slim Jim. Atop the dashboard was the picture of the character I had been working on, Bedlam Boy, looking slightly worse for wear. And on the radio, Linkin Park's futile plea for consideration, their song *Numb*, emanated from my car's boomin' system.

I got behind the wheel. And then: "Daddy?"

"What, sweetheart?"

"What's wrong?"

I hesitated, looking at my daughter's abstracted face.

"Nothing, sweetheart," I said. "Why do y'all have it tuned to this station?"

"I dunno," Danielle said, hunching her shoulders. "Jacob turned it to this station."

"Change it."

7

WEJANUARYSIXTH   3:36am

Today is Danielle's twelfth birthday. She's asleep. We're still at the Sleep Inn.

I have an important meeting later this morning re: the chapter 11 stuff. Another so-called 'meeting of creditors.'

I finally talked to Sherry yesterday. We spoke briefly after she pulled up (w/ Genevieve her assistant) in front of #701 where I was cleaning up. We talked about the email I sent weeks ago.

Yesterday, for the first time this year, I got back to my Psalm 119 meditations, getting all the way to verse 176. The last verse. It helped me to resist the urge to PMO. I had briefly returned to the hotel room, quickly going to my knees in prayer, as I sought the Father as to what my next move should be. Philip's father left a voicemail last night about some veterans' shelters he wanted me to investigate, but I only heard it less than an hour ago because, after the kids and I visited Dusty at China Grove yesterday (after school), I crashed for the night upon returning to our room.

The only friends who've shown a modicum of concern are Sloane and Paula. They've seen my posts. Thomas E. is also paying attention.

I know Claire must've seen them, too, but so far she's remained silent. But I am not bitter toward her or anyone. Also yesterday, President Obama announced an executive order around guns. It was controversial, but common sense stuff, in my opinion.

We stood in the hotel parking lot in the light drizzle that was coming down, just as the sun was coming up, standing by the Outlander as I motioned for Danielle to stand in front of it. She did as she was told. I had my iPad with me. I wanted to get a shot. My iPad took good photos. I don't know how many inches the screen was or anything, but it was a pretty good size, with megapixels and clarity out the ying-yang.

The rain pelted the dark gray hood as Danielle stood in front of it. She wore a purple cardigan, also of the zip-up variety, looking cute (I was biased, of course), but shabby compared to her normal standards. It had only been a couple days since I'd gone back to the Hotel Atwater to go get them and bring them with me instead. Anyway, Danielle had her black-rimmed glasses on and she shivered in the winter cold. Against the pallid colors of daybreak, her eyes looked like broken Christmas lights.

"Will you hurry up and take the picture, Daddy?"

"Okay," I said. "Here we go. Smile!"

I got the shot I wanted, and I took it. I was going to post this on my Facebook page. In addition to having a leather-bound journal—several of them, actually—that I'd chronicled the previous twenty years of my life in, I also was compiling, at least in my own mind, a visual chronicle of our lives online. I would come later on to regret that decision. You have no idea.

Anyway, I was also sad, within, because it was the morning of Danielle's birthday, and I couldn't afford to buy her anything or give her a party.

She pretended like she didn't care, but I know she did; and even if she didn't care, I did. Enough for the both of us.

She was taking it like a champ, though.

She liked the living in hotels part. They both did. Hotels, at least the first few we stayed in before we started living in the car, were always immaculately kept and pristine, especially when you swung the door open and walked in for the first time. There was a large indoor pool at the first one, and I walked back and forth from our room to it as they played in the water, afraid to leave them unattended.

"Okay, get in the car, guys. School starts soon. We gotta go," I said.

Jacob flipped his hood, and his shoulders hunched as a stiff gust blew. He reached for the back door handle. He and Danielle got in the back seat. I started the car, and we glided through the wet, early morning streets through rush hour traffic on the way to what the Mexicans, who comprised the largest percentage of the population in San Antonio, called *esquela*. I'd learned that crossing back and forth from the living room to the stairs back in the townhouse when the kids were little as a young Latina named Dora, who liked to explore things, introduced multiculturalism to them, flashing in front of them on the oversize big-screen console inches away, while they sat Indian-style before it. I had learned more Spanish words, however, from my best friend in the whole world, Claire—not the girl from Ipanema, but from Ecuador—and who I'd met in Chicago twenty years prior and who still lived there. I might tell you more about her if I get a chance because she's an important part of my life. I don't know if I'll have time before I have to go.

Hell, even a garbage can gets a steak every now and then. When was it gonna be my turn? *Great, Tony,* I thought to myself. *Now you're comparing yourself to a garbage can.* I was running out of money, but I was also resourceful, and I kept believing that something good was going to happen for us which would allow us to remain entirely independent of my mother's help. I was going to show her, I remember thinking. I hadn't seen or spoken to her since the night I'd stormed out. When I had gone back to get the kids, she wasn't there. That had been a relief.

Now you got me started. I mentioned feeding the kids in the living room, and now that's all I can think about. Thanks a lot. All those countless mornings and afternoons I spent, watching the children while their mother was at work, serving them Totino's pizza rolls and Hot Pockets and White Castle cheeseburgers from the microwave, reclining on the sectional behind them as they sat on the floor, watching cartoons for what seemed like temporary forevers split into innumerable ten hour daily increments. Many times I'd turn my back to them to bury my head in the cushions and try to make the world go away. I had often dreaded Darlene's long hours at work. As much as I loved my own children, I didn't always relish the prospect—especially on those long and lazy summer days when they were out of school, and they'd spend them indoors because of San Antonio's oppressive temperatures—of taking care of them all day with no one to give me a break. It bothered me more than I liked to admit that I was a stay-at-home dad. As common as it had become among millions of men in America's shifting economy, the stigma of an unemployed father and husband being nothing more than a bum never quite went away, and it haunted me, manifesting itself as a continual and secret melancholy.

It was Groundhog Day every day for me back then. I'd either quit or had been fired from so many jobs over the years that I couldn't put a decent resume together. I began to think of myself as unemployable. I stayed home on Sundays—the only day that Darlene always had off every week consistently during the Walmart years—while the rest of the family went to church. I had nurtured a secret fear that a fellow parishioner might engage me in conversation, suddenly, catching me off guard—I couldn't spin tales as easily as George Constanza— and ask me what I did for a living. And so, for that reason, I usually remained back and watched football.

Like I said, I'm not a good liar. I'd been caught off guard one time in the aisles of a grocery store by a former co-worker who'd asked what I was doing now, and I stuttered and fumbled for an answer before I came up with some company whose name I can't remember. I cringed, within, as I walked out of the sliding automatic doors back to my car. She had probably known I was lying my ass off, I remember thinking. So, I did my best over the years to keep humiliations like that to a minimum.

We came to a red light. When it turned green, I made a left down Potranco Road. School was just minutes away. I looked at the kids in the rear view mirror and the self-loathing backed up in my throat as a bitter aftertaste, even stronger than the taste of coffee and weed that I'd started the morning with behind the closed hotel bathroom door before I'd awoken the kids. Those were the times that my mind would reflect thoughtfully and sanely on the fact that I abhorred guns.

I glanced at the odometer. The gas was at a quarter of a tank. I was worried. I didn't have enough to fill the tank and also stay at the Sleep Inn another night. I had to make good use of the time the kids were in school and come up with a plan to get my hands on some cash. I had established a good rapport with the front desk clerk when we'd checked in, and I inquired if they were looking for a night auditor. Someone to work in the front in the middle of the night and run the relevant nightly reports to balance the books. I'd done a job like that before, in Chicago, during the late 90s, at a downtown European-boutique-style hotel located right across the street from the John Hancock Building. It was called The Seneca. I had enjoyed working the graveyard shift, using the solitude and isolation of the wee hours as another opportunity to tinker with yet another idea for a novel that never came to fruition.

During my time there I did, however, meet the young woman who would later become the second face on my Mount Rushmore of Great Loves of My Life.

(*Masara*)

I commandeered the radio and switched it from the mindless rap the kids had been listening to. I scanned the FM stations. It didn't take me very long to find something that fit my mood. On one of the adult contemporary channels, Gino Vannelli's masculine yet vulnerable voice sang a bittersweet and haunting ballad called *Living Inside Myself* that I'd always had a special, if not morbid, affinity for.

I turned my head to face the rain-splattered driver's side window as my eyes silently filled with tears. A single teardrop slid down my cheek from underneath my dark shades as the chorus came on.

I brought my hand up and wiped away the single tear, despising the shame. I glanced upward again at the kids' faces in the rear view mirror. *Good,* I thought to myself. As far as the pity party I'd just had was concerned, the kids were none the wiser. I knew that they probably hadn't enjoyed that song, but they had indulged me, because even though they were too young to understand, I think they could tell that it was something about the lyrics and the melody of that tune that held a special resonance for their Daddy.

"Okay, we're here, kids," I announced as our motoring chariot pulled up in front of Luna Middle School. "Make sure you have everything. Jacob, did you remember to bring your homework?"

"Yes, Daddy," he said, clutching the backpack on his lap as if to indicate his assignment was inside. Even though he was a special needs child, he and his sister attended the same schools growing up. I was grateful for that.

"And Danielle, do you have everything?"

"Yup," she said.

"Is there anything I need to know about...stuff going on after school, rehearsals, or anything like that?"

"No," they said in unison.

"Good. Okay. Out you go. I love you. Have a good day."

They said the same as they shuffled out of the back seat and up the walkway, finally entering the school doors and disappearing from my sight. The driver of the car behind me seemed a little impatient as I waited for them to go in, but I didn't care.

8

I am alone.

I've spent the last five nights sleeping in a dark, cold apartment with no electricity or heating on top of two soiled mattresses on the floor of (first, Danielle's) Jacob's old room on the second floor. I had never turned in the key, and I've been sneaking in late at night to sleep here. You'd think it couldn't get as cold as it does here, in a town that regularly gets over 100 degrees in the summer. But it does, and it's too cold to sleep in the car. I've wept a couple times. I've been scraping by with very little money, spending hours at Starbucks charging my devices while creating some of the best artwork I've made so far on my iPad.

I had to bite the bullet and send the kids back to be with my mother. I had no choice. I ran out of money. But I won't go back there, and so here I am. No one knows where I am. I'm off the grid. I've been picking them up for school every morning, though, without fail. The last thing I want is to hear her mouth if I neglected to do that. So, every morning I rise before dawn on the floor of Jacob's old room. The old carpet is soiled, the blinds are all torn to shreds, the walls are damaged. I can't believe it's come to this.

I could get in trouble for this if I'm not careful. If I were to get caught staying here, it would be bad because this place is not really fit for human habitation. In the mornings, before the sun comes up, it's so cold that I have to play these mental games with myself about the right moment to fling the covers off and suddenly rise from the soiled twin-size mattress and face the thirty-degree temperatures in earnest. It's like getting into a cold pool for the first time, or a scalding hot bath.

I have very little money, the car interior is/has been a mess, my T-Mobile bill remains sky high and unpaid and liable to be cut off (again) at any time, and I miss Dusty. I have a runny nose, and I'm sneezing as a result of sleeping in the freezing cold every night, and my first payment to the trustee bounced. But I knew that was going to happen.

Several notable news items: "El Chapo" Guzman—King of Tunnels—the world's most famous (or infamous) drug cartel kingpin, was recaptured over the weekend, after a daring underground escape from a Mexican prison last year. Recent celebrity deaths: (last year) Natalie Cole, and (yesterday) David Bowie, 69, arguably the world's first icon of androgyny. The primary season hasn't started yet, but I have a feeling it's going to end up coming down to Trump and Hillary. A choice between political malaria and political Ebola. I like Bernie.

Oil is down to about $30/barrel. It's $1.50/gal at the Neighbor Mini-Mart on Horal near Highway 90. Republicans strangely silent as gas in U.S. becomes cheaper than bottled water under Obama. The 'secret Muslim bent on destroying the Republic.' I wonder what Esperanza thinks about all this. I haven't talked to her in a while. Anyway, Trump makes me sick. He is the George Wallace of 21st-century American politics. When a faithfully married black president who was the son of a single-mother, the first black editor of Harvard Law review and a professor of constitutional law is considered un-intelligent, immoral, and anti-American by the Right WHILE a *xenophobic, misogynistic, serially philandering trust fund baby who quotes from the National Enquirer, peddles conspiracy theories, routinely calls women fat and bimbos, calls John McCain—a bona fide war hero—a loser for having been a prisoner of war, and who has advocated torture and the bombing of women and children has captured the hearts of a majority of Republicans—that is white supremacy, folks. Plain and simple. Vanilla ISIS, I call 'em. I hate to say that because my kids are half-white, and I'm probably the whitest-acting black guy you ever met; with the exception of Bryant Gumble. In fact, that's been the rap on me my whole life.*

Racism is an inescapable fact of American life. I remember the night of my junior prom is '88. I was with my date, and Richard was there, and we had another guy named Winston there with his date. We were dressed in tuxedos and cummerbunds, and the girls were in fancy dresses, of course, at some steak restaurant on the outskirts of Chicago. The Purple Steer. Anyway, as we ended the meal and were walking out, I remember very clearly a white man sitting in a booth saying, "Yeah, y'all niggers push on." I was the only one who'd heard it. I was the last person in the entourage as we were filing out. I remember stopping. I remember looking at him. Everything else is kind of fuzzy after that. I like to think that I got the guys involved and scared the shit out of the man, but honestly, I don't recall.

Even though being called a nigger by a white man—the real word, not the one that my own people use—felt like the worst thing in the world at the time, yet over the years it has become to me a badge of honor.

The black man is probably the most neurotic, schizophrenic, confused, problematical, byzantine specimen of mankind in the history of the world. Feared by many, understood by few. I don't understand myself, sometimes. At the center of my inner conflict has always been my relationship to that other marginalized class—white women. Although two of the faces on my Mount Rushmore (Madison, Masara) are black, it doesn't change the fact that I've always loved, reviled, and tried to control a great many white women. Madison was a strong black woman when I knew her. In the antebellum South, she would've been considered an octoroon, perhaps whiter. I remember looking at her as a white woman who had suffered a long siege of illness. Yet, Masara was the exact opposite. Masara—from the day she first walked into the Seneca Hotel—was the most beautiful brownskin girl I had ever seen. Danielle will not suffer Madison's problem. Her skin tone is the same as mine.

I have fetishized white women in my life, seeing them sometimes, not as people, but as props in my own ongoing drama. Except with Darlene, it's different because I often feel more like a father to her than a husband. We've gotten into so many fights over the years because she won't study to pass the damn GED so she can get better jobs than being a fuckin' cashier at Walmart her whole damn life. "Is this the example you want to set for Danielle?" I've asked her often over the years. "Do you want her to grow up having a mother who doesn't appreciate the value of education? Do you want Danielle to get all the way to twelfth grade and you still not have your GED?"

I learned the hard way over the years that school and books and stuff are not for everybody. I've even often wondered if Jacob's autism is somehow inherited from his mother because she seems to have some learning disability that I can't put my finger on. Anyway, I'm not proud of how I've lost it sometimes with Darlene. I've put my hands on her before, but she's always forgiven me. Sometimes I wonder if the final answer of any black man to a white woman with whom he lives in a white society is violence. My resentment toward my mother has often spilled over into my relationship with Darlene. She is an over-bearing mother and clawing child all in one. Sometimes I just want her to shut the fuck up.

Stop it, Tony.

I've had a little bud since Friday when I copped after a quick stop to Philip's. Finally, last night I saw Paula Bradshaw again for the first time in over a decade. She gave me a gift to give to Danielle for her birthday—a pkg of Katy Perry perfume for girls.

Danielle loved it.

9

DAYS PASSED. Darlene and I didn't speak much. But I knew she was still at the Hotel Atwater, still working. As for me, I was still living like a washed-up celebrity. I turned to a daily staple of coffee and bananas for sustenance. One day I ate a whole cluster of bananas and then raced to the bathroom and vomited it up because they hadn't been sweet enough. The level of petrol in the gas tank wasn't getting any higher. I was quickly getting down to my last few pennies.

The worst moment of the day had come before the sun was up. I had to be out of the townhouse before I was spotted, for one thing. The weather was frigid, the heat and electricity were shut off, and the sky outside still dark. If I was lucky, the temps would be in the mid-forties, instead of hovering around the low-thirties. There was always a moment when I had to stop playing games and fling the covers off and expose my bare extremities to the freezing air. But it lasted only a second. And it got warmer as the sun came up.

It happened on the fourteenth of January. I was still waiting for those black-eyed peas to take effect. The fourteenth of

January fell on a Thursday, which was Darlene's payday. I had been greatly looking forward to it, not only because several outstanding bills—including the one to the vet—were set to be automatically debited from our joint account that day, but also because I'd desperately wanted—and needed—to have cash in my pocket again. I wanted to eat a decent meal. It had seemed like forever since I'd had one. I had begun losing weight. I was already thin as a wisp as it was, but now I had to literally tighten my belt just to keep my pants up. My stomach growled often.

I comforted myself with the knowledge that Darlene's check would soon enable me to eat a king's breakfast. And that it would take place, she'd told me, sometime before noon. I snuck out of #701 humming, even though I had that balsamouth feeling that comes from too many bananas.

It was a bitter-cold day, the kind that turns your hands to stone, and after I got to Starbucks, I plugged the iPad into one of their outlets and sat at a table sipping from my Thermos. Only trouble was, there was no coffee in it. I had finally reached the point where I had to choose between a cup of Joe and a gallon of petrol for the tank. I chose the latter.

Looking back, it was a wise decision.

Hours passed. I kept checking the account on my smartphone, hoping desperately each time I did that the screen would show a deposit of slightly more than eleven hundred dollars had just been made. Nothing. Zilch. Goose eggs. I was so broke I couldn't spend a lovely evening. Then I decided to send Darlene a text via Facebook Messenger and pray she'd see it. I had known she was probably behind the wheel of her charter bus, and company rules forbid the use of her cell phone while she was driving. To my surprise, she responded.

"Hi," her message simply said.

"It's taking forever for your job to post your deposit for some reason. I like your job, but I wish they could be like Walmart and release your pay stub days in advance. I'm sitting here in the car with no money and needing to get a lot done, and I have no idea when or if it's going to be deposited today."

Crickets.

"Hello?" I finally texted.

"I'm at a meeting. A driver's meeting."

"What the hell is going on? How long does it take for them to post your damn check——I need to do a budget! And not to mention," I said, *"get a lot of stuff done, which I cannot do without money. You said it would post by now."*

"It's not finalized yet."

"Do you have any idea how long it's going to take because...I don't even know what you're going to get."

She didn't respond. Finally, I got tired of sitting there, in the cramped and messy confines of my car, and having to pee in empty beer bottles (because I was too lazy to go into public places, or it was too much of an emergency) and have to listen to my stomach grumbling over and over again. So, I sent Darlene another message.

"You are too damn passive. You need to make it clear to your bosses that you worked the hours you expected, and now you expect to get paid! You know I don't have a problem speaking my mind and letting people know, even if they are my bosses, what I expect of them because they have no problem making it clear what they expect from you. But you are afraid of people."

"No," she responded. *"I already spoke to the supervisor. If it isn't ready. Then I'll have to wait. And so will you. This is my job. Not yours. So don't get upset that it hasn't happened yet."*

I felt that warm rain on my foot again.

"I need to focus on what I have to do," she continued. *"And not you. You're making me upset. I have to leave in an hour."*

She went radio silent after that.

The time was 1:17.

After it was clear she wasn't going to say anything else, I sat in the car for a while in the middle of Kohl's parking lot and smoked a couple of roaches. At least I'd had that. It was a bright, sunny day outside. Boy, I felt miserable. I felt so sad you can't imagine. I started reminiscing about a time in my marriage, several years before, when things were really bad, and I had almost divorced Darlene. That had been in 2008. I'd been working at the government travel agency at the time, aware of the fact that, in a couple more months, I would do something I'd never done in my twenty years of working various jobs: I would reach my two-year anniversary at one place of employment. I was excited. As happy as I was at work, my domestic life was hell. Darlene had just been fired from her first stint at a newly-built Walmart walking distance from our townhome—a job I basically got for her, more or less, since I'd taken the online aptitude test in her stead after her repeated failures—just a few months prior. And that had been just a few weeks after I'd gotten a call one day, out of the blue, from a young woman named Vicki who said she wanted me to know that Darlene was cheating on me with her boyfriend, a co-worker.

That had been the same year Obama was running for president the first time. He and Hillary Clinton were still duking it out in the primaries. Even though I had voted for Bush in '04, I was an early and enthusiastic supporter of Obama in the primaries. When it was our turn to vote in Texas, my mom and I went together. The polling place, at the local school library, was wall-to-wall liberals. A minority in Texas. Clinton's supporters lined one side of the room; Obama's, the other. And then, wouldn't you know, Carol Clark's son was hand-picked to represent Barack Obama at the state Democratic Convention, a couple months away, as an alternate delegate. Mama had been so proud. It just so turned out, to my delighted surprise, they were pairing me up to travel to Austin with a Hillary delegate, an attractive young Hispanic woman. This meant we were probably going to have to stay in touch, drive up to Austin together, and maybe even share a hotel room.

It didn't hurt matters any that she didn't look like Ernest Borgnine.

There was a sudden rise in the sound of voices in the room, and I looked toward the front and saw the fetching Hillary delegate stepping through the throng, gliding in my direction at a regal, stately pace with high-heels clicking that I could hear, even above the cacophony. I felt so grateful that it seemed she was going to be the one to initiate a conversation. But before she got to me, she was cut off by a weird-looking man in a dark trench coat. He looked like a person of interest in a statutory rape case. He bumped into her, actually, but I could tell it was a ruse. He wasted no time engaging her in conversation. *Ok now she's giggling with an ugly guy...what the hell's this shit about*, I remember thinking.

They were close enough for me to overhear what they were saying. "I'm Esperanza—" and then something like "Juarez" that I couldn't make out. The noise level in the library was loud.

They got into a conversation about race and class. Actually, he was a pretty smart guy. I was becoming envious as she laughed at a few of the man's observations, and begun looking for a way to weasel my way into the conversation. She had been paired with me, anyway, not you buddy-boy, so back the hell up.

I didn't have to, however. Some idiot bumped into me from behind, and I jumped, and—oh, *great*.

Jostled against her drink. Spilled it all down her front.

"Dammit!" I said. "I'm so—dammit! I'm such a klutz."

"That's all right," she said. Her sleeve was wet. She raised one hand in the air, at the same time holding on to her coffee with the other. "Let me," I said, and I took the coffee away from her so that she could get a Kleenex out of her purse. She did. "I could kick myself," I said. I could tell through the cup's material that the coffee was scalding, which made things all the worse. "I hope you didn't get burned," I told her.

She replied, "No," and halted, putting the tissue back in her purse. In an amicable tone, she said, "Really. It's fine."

"Oh—sorry. My name's Tony Hill. Apparently, we've been partnered up to go to the convention together." Take that, Mr. Trench Coat.

"Esperanza Torres," she told me.

When we were alone later, I asked her, "You're not here undercover, are you? A reporter for Fox News?"

"No," she had replied.

"Strange," I said to her. "You're looking awfully fair and balanced."

And the library: the three of us became deeply embedded in conversation. The best kind. Stimulating. It turned out Mr. Trench Coat had known a thing or two about several subjects, to my chagrin. He did seem flabbergasted about one thing, however. "I'd love to know what a superdelegate is," he was saying, "because that seems undemocratic."

The topic turned to the primary and the reason we were supporting our respective candidates. "I guess I'll support my former boss," Esperanza said. "I was an intern for Hillary five years ago. I spent a summer working in her mailroom, which is not as glamorous as you might think.

"That was the era of the Anthrax scares."

"Ohhh," I said to her, laughing, "and they hired the brown girl to open up the envelopes."

"Yes," she confessed without an ounce of shame. "And in spite of that, I would still vote for her. I would vote for her in spite of the fact that we were forced to call each other 'Clinterns.' "

I gasped. I said, "That's weird cause that also sounds dirty."

We all laughed. "Yeah, I know!" Esperanza said. "There were a lot of things about that that bothered me. Also, being a Clinton intern in 2003—it didn't matter that I was interning for Hillary—people would say stuff like, 'Oh, you better get knee pads, you better get knee pads...uh, cause, y'know, cause you're Hillary Clinton's intern...' And I'd say, 'Why, am I going to suck Hillary Clinton's penis or something?' 'No! You should still get kneepads, though! Cause o' what happened, y'know, seven years ago.' "

More laughter. This chick was hilarious.

"Still, I'll vote for her."

"What were we talking about before?" I said once the hilarity had subsided.

The man in the trench coat said, "Dog-whistling. The generic meaning of the term 'dog-whistling' is speaking in a coded speech that your target audience can identify, but others can't. Okay, that happens all the time. That's just called political speech. But when we're talking about race or about gender what we're really talking about is a dynamic in which politicians are saying things that are socially offensive—and would be widely repudiated—if they were clearly understood. So, they use coded phrases that trigger social anxiety and social revulsion, that trigger racism and sexism, but at the same time allows them to deny that they are doing any such thing."

"Interesting," Esperanza said. I admit I was also intrigued. She asked, "So, can you explain the history of dog-whistling and where it comes from in this country?"

"George Wallace," he continued, "is this phenomenal figure, because he first ran for governor in 1958. And when he did so, he was actually a racial moderate. He was endorsed by the NAACP; his opponent by the Klan. He lost. And he realized that he lost because of racial anxiety, and he had this incredible quote. He was about to go out to deliver his concession on the night he lost, and he turned to some of his cronies, and he said, *'No sonofabitch is ever gonna out-nigger me again.'* "

Esperanza and I said, "Whoa!" in unison, and a few heads turned our way.

He went on. "And what he meant is, *'I'm* gonna start using the n-word, *I'm* gonna start being the racial reactionary, and that's how I'm gonna get elected.' And that's precisely what he did!" And with that, the man, who was white and who'd said his name was Aubrey, quickly excused himself to find the little boys' room.

I was grateful to have Esperanza all to myself, at least for a moment or two. I turned to her. "So," I said, "was it weird for you when he dropped the n-bomb like that?"

"Yeah," she admitted.

I said, "I know it's one of those things, like, 'Yeah, I know he's on my team, and I know what he meant,' but I was still like, 'Whoa!' "

"I kept waitin' for him to whisper, like, 'Don't worry, I'm one-eighteenth black,' " she said. We were both cracking up now. I had always loved an intelligent woman with a good sense of humor. "I just kept waiting. I was like, 'Please say that, sir, give me something, sir!'"

"Now, to be fair, when he walked in the room, I did say, 'Nigger, sit down.' So I started it," I said.

She was really laughing now, a genuine smile showing across her face. Just then Aubrey returned and picked up where he'd left off without missing a beat. I was starting to suspect this guy was fond of hearing himself talk. Still, I was enthralled. We both were. "So," he continued, "George Wallace gets elected governor of Alabama in 1962 by being this staunch segregationist, even though he had been a racial moderate. Being a racial moderate didn't work to get him elected, so he became this racial firebrand. But at the same time, he was elected in 1962, and, nationally, had become a bit of a laughingstock, because he came to personify the sort of red-faced, bellowing, um, spittle-laced Southern politician, spewing hatred about blacks. And then he began another shift.

"He began to shift away from white supremacy—y'know, 'segregation today, tomorrow, and forever'—to states' rights. And freedom of association. These coded terms. He really pioneered the expression of white supremacy in coded terms that could be defended as race-neutral.

"And then he pioneered in another area," he said ominously. "He pioneered the idea that you could flip the script on people who accuse you of racism. And you could accuse them of being the real racists."

"Wow," I said incredulously. "That came from George Wallace? I thought that came from Reddit."

Esperanza giggled. The hook had been baited.

"George Wallace in 1968 started saying, 'You know who the biggest bigots in the world are? They're the ones who accuse others of being bigots!' "

"So, is the GOP a modern-day George Wallace?" Esperanza asked.

"Pretty much," Aubrey said. "Yeah. Not just in the sense that they engage in race-baiting. But in the sense that many of them are social moderates shifting to the Right, because it's effective."

As I sat in my car, remembering these things, I couldn't help but think about Trump. Mr. Trench Coat had described the Donald to a T eight years before his run. Trump came across as an immigration-bashing carnival barker. But that's not who he was in fact, I'd always suspected. In fact, he was a thoughtful, strategic businessman who excelled at selling stuff. It was even more interesting to me because it felt like Trump was doubling-down. Like, I felt like other candidates would say one thing, and then they'd dog-whistle. And then you'd be like, 'Wow, he seems like a decent person, sure, he *says* certain stuff, but you know he's only talking about this.' With Trump, however, when he said that he wanted to build a wall, you know, and he gets challenged on it, he'd say, 'I'm gonna build it twice as high now that you challenged me!' Most politicians, when they got caught dog-whistling, start to backpedal.

Not Trump. It was quite blunt what he was doing, but it was still dog-whistling. Then I suddenly remembered the time, only a few weeks prior, when Trump, on CNN, feigned ignorance of having knowledge of the former grand wizard of the Ku Klux Klan. "Well, I have to look at the group," the former host of *The Apprentice* had said in his usual word salad, as CNN's Jake Tapper peppered him with probing questions.

"I'm just talking about David Duke and the Ku Klux Klan," Tapper had replied, amazingly, with a straight face.

Do you need a minute, Donald? I remember wanting Tapper to ask him. *Tell you what, why don't we go to commercial while Trump Googles 'K-K-K,' and we'll be back to discuss it.*

By the time it turned eight, we'd progressed to other subjects. Eventually, Mr. Trench Coat looked at his watch and excused himself politely. Now it was just Esperanza and me. My mother, who'd been occupied in another part of the room most of that evening, motioned to me as if to say it was time to go. In the library, I turned and faced the young woman, wondering how to ask for her number without seeming too eager. I never wore a wedding ring, anyway, so no worries there. "Well," I said, "I enjoyed our conversation."

"Yes! Me too!" she told me. But she continued talking, and so I was forced to listen. Not that I minded. She said, "I thought that was so fascinating about George Wallace. What do you do for a living?"

"What do I do," I repeated, sounding like a moron.

"Are you working right now?"

"Oh, yes. I work as a travel agent for federal government employees."

"That sounds interesting."

"It is."

It had been a time when I had been proud to answer that question. I hadn't known at the time that I'd be fired from that job just a few weeks later. I said, "I consider it the best job I've ever had."

"Cool. I work in a bank. Equity loan department," she said. And while I was processing this, she gave a little laugh and said, "Doesn't sound half as interesting as what you do!"

"Well, I don't like to brag," I said. "I do talk to some bigwigs in the upper echelons of power every now and then, though."

She made a face, you'd think she'd just been tasered. "And you make their reservations for them?" she asked.

"Flight, car, and hotel. We usually deal with employees of the Department of Labor, Bureau of Indian Affairs, that sort of stuff," I told her.

"What do you like to do in your spare time?"

"Oh, I like to collect comic books and draw," I told her. Then it dawned on me that that hadn't sounded badass enough, so I added, "I also dabble in writing. I'm sort of a double threat."

"Comic books, eh? Wow...you're really letting your nerd flag fly, huh?"

"Actually, it's a geek flag," I said knowledgeably. "Nerds are more academically-inclined, while we geeks are just superpassionate about our hobbies."

"I see. And the people who know and care about this difference are called...?"

"I believe 'dork' is the preferred nomenclature."

Esperanza laughed then, tilting her head back. I took in the moment, reflecting on the fact that this was the kind of conversation I could never have with my wife. It wasn't Darlene's fault, though, in all fairness. I put on an expression that I hoped would hide the pain.

"So," she said, finally. "You're from Chicago?"

I had wanted to ask her more about what it was like to support a bossypants feminist who showed open contempt for traditional models of womanhood, but it was getting late. "Huh?" I said, again sounding like an idiot. Then I realized she was looking at my White Sox cap. "Yes, originally," I told her.

Damn, I wanted to talk to her longer! I glanced at her ring finger. Nada. In a funny way, though, that made me feel even worse. My chest got a hurtful, heavy feeling that settled around my heart. She was a clock, I thought to myself, with hands above my world. There was some dark genie inside me that I very much hesitate to call a disease which drove me to flirt. Even though I had toddlers at home and a young wife whom I'd been teaching to drive a car around that time. All of a sudden, the hauntingly suave words and melody of Donell Jones's R&B ode to needing a breather, called *Where I Wanna Be*, floated through my head involuntarily.

Weeks passed after our meet-cute, and the two of us, Esperanza and I—she'd told me to call her *Q* for short, because of her maiden name, Quarrelah—managed to navigate our way through a flirtation of sorts in the days leading up to the convention. I sensed its ultimate doom, but craved the new attention. Things began to get serious. Then the firing. I had lost my job again, this time, a good-paying one. My already fragile confidence was decimated. We did end up sharing a hotel room for the convention in June, but the entire trip was a disaster. I don't know what I had been expecting, but I'll take the blame. After the convention, we drove back to San Antonio in her car in complete and memorably awkward silence.

Yet, many years later, we would bury the hatchet and become close again, and today I count her as one of my dearest friends.

Still, at that time, as far as I was convinced, Pink Floyd had been wrong. *"Hanging on in quiet* desperation" was not just an English thing.

At 11:31 that night, I was still sitting in the front seat of the Outlander. Starvin' like Marvin, stuck like Chuck. It was dark and cold outside. I looked at my smartphone's battery life. It said twelve percent. The iPad was even worse at eight percent. Darlene's check still had not been deposited, contrary to expectations, and pretty soon I wasn't going to be able to communicate with her, or anybody, for that matter. I glanced at the odometer. The little digital blue line that indicated the level of gas in the tank was non-existent. I'd been reluctant to turn on the ignition and get some heat flowing through the car, as cold as it was, fearing that I'd deplete whatever gasoline I still had in the tank.

As it was, I knew, at the very least, that my eight-day streak of picking up my kids in front of Mama's house each morning, without fail, was going to be broken the next morning. I couldn't get them to their school on Friday driving on fumes. So, there was that. On top of that, Darlene had been giving me the runaround all day, insisting she had no idea why her paycheck had never been deposited to our debit card. I was, truly, at the end of my tether.

And hungry as fuck.

Throughout the afternoon and evening, my several texts to Darlene, via Messenger, seemed to fall on deaf ears. At 8:28 that night, just a few hours earlier, I'd sent her the following message: *"Sorry. I know it's not your fault. I guess I'm still getting used to the fact that with this job for some reason they don't release your checks like Walmart used to do. After today, I'm going to stop getting my hopes up that it will ever come like it's supposed to. Is everything ok over there? Are you off tomorrow, because we need to go get the taxes done."*

She had replied, at long last. *"In the afternoon,"* she texted back. *"Tomorrow is my mandatory work day."*

"You work in the afternoon, or you're off in the afternoon?"

"I'm off in the afternoon."

"Ok," I said.

At 9:26, I texted, *"Are the kids ok?"*

"Yes, honey," Darlene replied.

More silence.

By this time it was obvious: there wasn't going to be any check. At least not today, I remember thinking, in the few minutes of that day that were left. And my eating that day had not been like either a rich man or a poor one—I wasn't eating, *period*. Darlene had missed her calling, I thought. She should've been a politician, as good as she was at stonewalling.

Given the waning power of my devices, and the fact that I was going to soon be incognito as a result—or, in my case, incog-*Negro*—I decided to make one last valiant attempt to find out what the hell was going on with my wife's check. I knew she had to be at work before dawn, as usual, the following day. At 11:17, I texted:

"Are you awake?"

"I'm trying to sleep," she replied.

"I need to talk to you," I wrote.

"I have a 3:55 clock-in."

"Can you just answer the phone please when I call?"

There was no reply, so I took it as a Yes. I dialed her number. Each ring seemed to go on forever. Finally, she picked up. There was silence on the other end. I said, "Hello?"

"Hello."

"What the hell is going on, Darlene? You know I'm out here with no gas and no food and my devices are just about out of power. I'm not going to be able to pick the kids up for school in the morning! Tell me, one more time, what your supervisor told you about why your check didn't come today."

I'll tell the truth. I can't really remember her exact answer. It was some gibberish, if memory serves, about some technical problem. It wasn't a long conversation, I know that. Her voice, groggy and tired, was barely understandable. I sat there in the empty parking lot of Kohl's, the clothing store, up to my neck in junk, the kind you accumulate when your car becomes your de facto residence in between more permanent—and suitable—places of habitation.

She waved my words away. Invisible, callous hands, unmoved by my plight. "I have to get some sleep," she said. "Goodnight."

She ended the call.

From the passenger seat, I lifted my iPad—the most expensive thing I had in my possession. I could've pawned it for quick cash (I'd paid a grip for it and could get some decent coin for it if I had), but I liked carrying it around. Besides, there were no pawn shops open at that hour, anyway.

Something wasn't right. Something didn't add up. That warm rain on my foot had become a deluge. I was swimming in piss. Even John Stockton couldn't assist me. I suddenly felt bad, almost crying bad.

I opened up the employee app for Darlene's job that I had on my phone. I'd been checking it all day, but this time, I decided to look at it again. If it isn't ready. Then I'll have to wait. And so will you. This is my job. Not yours. Her password remained permanently populated below her username, so I had no issues getting access to her pay stub information. It opened. To the left, there were several links: Employee Overview, Check Stub, Payroll Summary, Benefits Summary, Password Change. Stuff like that. I clicked on the link which said Direct Deposit.

I was jolted out my despondency by what appeared. Darlene and I had always shared our finances, mind you. *Mi income es su income.* Whether they were my disability benefits or her hard-earned paychecks, whatever funds were left over after all the bills had been paid belonged to both of us, regardless of its origin. Ultimately, it was for the children. Yet here I was, looking at my phone's screen near midnight, alone and famished, maybe confused or just refusing to believe what I was seeing. The sight brought me dangerously close to tears again, and while I fought them off, I looked at my iPad, verified our joint account number, and checked it against the one on my smartphone's screen.

Next to our account and routing number within the Direct Deposit link, the word 'Inactive' was displayed, over to the right, in the same row under a column titled Account Status. And below our account information was another account which I didn't recognize. At first.

Over to the right in that row, under Account Status, was the word 'Active.'

And then I knew.

It hit me like a gut punch. Staring back at me, from my phone's screen, was the clearest evidence yet—not that I needed any, having been married to her for so long—of my wife's horrifically difficult relationship with the truth.

And the person, her eager and unlikely accomplice, who'd conspired with her to divert the money to a place where I didn't have access, leaving me to rot.

Mama.

10

I WAS WAY EARLY when I got there, so I just parked in front on the curb near where Darlene's car was and watched the house. A lot of the houses on the street were still under construction, and there were about a million pieces of lumber lying around waiting for the Mexicans to show up and assemble them. Some of the homes, though, were occupied already. Houses with two stories, houses with verandas, houses with sun porches, houses with stoops and railings, houses that looked like their owners would be assholes if you knew them. It was a really nice neighborhood, though. In a way, it was kind of depressing, too, because you kept wondering how much better their lives probably were. You figured most of them had decent credit. Folks that always talk about how much money they have in their 401(k)s. Folks that attend NASCAR and eat happily at Applebee's and scream "*Lock her up!*" at Trump rallies. Folks who use the word *summer* as a verb, in houses where they keep their summer condoms, citrusy-flavored for a more refreshing summer experience. Folks that blame the victim whenever a black guy gets shot in the back while face-down on the ground by a cop over a traffic stop. Folks that would certainly call the police on my ass if they woke up and looked out their front windows to see a black man arguing with a white woman in the middle of the night on my mother's front lawn—But I have to be careful about that. I mean about thinking certain people are racists. Especially cops. When I was in Chicago, before I entered the Navy, I lived briefly with the second face on my Mount Rushmore of Great Loves of My Life, Masara Cunningham. She was the most beautiful brownskin girl I'd ever seen and all, but her mother had been a raging alcoholic. Masara had a six-year-old daughter named Ashley, and she lived with us, too, in the very first apartment I'd ever had: a studio efficiency across the street from Chicago's famous Museum of Science and Industry. Naturally, I never told Masara I thought her mother had a drinking problem. I mean you don't just go up to your girlfriend of a few weeks and say, "Your mother is a falling down drunk." But I shared my studio with Masara and her young daughter for a whole summer, even though they drove me half crazy, just because the mother was such a terrific lay, the best I'd ever had up to that point. One day, Masara's mother stole five eggs to feed herself and her other grandchildren. Instead of arresting her, this white cop and his colleagues gave her two truckloads of food for her and the grandkids. So, I don't know about cops. Maybe you shouldn't assume all of them would just throw you in jail soon as look at you. They serve and protect us, most of them, and maybe they're secretly all good Samaritans or something. Who the hell knows? Not me.

I sat on the driver's side bolted to the seat, trying to stay awake. I was cold and hungry. There hadn't been enough gas in the tank for me to turn on the engine and run the heat for very long during the day. The tips of my toes and fingers were already numb, and every time I exhaled, my breath came out like little clouds. My body odor rose to my face and, mingled with the stench of urine and sweat flaring my nostrils, nauseated me. I felt fricasseed.

Finally, Darlene started waking up to get ready for work. I knew because I saw her turn on the light in the guest room, which faced the front of the house. I knew her routine. After all, I'd lived there myself just a few weeks before. I just had to see for myself. I had to see if she was actually going to come out of the house, walk to her car, and drive off to work, all the while knowing (or *thinking*, anyway) her husband was out there somewhere with no food, no gas, on the outside looking in. The funny part was, I felt like Michael Corleone. I'm crazy. Sitting outside the house in my car for about three hours, I felt angrier with her than I'd ever been. I rehearsed over and over again what I'd say to her when she finally did emerge, and how I'd say it. If ever there was a time I needed to remain self-controlled, this was it.

I was getting tired; the closer it came time to confront Darlene, the more a sense of fatigue enveloped me. I looked down at my clothes; they were damp and crumpled. I was shivering.

I saw Darlene through the blinds: blond hair, blue eyes; a sturdy, innocent face often afflicted by rosacea. Hate flooded me as I looked at her Outlander Sport, just one year older than mine, parked a few feet in front of me, thinking how different—and better—her life had been since I'd come into the picture so many years before. And how she had replied when I'd asked if the kids were okay. Yes, honey.

Honey, my ass.

At 3:06 in the morning, the moment of truth had arrived. Darlene turned off the light in the guest room and prepared to leave the house. I exited my car and took a spot in a chair just outside the guest room window. It was positioned in such a way as to preclude being noticed in the dark if you didn't have a reason to look that way as you were going to your car.

She came out of the house. I heard the front door shut. Then I saw her walk toward her vehicle.

I got up from the chair I'd been sitting in. As she walked across the grass to the curb, I drew up close behind her. The wind swept against the cars and the house, whistling, then whispered into silence. Except for the streetlamps, it was pitch black outside. And dead quiet. When she was almost to her car, I opened my mouth and shattered the stillness.

"You and my mother have to answer for your lies, Darlene."

She whirled around. I saw her bewildered eyes. She stood staring, mouth open. Her teeth nearly fell out of her mouth. In the pallid yellow glimmer of the street lamp we faced each other. A stiff gust of winter wind blew over us, rustling our clothes. I had my hand behind my back, holding the iPad. Darlene stopped.

"Goodness! Don't be afraid. I'm not going to hurt you."

She looked guilty as hell. My very presence condemned her. Yet her expression held no trace of wanting to atone for her guilt. There was no contrition, only fear.

"I don't want to talk to you," she mumbled.

"But what have I done to you?" I asked desperately.

I had done nothing to her, at least not recently; and it was my innocence—coupled with her indifference—that made my anger percolate even more. My hands clenched into fists.

"I don't want to talk to you," she said again.

I felt that if Darlene continued to stand there and pretend not to know why I was there, I might have to strangle her right there, in spite of myself, and tell the kids Mommy died. I began to tremble, all over; her lips parted and her eyes widened.

"Darlene, I'm going to ask you the same question I asked you almost four hours ago. I'm going to give you a chance to tell me the truth, something which I know is hard for you. But keep in mind before you do, though," I said, revealing the iPad, "I already have the truth right here on this screen.

"So be careful how you answer."

I swiftly moved behind her, in between her and her vehicle so she had to get past me to enter it. She whirled again, facing me. She stopped: her face was devoid of color.

"I'm going to ask you again: Do you know why your check never came?"

I don't really remember what she said next, to be honest. Whatever it was, it couldn't have been good, I can tell you that, based on what I did next. On her key chain, which she held down at her side, were keys to both her car and mine. Without thinking or knowing which key I was grabbing, I reached for the key ring in one rapid motion. We tussled for a moment, but I prevailed. Somehow a key came off and into my hand. Without knowing which one I had snatched—hers or mine—I raised my hand and depressed the Unlock button.

There was a *CHK-CHK* sound, and two yellow lights silently flashed twice behind me in the night.

It was hers. Thank you, God.

"Get in," I said. "I'm taking you to work."

"*Noo*," she said. She cared about that damn job more than anything else. I swear she did. I can't say I blamed her, actually. After years of working as a lowly cashier making peanuts, she was now getting more green than Earth Day, working as a driver, and her monthly income had been consistently exceeding mine. And she was feeling herself. She busted her hump working a lot of overtime, to be sure. She had the pay stubs to prove it. I'd soon learn that hadn't been all she'd been doing at work, however, and that my paranoia had not been without a basis. But, in this moment—as we stood there in the middle of the night on my mother's lawn like characters from a tragedy, our doomed roles predestined from, it felt like, before the world's foundation, the world entire completely oblivious to the sad saga that was presently unfolding under a night devoid of stars—I didn't know any of that. All I knew at that moment was that, at some point in the previous few weeks or months, she must've stopped giving a damn about me, and I had been too stupid to see it. Like Paul, the scales had fallen from my eyes, and my long road to Damascus was about to begin.

Obediently, she got in on the passenger side.

In me, as I sped down the highway, was a cold, driving will. Darlene had made her play. Now I was making mine. It was a thirty-minute drive to where she worked, which was located near the airport, so I had a lot of time to vent. This had been the first time we'd seen each other in almost two weeks. These were the rhythms of our marriage, playing themselves out over and over again: violence and apathy; moments of intense desire and abstract brooding; periods of white-hot anger and chilly silence. *This little bitch!* I thought. A hysterical rage seized me. I railed at her at the top of my lungs, at times going hoarse as I turned to scream at her while I clutched the steering wheel.

She still didn't say anything. That had been par for the course for most of our union whenever I lost my temper. I didn't like myself much in these moments. I'm a peaceful person. But there was something about Darlene that made me this way. It could've been the fact that somewhere deep inside I'd resented all the years I'd felt like a father to her more than a husband, all the years we'd been calling each other silly nicknames as a substitute for intelligent conversation, all the years I'd spent shackled to this woman laboring under the misplaced belief that a two-parent home was the only way to give my children a happy childhood.

The kind I'd always wanted.

I stared at her, recalling how she had lied to me for an entire day for no reason she cared to articulate. An image of blood had come before my eyes and terror rose in me hotly.

"You want me to hit you?"

I lifted my fist. She flinched.

"Tony, please! Please don't!"

"What! So you get to do whatever you want to me, and I'm supposed to just bend over and take it? You didn't think I had enough gas to get over here, did you? Surprise! What'd you expect, Darlene? You think I'm that stupid, that I wasn't going to figure out what you and Mama did? You insult my intelligence, and that makes me very angry."

Michael Corleone would never have gone off like this, but then again, I had dropped all pretense of trying to be him back at the crib. He always kept his cool, that one. Well, come to think of it, I guess he did have his moments. There was that time in the kitchen from *The Godfather Part III* where he said, 'Every time I try to get out, *they pull me back in!*" And there were a few other times like that. So I guess you could say I was in good company, depending on how you looked at it. Although I can't say aspiring to emulate and maintain the poise and equilibrium of a fictional murderer and La Cosa Nosta chieftain was anything to crow about.

"Darlene! Say something, dammit!"

There was no answer. She was huddled in the passenger seat, whiter than the dome of the U.S. Capitol. I clutched her arm and squeezed it tightly.

"You don't give a fuck about me anymore? Is that it?"

"Just get me to work."

My clenched fist suddenly swept upward in a tight arc and struck her square in her left eye.

She fell backward; the back of her head hit the passenger side window. She lifted her arms in self-defense as I raised my fist again in a menacing way.

"Don't! Tony, please! I'm sorry!"

"Oh, now you're sorry! You're sorry, all right. You are the worst mistake I've ever made. I wish I'd never met you."

A prominent bruise was becoming quickly visible around her eye socket, even in the darkness. A sensation of fear settled on me like a cloak, and it mingled with the fury while the shadow of an overpass loomed over us as we sped through the night.

"Put your shades on," I told her. "Now." She reached into her purse and produced these giant, Greta Garbo-type sunglasses with dark brown lenses the size of a small Buick. *They'll have to do, for now,* I thought. She put them on.

When we got to her job, I did something very childish and stupid. I was smoking a joint to try to calm my nerves, and when her hand reached for the door handle, I blew smoke in her face. I don't remember if I meant to, but I did it.

After she was gone, I'd started to feel bad about what I'd done. I felt a sense of foreboding, too, as I drove back to the

Hotel Atwater. Like it was going to come back to haunt me somehow. It wasn't a good feeling, particularly since traffic had slowed to a crawl under the pinkish sky and an endless sea of commuters clogged the 410 Loop as the sun steadily rose above the horizon line. My mother. What a piece of work. I'd deal with her. I suddenly had an idea for the title of my next book, if I ever got around to trying to write another one, and I'd call it *Get a Load of This Shit.*

The self-loathing which had begun to oppress me on my way to my mother's house had now become so acute that I longed somehow to part the traffic like Moses and drive off somewhere far away to escape the torture.

It wasn't all anger I felt, however. Sorrow and grief overshadowed me. I felt betrayed. As my hands gripped the steering wheel under a brightening sky, my mind helplessly drifted back to some of the good times Darlene and I had shared: sitting up in bed watching our recorded *stories*—a fridge full of groceries, enabling us to *eat like kings,* as she used to say— while Dusty nestled between us. Sunday dinners as a family at the townhouse, sitting at our perfectly square black dining room table while I led the four of us in the saying of grace, whatever car we had at the time during those eight bittersweet years parked just outside the broken blinds behind Madison's chair; watching Jacob in his miniature car—a Ford F-150, for which his mom and I'd paid $300—and the crunching, motoring sound it made as he drove happily up and down the narrow driveway between the low buildings of the complex we lived in.

We hadn't always been short on tenderness.

After I had gotten the kids to school, I drove to a local park to clear my mind. A cold wind gusted down Potranco

Road, and the wet rain had already started to fall. My toes felt numb in my shoes, and the hunger in my belly had started gnawing at me again. My nose was running. I wiped it on my sleeve, no longer caring how it looked. I must've looked like I'd been to hell and back because a passerby came over to me and gave me a dollar.

I looked up at him. "I'm not homeless," I told him squarely. "I'm married."

BOOK II

Free Agent

1

I WOKE UP ON THE THIRD DAY and looked around. The room had white walls, and there were blue-green curtains on the window. A flat screen TV was mounted high on the wall. The sheets smelled fresh, and there were several soft-cover Bibles, different versions, on the nightstand next to the bed. I felt my body. It was hard to tell it was still there because it wasn't cold and it wasn't aching. Not even my belly, which had been empty now for so long.

I felt like praying or something, while I was there in bed, but I couldn't do it. The previous year I had spent six months memorizing all one hundred seventy-six verses of Psalm 119 from the Bible. It had been one of the hardest things I'd ever undertaken. And one of my proudest accomplishments. I had probably spent hundreds of hours the previous year turning those verses over and over in my head, when I was going to sleep and when I was waking up, when I was depressed and when I was euphoric, when I was going out and when I was coming in. That is not to say I am an especially religious person. If you want to know the truth, I can't stand religious people. Take my mother, for instance. When you're in the car with her, she plays this AM station that plays all this old-timey Gospel music the way black people sing it. God, I hate that. They have all these Holy Ghost voices when they sing and sound so self-righteous. Even though I liked the idea of Christ, I could see how a lot of people thought the Bible was responsible for a lot of bad things in the world. Or maybe it's just us that keep getting it wrong. Maybe the Bible was the perfect Blueprint, what with its commands to love your neighbor and not covet your neighbor's wife and stuff, but we—His people—are about as much use to Him as a back pocket on a T-shirt. And then when you put your earbuds on to zone out and listen to your *own* music, she'd say, "Take those off, I like for people to listen to what *I'm* listening to when they're in my car." You had to sit there and listen to her try to sing the words even when you were feeling depressed. You'd end up feeling even more depressed, as you stare out the passenger side window getting some old-time religion of your own—by praying for deliverance.

Anyway, when I was in bed, I couldn't pray. What I did do was, I started thinking about that old 80s song by Michael McDonald and James Ingram, "Yah Mo B There." I'm crazy. I'm sure you've either heard it or know it from "The 40 Year Old Virgin." You know, the part where Paul Rudd tells the manager, "I would rather listen to Fran Drescher for eight hours than have to listen to Michael MacDonald. Nothing against him, but if I hear 'Yah Mo B There' one more time, I'm gonna *'yah mo'* burn this place to the ground!" I sat up in bed, thinking about it hard. Unlike the unwashed masses, I knew the song was actually a shout out to God. Yah is a shortened version of the name Yahweh, or YHWH, which means God in

Hebrew. So the song literally means, "God will be there," and can be interpreted as "God be with you." The idea behind the song was that nothing can save mankind except the Father in heaven. Now, I liked that idea, and I even fancied the quaint notion that I had somewhat of a middling-to-intimate relationship with this Person.

All of a sudden, while I was sitting there with my knees bent and resting on them, I started humming the tune under my breath.

I could get with the idea of a loving God, for some reason. Plus, that tune had a catchy beat, and it was easy to dance to. Yet, despite my joy of living in America in the age of Obama—and my confidence in his leadership—many said the end was near. Sometimes, it was hard to argue with them. America was having so many disasters and tragedies lately you'd've thought it was built on thousands of ancient Indian burial grounds or something! And, so, the idea of a loving Father who would come and save us from ourselves appealed to me, even though I still liked to believe we had a lot of time left to try to get it right. Besides, I wanted to be around decades from now to see what the general consensus of historians would be about Obama's two-term presidency. I was convinced he would one day be lionized like Lincoln and FDR, but it was going to take the perspective of history to render that verdict. In the meantime, I wanted this present system of things to stick around long enough to see what airports, what battleships, what aircraft carriers, what schools might be named after him, and privately wondered if he would one day be appointed by a future President to the Supreme Court. I even went so far as to mentally imagine his face being carved into the granite face of Mount Rushmore: men in hard hats, suspended hundreds of feet in the air, etching his already steely visage into the stone, upheld by the giant lattice work of metal scaffolding resembling a large, square iron spider's web. Some leading black intellectuals, like Cornell West, criticized him as a Republican in sheep's clothing—like he got Merrill Lynched or something—but not me. I was a big fan.

After I was gone, the Hotel Atwater was no doubt completely silent.

I would've bet you dollars to donuts that Mama was lingering in her bedroom, thinking only one thought: He's gone off the deep end. Out to pasture. Goodbye, sanity.

She'd walk slowly from her bedroom into the kitchen, thinking first that Satan had gotten into me, her son. She'd think she needed to double her time in her "war room," which is what she called this small closet in the second guest room where she often fasted and prayed. She thought of prayer as a gymnasium of the soul. She'd think she knew well the Spirit's power. She'd think she hadn't done anything wrong, and that her son was the crazy one for thinking a little head's up would've been nice before she and her daughter-in-law pulled the rug out from under him.

I imagined her congratulating herself on her subterfuge. "He brought this on himself," she was saying, but it came out sounding more holier-than-thou than empathetic. I pictured her sitting upright in bed with satisfaction as she stubbed out her joint in the overflowing ashtray.

Then I remembered where I was. I was at a hotel called the Quality Inn off 410. The kids were with me. They were presently down the hall looting the vending machine. When I had gotten them from school after dropping them off the previous Friday, I'd kept them with me. No way in hell was I taking them back to their grandmother's house, not after the stunt she'd just pulled.

Unsuccessfully, I might add. The money never ended up making it to her account, after all! It turned out Darlene's salary had been issued as a paper check that day since they hadn't made the switch in time for it to take effect. It was a good thing, too, because the little money I'd been able to keep from it—after first commandeering the paper check from my wife to clean up the mess they'd caused—had enabled me and the kids to stay here. Their mother had been with us the first night, that Friday.

That hadn't been a good night, either.

The kids heard Daddy screaming and yelling some things he'd much rather not repeat if you don't mind. All four of us in the same hotel room: two queen size beds, the kids and Mommy all sleeping in one; me, just inches away in the other.

If you can call what I did sleeping.

No, what I did actually end up doing was almost having a panic attack. Right there in the middle of the night with my family, the three of them, peacefully asleep only a few inches away.

The light from the TV threw a ghostly pall over the dark room, and all I could think about, as I lay awake, was how close my wife and mother had almost come to shutting me out of my kids' lives, forever.

And the thought filled me with horror.

I flung the covers off me violently when the thought hit home and paced the dark room back and forth hysterically, my heart beating like a hammer in my chest. I kept seeing my mother's face suspended in the dark like a Star Wars hologram of the Emperor, even recalling with dread the text I had received from her just as I was pulling up in front of her house in Darlene's car (while she was still ignorant of what'd happened on her lawn just a few hours earlier), which said: "*I have ten dollars. Do you need it this morning?*" To which I incredulously replied: "*Probably, considering the fact that the deposit that I was desperately waiting for yesterday was never going to come because my loving mother did not inform me that she and my wife had arranged to transfer it into your account. Once again thank you for the communication.*"

I also added, for good measure: "*And you knew full well that I was waiting for that because there are several bills that need to be paid and all the time you knew that I was never going to receive it.*"

I confess to disregarding the rules of good diction in that moment. As the disintegration of my family commenced in earnest, I may be forgiven if the proper placement of commas was not my chief concern. But contrary to what it may sound like from everything I've told you so far, I did love my mother. Really. I knew it hadn't been easy for her as a single mom, raising three very different kids from two different "baby daddies," and all the familial turmoil such an arrangement comes with. As an adult, I would unfailingly bawl whenever Tupac's *Dear Mama* came on the radio, or especially Boys II Men's simply titled *Mama*.

That one got me every time. I'm somewhat of a crybaby if you haven't already figured that out. The water cooler scuttlebutt was, for a straight guy, I sure did have my feminine side in a chokehold! Some might've even said I had "homosexual tendencies." Nothing, however, could have been further from the truth. I loved women. Idolized them. Fantasized about them. Trouble was, I never could seem to find the right one. Women are creatures I don't understand too hot. I mean, a lot of them wear fake nails, fake hair, fake tits, fake other stuff, but then say they want a *real* man. Okay. Good luck with that. I mean that's my biggest trouble. In my mind, I'm a pretty decent guy. The kind women said they wanted when they were girls. Somewhere along the line I'd found, however, many of them had switched their preference, opting to check off the "bad boy" box. Now, growing up I was many things, but bad boy definitely wasn't one of them. Damn stereotypes. It stinks that it's like that, but it just is.

Recently I'd made a rule for myself that I was through with the opposite sex because, in the end, they always break your heart. I broke that rule—or, rather, hadn't made it yet, the day after I had my panic attack.

On Saturday, I picked up my phone to find a text from a family acquaintance on Facebook Messenger. "*If you and the kids want to come over and do laundry, you can. Lizzie has an appointment at two for her eyes, but you all can come over and hang out.*"

Carrie Armstrong.

She was this blonde, dog-loving lady a whole lot different from my wife, and our daughters were classmates. And best friends. Or "besties," as they liked to call themselves. She'd seen my Facebook posts about the dire straits the kids and I had found ourselves in, and she was reaching out. I really liked Carrie, and so even though I wasn't in the best mood, I was eager to see if I could somehow move out of the friend zone she'd had me pinned in for the previous twelve months. "*Okay, thanks,*" I replied. "*I'll probably take you up on that.*"

"*Where's Darlene?*"

"*Don't know, don't care,*" I said. "*I'm going to divorce her, and nothing will change my mind this time.*"

"*I saw your posts on Facebook,*" she wrote. "*What the hell is going on?*"

"*It's a long story. Too much to go into over Messenger. Probably better if I tell you in person. Did you know 'dammit I'm mad' spelled backwards is still 'dammit I'm mad' ?*"

"*LOL,*" she replied. "*Surprised you had time to be on Facebook considering all you and the kids are going through.*"

"*Guilty as charged,*" I texted back. "*As much as I used to get on Darlene's case for always having her head in her phone, I'm no better. Smartphones really are revolutionizing the way people get hit by cars.*"

"*Ah. How are my godbabies?*"

Carrie was the unofficial godmother to my kids, too.

I said, "*They're fine. My kids are very resilient. Just like Lizzie. I know she's been through a lot, too. But this is breaking my heart. I never wanted this.*"

"*I have extra beds. You all can come here if you need a place to crash.*"

"*Aww, that's sweet. I'll have to let you know about that,*" I texted, "*because I have to let the front desk know soon if we're going to extend our stay, but you're giving me options, and I appreciate it.*"

"*I meant, if you all want to take a nap.*"

"*Oh! LOL. Okay, thank you! Duly noted.*"

"*Have to avoid the appearance of evil. I don't think you would like it if a male were staying at your house with Darlene while you were gone. He wouldn't either.*"

The *he* she was referring to was her live-in boyfriend, a beefy Hispanic guy named Louie. I'd never met him, just seen pictures. That's another thing that killed me. Whenever I came around, she was always talking about *the appearance of evil.* As professing Christians, we'd had a number of deep conversations about the nature of faith and stuff like that over the course of the previous year. Apparently, her concern about the appearance of evil didn't extend to the fact that she'd been living for many years with a man that was not her husband. Not that there was anything wrong with that. It just struck me as a little hypocritical, that's all.

"*No,*" I said, "*you're absolutely right. I misunderstood. No worries, we're on the same page.*"

Only we weren't on the same page. But I knew full well what Carrie's response to an advance would be; she had rebuffed me before.

I said, "*I was telling the kids we should make this a tradition, spending every MLK weekend at your house.*"

"*Oh, that's right!*" Carrie texted. "*I forgot. You all were here last year at this time.*"

"*That's the first time we ever came to your place. That was the same weekend as Danielle's birthday party.*"

"*Right. Time flies,*" she said. "*Well, get your butts over here.*"

Darlene had been with us that first time we'd gone to Carrie's; we'd gone as a family. This time, however, it would just be the kids and me. Carrie had not been stable herself, in many ways, with more issues than a *Sports Illustrated* subscription. That would've been good to remember before we went over there. But still, at least we'd found something to do with ourselves on Martin Luther King's Day.

The kids and I were staying at the Quality Inn, less than three miles from my mother's. Carrie lived on the outskirts of the city; it would take thirty-some minutes to get there. We were in no rush; besides, there was something I had to do. First,

I grabbed a Coke and returned to the room, where the kids were watching Cartoon Network. We had to check out by eleven, unless I could pony up eighty dollars for another night. The kids were oblivious, of course, as always. I never told them about things like that if I could help it. I felt like Atlas—the weight of the world on my shoulders—doing my best to shield them from the penalty for my pride.

But to them I was Superman.

By now the sky had become cloudy. I set my Coke can on the nightstand between the two beds and swung my legs to the floor. "Hey kids," I said. "Daddy has to leave the room for a few minutes."

"Where are you going?" Danielle asked.

"I have to go see a man about a dog."

"*Nooo!*" Jacob said. He had an inordinate fear of dogs. Cats weren't too high on his list, either.

"I'm just kidding," I said. "I'm just going down the hall to talk to the manager. I might start working here soon. Wouldn't that be cool?"

"Yeah," Danielle said, smiling.

"You all gonna be fine by yourselves for a few minutes?"

"Can I be in charge?" Jacob asked.

"You're the oldest," I said. Usually, I'd put Danielle in charge, but he'd asked first; it was only fair.

I walked down the heavily carpeted hallway to the front desk. This was my third time trying to get a sit-down with the manager. Apparently, he was a busy man. I was hoping, frankly, to get a job there on the strength of my good looks and winning personality because, let's be honest, my resume had more gaps in it than the Grand Canyon. Not to mention I could, if they hired me, pay my past due room bill out of my first check. So I had the front desk clerk, Jerry, tell his manager about me. Eventually, he'd persuaded said manager to give me a brief interview. I'd only seen him once and in passing. He was Pakistani or something, I knew, but from what I'd gathered he spoke fluent English.

After a few minutes, he emerged from a door and motioned for me enter. He led me down a short hall to his office. If you could call it that. We were its only occupants. The small space was cluttered with outdated, unmeaning furniture, and crowded by hoarded, mismatched memorabilia. I had been hoping my balance had been the furthest thing from his mind.

I was out of luck.

"Mr. Hill," he said, closing the door behind us, "you gotta another payment for us?"

I entered after him, grinning like a schoolboy. "Yup," I said, "a one hundred fifty pound deposit of Tony Hill!"

"What?"

"Jerry told me you need a night auditor. That's right up my alley. *Shall we discuss compensation?* " I asked *way* too presumptuously.

He was playing ball, though, crossing briskly to his desk like a man about to get down to brass tacks.

I took a seat across from him, saying as I did (again presumptively), "It would be great if I could get off at seven in the morning, and not eight, y'know, so I can get my kids to school. But, hey, it's not a deal breaker."

"Right," he said, poker-faced. "So, why should the Quality Inn hire Tony Hill?"

I paused a moment, and then said, "What?"

"What would a Tony Hill bring to the Quality Inn?"

I laughed nervously. "I'd bring myself," I stuttered, "a-and my kids if I can't get off at seven." More nervous laughter. Maybe this guy didn't like the cut of my jib. He didn't say anything, so I continued babbling. "I'm a...I'm a real dependable employee, you know, um, I've got a pleasant personality, I'm relatively stable, and I've been told I'm quite the comedian."

"Comedian," he mumbled absently as he jotted something down on a notepad. And then I heard him say in an undertone, "Stable is a place where horses live." He looked back at me again and asked, "And, uh, where do you see yourself in five years? You got a five-year plan?"

Man, this immigrant had assimilated well! Apparently he had been expecting me to pull a bunny out of my hat, not just bring a bunny. "Five years? Uh, yeah, I hope to still be night auditing, only with a clone so he could sit in for me some nights." I followed this up with a lame attempt to mimic what I thought a clone might sound like. It was such a reach.

He leaned forward, folding his fingers together. He had one of those regretful looks on his face like how a politician looks when he gets caught in a sex scandal and has a press conference. "You are quite the comedian," he said. "Here's the thing, though. We're really not hiring at the moment."

"What?"

"Yeah, we're runnin' a tight ship right now."

"But Jerry told me you needed a night auditor right away!"

"He was just blowin' smoke up your ass," the manager said. "What's he gonna say, 'Your room bill is sky high and tomorrow you're out on your ass' in front of those beautiful kids of yours?"

"But I'm out of money!"

He slid away from his desk in his wheeled chair, getting up hastily. He crossed to his door and left me to trail behind him, begging for a second chance to make first impression. He said, throwing his words to me behind his back, "Tell you what. We'll keep your application on file."

"I don't want my application on file," I said desperately. Man, that's job search limbo! Look, uh, *macaca*," I said, dispensing with political correctness and racing to keep up with his brisk pace, "I want this job! I can do this job!" I swept in front of him, cutting him off, forcing him to stop and look at me. "Look, see," I said, flashing my biggest, phoniest smile, and adding a thumbs up for good measure, "Welcome to Quality Inn—how may I help you!"

Unconvinced, he tried to step past me, but I blocked him again. I lightly grabbed him by his shoulders and removed my Ray Bans so he could look me directly in the eyes. I pleaded, "Macaca, man, I am not leaving this hotel until you hire me! Now, we both know that I am the man for this job. *Look in my eyes!* You see my can-do spirit? Now I know you're thinkin'," I said with a gleam in my eye," *'Deep down inside, I know you're sayin', I'm gonna help this guy out of a jam!'* "

There was a phone on the wall nearby. He quietly turned away, picked it up, and said into it while looking at me, "Security."

2

BY THE TIME I GOT BACK to the room it was overcast, and a chilly rain was falling. The kids and I had to get the hell out of Dodge—with the Quality Inn in the role of Dodge. While the children packed, I texted Carrie and told her we were coming over sooner than expected. We loaded our things into the car, and we stole away like we, er, well, stole something. I adjusted the rear view mirror, glancing back at the kids, and said, "We're off!"

I gripped the steering wheel. It was easy to picture Carrie, smoky-eyed, breezy, with her ample bosom, full of smiles, which I knew covered a trace of sadness, the residue from the mysterious death of her autistic son, Christopher, just a few years earlier. She had helped me deal with Jacob's meltdowns many times, and his fear of dogs, which she kept as service animals to assist her in her own ongoing battle with mental illness. We had a lot in common. My funny Carrie, in whom I had confided, my legs looped over the couch cushions as I typed responses to her many messages, as Darlene and the kids also sat in the living room, absorbed in their devices, and oblivious.

Carrie, who had once driven me to the blood bank to show me how to get started donating my plasma for a little extra cash on the side, and who claimed, occasionally, to love me.

As a friend, of course.

How I became Carrie's friend: Danielle was having her eleventh birthday party—a sleepover—and Lizzie had been invited. Her mother brought her. Prior to that, I didn't know either of them from Adam's cat. Immediately when Carrie walks in our place she starts talking to Darlene and me a mile a minute about people we didn't know and situations we didn't understand. Eventually, however, we did learn the names of the main players in her soap opera: Steven and Melissa, her ex-husband and his new wife, with whom she was involved in a nasty custody battle.

Later, when she got to know me better, she said it was because I was, in her words, "a godly man" that she had let down her guard and shared with me her most intimate secrets. She said Louie abused her sometimes. A few months before, she had asked me, "Do they have any vacant units where you live?" She was finally going to leave him, and she had wanted my help. We fell out, though, during the planning stages, and we stopped talking. This was going to be the first time the kids and I had seen them in quite a while.

She had no clue how much I had hoped it—the move—would happen. An entree is always better with a side piece, was my thinking at the time. Thinking of my marriage the same way I thought of the number two combo at Popeye's. My illness—rearing its ugly head again.

Carrie lived in Alamo Heights, in a white clapboard Colonial that was a pretty decent size but shabby, on account of the small menagerie of dogs she had living rent-free there.

Even though I had only seen a glimpse of her face, I saw enough to notice she had cut her hair. Then, pulling into the driveway, I saw her. It was instant, simple as that.

It was Carrie Armstrong, who lived in the cul-de-sac on Bell Avenue. If there had been any question in my mind, it was answered by the way she looked when our eyes met. Her face was both plain and sultry, but it was marred, even while she anticipated our arrival, by an incessant grimace. Yet years of prayer and fasting had vanquished the proclivity to violence, leaving only the residue of passion readable in the contours of her face. *She must stand up to him*, I thought, while we exited the car and walked up the steps to the front door.

She looked worried and irritated. I started to speak to her. "We don't have a pot to piss in or a window to throw it out of," I was going to say in an undertone to prevent the kids from hearing. Then I stopped because I saw that she was not alone. She was with her daughter, Lizzie.

We all scampered inside.

The couch was a sleeper couch, still folded out from last night apparently, the blankets all twisted and disheveled. Someone was in the doghouse, in more ways than one. The sound of dogs' nails clicking and scratching against her hardwood floor was a constant sound. Background noise, really. She had a flat screen TV kitty-cornered over yonder surrounded on either side by a stand that held about fifty million DVDs of various Hollywood blockbusters. Two large metal cages filled with bowls of food for man's best friend, one in the living room and one in the kitchen, were on the lower level. The smell of wet canine nearly asphyxiated me.

Well, I make it sound worse than it was. It wasn't so bad. I think I was just at a low point that day. *Here I am*, I thought, *unable to feed my children, or myself, and with nowhere to go. Except here, where my only friend is a girl, one I'm secretly attracted to and afraid I might cross the line with.*

And destroy the friendship in the process. It had already happened once.

I think that had been my fault. She had been sending mixed signals, and I kept misinterpreting them. Or maybe she hadn't been sending mixed messages, and I was just a moron. And a dog. (But she was such a bone.) We had met at the crossroads of circumstance, back in those imprudent years when I was still on the hunt for the ideal (but secret) female friend—a willing culprit—with benefit package, often sabotaging myself in fruitless and never-ending attempts to merge just the right estrogen with my demanding and finicky testosterone.

My only goal in those foolhardy days was finding someone (other than my wife) who looked at me the same way Monica Lewinsky looked at Bill Clinton.

I told Carrie when we were alone, "Last Thursday, the reason Darlene's paycheck never came is because my mother and wife had secretly days before moved to have her paychecks deposited into my mother's account."

"Whoa! Are you serious?"

"As cancer. My mother said I brought it on myself because I stormed out of there two weeks ago," I said.

"Yeah, right."

And then...I don't know why I said this next thing. I'd been planning to tell the story just the way it happened, I swear. But what I said was, "And that's the reason I'm broke as a joke."

"Seriously?"

"Hell yeah!" I said. (For a second, I thought she was doubting my word. Better than telling her I had actually recovered the check and was already destitute again because I was terrible with money.)

"Your mother is a piece of work," Carrie said.

"Well, obviously they didn't succeed," I said, "in terms of them keeping it a secret. I can't believe Darlene did this to me. We were all looking forward to getting our tax return in a couple of weeks and getting our own place again, and being a family. Now she—they—have blown it all up."

We turned and sat down at the kitchen table. Her patio lights lit the backyard like glowing strands of yarn.

"So anyway," I said, sighing.

I felt this inward kind of despair, all at once, like, *What does it all mean? What does it all* mean? Then, in my vision, just for a moment, I saw a large mountain looming before me—the summit seemed unreachable. Then, as quickly as it appeared, it went away. "The kids are with me now," I said, quickly forgetting what I'd just seen, "and Darlene, as far as I know, has gone back to my mother's house. And that's that."

Carrie had served some coffee now, and she was facing me. For a woman with such a boyish figure, she had awfully large breasts, a long, fleshy line of cleavage showing through her tank top—to the point that if we'd been playing Monopoly she'd definitely bogard the Community Chest—and her eyebrows were thin, arched, above her bright blue eyes. She said, "Tony. Would you like to stay the night?"

"Who, me? Us?"

"You know I'd love to have you. You can help me take the dogs to get their shots in the morning."

(*I'd love for you to have me, too*)

"I appreciate it," I said. "And I'd be happy to help you."

Then I took her folded hands in mine and squeezed as a sign of gratitude and got up from the table.

Slick, Willy

"*Something tragic has happened,*" I texted Carrie later, after I'd taken the kids out for ice cream. I was driving.

Twenty minutes later, she responded. "*I'm on a dinner date. What's up?*"

"*It's too much to go into if you're busy. I'll have to tell you when you have time.*" I may have been exaggerating, blowing things out of proportion, but I'd gotten a text from my mother that evening saying Darlene hadn't come home the night before, and she was just now telling me. I texted Carrie, "*I can tell you're busy. I don't know what's going to happen to me and the kids. Goodbye.*"

Two hours later, she responded, "*Ok, headed home. What's going on?*"

"*Your dinner date seemed more important than the tragedy the kids and I are dealing with.*"

"*Wow. I have been there this weekend for you and I take one day for my relationship and legal issues, and you act like I don't give a shit.*"

I was steering with my left hand, and I'm right-handed. The kids said there had been a yellow caution sign, but I was going too fast to notice.

"*The kids and I are dealing with a tragedy regarding their mom,*" I added, as Danielle gripped the dashboard. "*It's ok. Your business is important, I know. But I assure you when I used the word* 'tragic' I wasn't exaggerating. I don't know if your dinner date was as important as what we learned today. But when your godbabies asked, I had to tell them the truth, which was that you were busy. It's fine. At the end of the day, everyone has his or her own lives. But we're dealing with life and death here."

"So do you want to continue being overdramatic or do you want to tell me what the hell's going on. You know you have a lot of words to say but you're not telling me what the hell's going on."

I was showing Jacob her message instead of looking at the road. "Not anymore. Jacob just read your message, though, and asked why you are being mean. He literally just said, 'That breaks my heart.' We're on our own now. This is worse than what I told you Sunday. But I'm not going to confide this when you seem to be either stressed or have an attitude. But if you knew what we were dealing with, you would feel ashamed for calling me overdramatic."

Why did I subject my kids to this? Every time the Outlander cut around a curve, I'm sure they thought they were going to die. I know I did.

"Like I said, you have a lot of words to tell me but you're not telling me what is truly going on.

"Well, yeah," Carrie added, "you are being overdramatic because you're having a lot of words to say but you're not telling me what's going on with you guys! And because you couldn't chill while Louie and I had our first dinner date in months. You're not welcome in our home anymore. Because the whole time I was on the date you wouldn't just chill for a minute and tell me what the hell's going on so we can help you. So, Louie has made it very clear that you're not able to crash on the couch anymore, and you're the one that caused this, so you can't blame anyone but yourself. After we opened up our home and let the godbabies stay here and you crash on the couch! And you couldn't give us one dinner date."

"*I'm not going to tell you when you're like this,*" I replied. "*Ok. That's fine. Farewell, and thanks for what you did for us. But the kids are seeing your messages. Danielle's crying. Goodbye, Carrie.*"

"*You did this, not me,*" she shot back. "*Stop blaming me. I have been asking you what is going on and you want to tell me everything else but what IS going on. I opened up my home when you had no-where else to go. I have given from my heart, asking for nothing in return, and this is the thanks I get. I have asked you over and over what is going on.*"

I told her, finally, "*Darlene has gone missing. My mother sent me a message saying she didn't come home last night. And her car is still parked out front. She has no money, and no vehicle. That's all I'll say. She could end up...never mind...Enjoy your night.*"

"*What are the police doing? You have her cell phone or does she have her cell phone on her? Even if the cell phone is turned off they can still get a signal if her phone is charged.*"

"*The kids and I have no money and no place to stay. I guess you've forgotten that our cells don't work as a result of what she and my mother did. It doesn't matter because her cell isn't on anyway. I would drive the kids back out there with the little gas I have left, but I will not let them stay anyplace where I'm not welcome. So we're on our own. Goodnight.*"

"*And you have no one to blame in this,*" she told me again. "*You're blaming everyone else except your own actions.*"

"*Ok. You sound like my mother.*"

"*Well I am a mother.*"

I was tired of driving in circles, literally and figuratively. I pulled into an abandoned parking lot. "*Goodnight.*"

"*Do you not remember promising me,*" she said, "*that you were going to help me with the dogs tomorrow? So don't drop by the house. I'll be out doing what you said you were going to help me with.*"

She added, "*After I have been helping you out you promised to help me out, but I take it you're not going to.*"

"*I still had every intention of doing that!*" I said. "*Nothing has changed. But you said Louie doesn't want me there, so what am I supposed to do? The kids don't want to be anywhere where their daddy isn't welcome. If you could please leave the clothes in a bag on the doorstep, Danielle would appreciate it. She really wants them. We will pick them up first thing in the morning.*"

"*No. I'll send them to school with Elizabeth. I would rather not deal with this drama. You have a lot going on in your life and I have a lot going on in mine, and after helping you out you act this way...I'm sorry I let you back in.*"

Several minutes went by. Then Carrie wrote, "*Your wife has not disappeared. I just got through talking to her. You two need to talk.*"

She added, "*Your kids deserve better.*"

"*You said I was no longer welcome, Carrie. What do you want me to say?*"

"*You're not welcome because you had no respect for my time and lied to me. Those are your actions. You lied to me by saying this would never happen again. And the sad part is the kids are paying for your actions. I wish you and your family the best. But for every action is a reaction.*"

I wasn't exactly in the mood for a physics lesson.

I didn't hear anything else from her that night. I found a place to park that was deserted, pulled down the rear seats to give the kids room to lie down, and told them to get some sleep.

Or try to.

That was the first night the three us slept in the car. Yet, it wouldn't be the last. Not by a long shot.

That night, in the car, I dreamed of that mountain I had imagined earlier.

It was nighttime. The mountain's pinnacle was moved by some terrific power, at a terrible speed. It was indiscernible in the blackness; I had an intuition that we were headed toward the peak. No one else seemed to be in my climbing party; there were no equipment bearers. I was very fearfully aware of my...isolation.

I could be broke and keep a million dollar smile, were it not that I have bad dreams. I figured it was the speed that alarmed me; I'm used to going a gradual pace.

The next morning, as soon as the pawnshops were open, I put the iPad in hock—something my fool tail should've probably done far earlier, now that I think about it—and got enough back to check into a room. We were good again. At least for the next couple of days. The kids and I were so exhausted we threw our dirty clothes from the car on the floor of the new room and immediately hit the sack.

Then, I got a text from Carrie. I might not have liked to admit it, but I had been glad she had still been concerned. Even if it was more about my children than me. She texted, *"How are the kids?"*

"We're fine. Thank you for asking. We're at a Red Roof Inn."

"Which one?"

"Across from Ingram Mall...but we were about to step out because they're hungry and I was going to get some microwaveable meals from the grocery store."

"Oh, ok."

"If you would like me to wait you till you get here, maybe I could do that."

"No. You go get the kids something to eat and we can meet up later."

"Ok. Thank you."

"I wish they were still here," she told me, *"but I respect your decision as their father."*

"I will," I texted her. *"I appreciate that, Carrie. And I respect you and Louie's decision because it's your home. And I hope that you understand that I separated from my children once, and I nearly lost them; I can't do that again. We're a package deal.*

"We'll talk later."

"Talk to you later."

Things were good between us again, and I was glad. Relieved, actually. Part of me was just happy to have Carrie as a friend, period. Especially then. Benefit package or not.

I should've known it was too good to be true.

The kids and I departed the room. We bought food. On our way back, I received a message from Mama inviting us to come pick up the rest of the kids' clothes. My mother and I still weren't speaking, but I figured, what the hell. They needed those clothes. I could just stay in the car while they got them.

So I texted Carrie: *"Your godchildren and I are leaving now to pick up clothes from their grandmother's and will be out of touch. I will try to keep you posted whenever possible. Bye for now. P.S. I hope you were able to accomplish what you needed to with the dogs. I love them very much now,"* I said.

Now, maybe I was tired, but I still should've realized the import of what she told me next, about an hour later. She wrote: *"Spuds has gone to heaven."*

Spuds had been one of her favorite dogs. I was so distracted by my own problems I forgot momentarily. I did have enough sense, though, to reply, "*I'm sorry. I know that must be very painful to you.*"

I guessed since her text message didn't resonate I'd pick up the phone and dial her number. This was too important to talk about over texts. She picked up. I said, "Did they get their shots today?"

She was so distraught she didn't answer. She said, "It's just painful watching her die in my arms. I put them out in the back where they were fine, jumping and playing. I go out an hour later, Spuds is dead and Squeaker is fighting to live. I think our new neighbor poisoned them."

"I feel bad for saying this," I said, "but if I had been allowed to stay there last night, if *we* had been allowed to stay, this might not have happened."

"What the fuck."

"I'm just saying, if I had been there to help you as we planned, the day would've gone differently."

"Louie was here. You know what? That was really insensitive to say."

"I can't say anything right," I said to her. "Goodnight. If you could just send the clothes to school as you said originally, I'd appreciate it! Danielle really wants and needs them back. Thank you. I didn't mean to hurt your feelings. You are so easily offended!"

"You really want to bring that up right now when I have a dying puppy in my hands. That's being an asshole."

She added, "And you're a *psychotic* asshole."

I said, "Good. Night."

"You know what you don't deserve those wonderful beautiful children. You're an asshole."

Click.

I never heard from her again.

Now, why did this next thought occur to me?

I don't know, but it did.

Bedlam Boy. The name of the superhero I'd been working on. Suppose *I* was Bedlam Boy.

Silly, of course. We had nothing in common, save for the fact that we both left burned bridges and fresh enemies in our wake. My *dis*sent was causing my *de*scent. If that was not me in a nutcase, I mean, nutshell: imagining myself as one of my characters!

But still.

I saw his gold cape, his utility belt, his dark shades that were not so unlike (it occurred to me now) my tinted prescription Ray Bans.

The trouble was, I seemed to be the first superhero in history who didn't have a clue what to do with his powers

3

*T*ruly *Jehovah orders my steps. Everything that has happened in the last few days has done so in divine order.*
They tried to take my children away from me. Again.
I prevailed, again.

In this case, Mama and Darlene tried to lure me into a trap, as two San Antonio squad cars were parked in front of Mama's house the day the kids and I went by there to pick up their clothes. Somewhat curiously, before we left our room (215) at the Red Roof Inn to go there, I'd had Danielle lay hands on me in prayer. I had Jacob take a photo of it on my phone. I posted it on Facebook.

They—Mama and Darlene—were trying to get me arrested. Or institutionalized, either one. The kids, who'd gone inside to get their stuff (on strict orders by me to be in and out in ten minutes), were trapped—my mother wouldn't let them out. Finally, after talking to the officers outside for what seemed like forever—and they could see I was calm and reasonable—I asked them if they would let the kids come to the door so I could say something to them, at least, before I left. And when they did, I asked them, in front of my mother and the police and whatever neighbors were watching, "What would you rather do—stay here at Grandma's or come with Daddy?" And Danielle, speaking for both of them, said, "Come with you, Daddy." No sooner had she uttered the words than we were walking swiftly and silently back to the car, driving off.

It was an incredible feeling.

I also found out a few days later that, apparently, Darlene has a boyfriend. He works at Star Shuttle, too, and no one knows where they're staying. My children's mother is very unprepared, to say the least, to manage her affairs and strike out on her own. I'm afraid she's going to fall flat on her face.

We've been staying at the Red Roof for the last week or so. It's been nice, but we're out of money now, again. But I have an idea about a place we can stay tonight (other than the car) that would be indoors and wouldn't cost anything.

I don't know why I haven't thought of it before.

The Townhomes at Westcreek, the residential complex we had lived in for eight and a half years before our exile, when our family of four had still been intact and relatively content, if not always happy, had about five hundred something units in it, and was enterable from 1604, a main artery that encircled the entire city in one giant loop. It was larger than the 410 Loop, which was within it. Anyway, it had been our home for many years, and I was thinking of that as the three of us approached, at a slow rate of speed, the front gate of the complex around eleven at night.

I had stayed there before, after our eviction—I mean, that's basically what it was, let's be honest, we just beat 'em to the punch—for eight days and eight nights. That had been over two weeks ago now. It had been a harrowing experience, to say the least, going that long without the basic essentials: heat, electricity, lights, and other things you take for granted when everything's going well—and now I was having to drag my kids into it. You can imagine how I felt. Now we were returning, not as tenants, but as looters: *This is a stick up. Hands on the hood and spread 'em.* As I punched in the numbers of our (former) gate code into the keypad and cruised through the sliding gates, winding our way over speed bumps, taking slow lefts and even slower rights, watching for any kid that might dart from out of nowhere in front of the car, I thought about how we had used to just follow the path until we reached our unit.

#701.

The trouble was, we couldn't do that now. Those were the olden days now. Plus, I had to park the car far away from it so our old neighbors wouldn't spot us there that late. Or at all. They knew what our car looked like. And parking spaces were always hard to find this hour of the night. *I can't believe this*, I said to myself.

The low buildings, connecting unit after unit of townhomes—about five or so per building—formed an unmeaning assembly of dozens of randomly placed rectangular shapes if looked at from above, interspersed with the winding snake which was the driveway that connected the left side of the massive complex to the right, which was threaded in one long unbroken line through it. We'd had a garage. Some didn't. As we found an empty space and slid into it, I killed the lights, and I couldn't help but think of that lady that used to sit at that piano with Carroll O'Connor singing *Those Were The Days*. It came out of nowhere, I swear.

*Boy, the way Glenn Miller played Songs that made
the hit parade! Guys like us we had it made Those
were the days*

You bet guys like you had it made back then, I thought to myself
as we carefully approached the back patio door. Anything to
distract myself from the self-loathing which had settled on my
palate again. And guess what it tasted like. Meet the new boss,
same as the old boss.

Now, our old townhouse was about to become yet another
character in this unfortunate melodrama, the worst January
I'd ever had, and we'd be affected by its whims just like we
were affected by other people, try as we might to avoid it—
subject to its confinements, its darkness, its coldness, its tan-
trums...its *voidness,* if I can use that word.

We penetrated our old unit—it wasn't exactly impregnable—
and I led them up the dark hallway of heavily carpeted and
traffic-worn stairs. We entered Jacob's old room, the one I had
used myself weeks earlier, and now the three of us were its
only occupants. Danielle's room was larger, but again, like I
told you, couldn't afford to be spotted.

A typical day in the life at home in better days: You arrive
home at three-thirty, having scooped the munchkins from
school, you turn on the TV, which for many years had been a
large console floor model even after flat screens had been out
for a while (although you finally did catch up to the Joneses in
that department in the latter years), vote on the show you want.
The boy favors *Dexter's Laboratory,* but not *Dora the Explorer;* the

girl, *Gravity Falls.* Stick a finger in the air, see which way the wind is blowing, vote with whoever's behaving better that day, creating a majority, walk to the kitchen, crack open a can of Miller High Life, pop some pizza rolls in the microwave, and serve them with Capri-Sun juice packets on plastic trays. Your mind plays tricks on you. You've been up too long. You get irritated easily. You plop down on the sectional behind the kids and let them watch what they want till eight. You bury your face in the cushions, in the meantime. You finally tell them to march upstairs and put on their pajamas, that they can stay up one more hour and watch TV in their own rooms. You are grateful they each have one and that they're not in the pawn shops for once. You now get to watch what *you* want while you wait for your wife to get home from her nine hour shift—endless reruns of *The King of Queens* (your favorite show), cable news, see what good movies are coming on later, pop open another beer, and check one more time to make sure you've recorded your wife's favorite programs, like *NCIS* and *Person of Interest*, go in the bedroom and wait in there, face listless but for the brightness of the potential which, though dormant, still burns within like fire shut up in your bones and the sharpness of the line of your jaw.

Or, alternatively, get into the car parked out front and cruise the streets of San Antonio: an 18th century Spanish mission, a 750-ft Tower (of the Americas) overlooking downtown, a perennially competitive championship basketball team's arena, Sea World...But, alas, the kids have seen it all before and want to go home.

Home is #701.

What's for dinner? Talk about it. Maybe the wife emerges victorious (Hamburger Helper), and you sit there, staring into space, thinking, *This is it, this is domestic life in America 21st century-style, a kingdom of dysfunction, one car under Mama, indivisible, with porn sites and food stamps for all.*

And then, suddenly—as we were preparing to get some shut-eye (kids on the twin size unsheeted mattress, me on the floor) after our bodies had acclimated to the cold, something miraculous happened. I wouldn't blame you if you didn't believe it. Hell, I didn't myself and *I* witnessed it. I still can't explain it.

The lights came on.

Next, the hum of the townhome's air conditioning unit, and I knew the thermostat must've been on, too. The house came to life. What just seconds ago had been draped in darkness was now bathed in the yellow light under the slowly spinning fan on the ceiling. We were still standing in the middle of an eyesore, but it was the most beautifullest eyesore I had ever seen. It was 11:17.

I went downstairs and set the thermostat to eighty degrees.

I hurried back upstairs. Danielle said, "What happened, Daddy?"

"I don't know, sweetheart. I don't know."

Jacob's face lit up and he stepped toward me, giving me kind of a half-hug, his face looking at me to see if he'd be hugged back. He was. He said, "Are you happy, Daddy?"

"Yes, I am, son."

"I love you, Daddy."

"I love you too, Jacob, and I'm sorry for what I did."

We were all hugging in a tight circle now. I said, "And Daddy's sorry I got us into this mess in the first place. And I'm going to fix this, you'll see. But I want you to know it meant a lot to me what you did, choosing to live in poverty with your father rather than enjoy the riches of Egypt."

"What does that mean, Daddy?" Jacob asked.

"I know," Danielle said.

I already knew she did. "Tell me," I said.

"It means how Moses left Egypt and went into the wilderness for forty years, rather than stay in the palaces of the Pharaoh, where he was a prince."

"So Grandma is Egypt?" Jacob said.

"Kinda sorta. She's got that big ol' house with all those TVs and stuff. You could've been there right now instead of here, but you chose your daddy. That means a lot to me."

Then I said, "Danielle, do you remember the first verse of Psalm 119?"

" *'You're blessed when you stay the course, walking steadily on the road revealed by God.'* "

"That's right. And, Jacob, do you remember yours?"

"Yes!"

"Let's hear it."

" *'Take delight in the Lord, and He will give you the desires of your heart.'* "

"Bonus points if you can say the rest."

"'*Commit your way also to Him; trust in Him, and He will do it.'* "

I embraced him again. I looked at him, his round, cherubic face, so much like his mother's, and those magnificent eyes!—which I can only describe as pure ocean against the backdrop of a cloudless azure horizon.

"As I was saying, Daddy's sorry he got us into this mess. And, I promise you, it's not always going to be like this. Trouble, don't last always."

"You're welcome, Daddy," they said in unison. Standing there, under the dust-covered fan, once dead, now brimming with life, baptized in the light, we were a Republic of Three.

Something, somewhere, Some*one* Who'd actually had the power to *do* something—at that late hour, no less, for three souls who'd thought they were invisible to the world, as far as they knew—must've seen us, seen *me*, driving back there, about to subject my children to yet another terrible experience because of my pride, about to crash land.

Instead, what we got was a soft place to fall. That night, I, again, dreamt of mountains.

4

THE PAST NEVER TRULY leaves us. Its tendrils extend far from a bottomless abyss, into the Now, wrapping and encircling us with its tentacles. It doesn't matter where you go, you can never get away from it.

As January turned to February, I still would've hotly denied that I myself was acting in complicity with the forces of darkness and division, but gradually, to my horror, I realized I was; not that a great injustice hadn't been done to me—it had been, and there were more coming—only to say that regarding the things which led to my once relatively happy family's swift and sudden cataclysm, I was not wholly innocent. And, even after that night in the empty townhouse with the kids, I still wasn't done making mistakes.

There had to be a few more first for it to finally sink in.

My next one, though, would be my favorite. I'll tell you about it. The first one, though—the first real original sin in the marriage—had been mine. It was I who first planted those malevolent kernels that, once mature, would grow up to sprout leaves of emotional anthrax for which neither of us were wearing full metal jackets or hazmat suits, obliterating any potential for long-term happiness our young family would ever have. It doesn't make me proud to tell you, but, ten years prior, I *had* found that willing culprit, a co-worker, an office spouse, the woman of my dreams.

I cheated on my Darlene.

Worse, I fell passionately in love with this woman, who is the third face on my Mount Rushmore, and, up until my next mistake, the one I'm about to tell you about, had been the love of my life.

Tessa.

I couldn't dwell on her now, either, though. Three and a half weeks had passed since that night with the kids in the old townhouse, when the lights had suddenly and inexplicably come on. It was almost March now, and my mother and I were still waging a contest of wills, each side waiting for the other to break under the pressure. I had lost a tactical skirmish, however, during my campaign. After spending several nights in the car with the kids for most of the month—I'll tell you why—sleeping in an abandoned parking lot and skimming unsecured Wi-Fi from a nearby Jack in the Crack, I finally relented one day and sent them back, a second time, to stay at Grandma's.

I was alone. All was not lost, however.

I had reclaimed Dusty, and he was with me in this...place.

This fleabag hotel off Loop 410—$39/night, you get what you pay for, right?—so unsafe the door frame was all splintered to hell since someone had obviously had a real hard-on about getting in here, and the management had never repaired it. Probably didn't have the money to, I said to myself as I craned my head and gave the room a once-over from floor to ceiling. A big 80s model TV sat atop a cheesy dresser drawer that looked like it'd just come from a garage sale. The time on the alarm clock was 1:07. I was in bed with the remote in my hand, channel surfing. The reception sucked, as you would expect.

What I was going to tell you, was that in order to regain possession of Dusty, I had to fork over damn near my entire disability check at the beginning of the month, as a result of the bill being late because of my mother and Darlene's she-nanigans in January. (And yes, there are brothas who use the word 'shenanigans.') Money that could've gone to ensuring the kids and I had decent lodging for the entire month. The thing was, the bill to the vet had gotten so high that they had been about to get rid of ol' Dusty, so I settled the debt—$1,016. Most of my check. It had been either that, or a month in some hotel with no worries.

But, also no kitty.

I had sacrificed me and my children's ability to get through the month worry-free...for a cat. I don't have to tell you, or at least I shouldn't, what my mother thought when she found out. *What? How could you do that? You chose an an-imal over your kids? You got them kids sleepin' in that car*—or "cah," was how she said it—*with junk and cat litter everywhere! I woulda told the vet, like, 'Look, I'm sorry, but my kids and I are homeless and I need this money to get us a place to stay.'* And me yelling back at her: *I wouldn't even be in this position if you and Darlene hadn't done what you did in the first goddamn place! Do you know what you two did? Do you? We had a plan! We were going to move out soon, and be a family again! You've destroyed my family!* We were at an impasse, with neither side willing to admit it was in the wrong.

I looked at the tattered calendar on the wall. It had the wrong month displayed, but I had known what the date really was, anyway—February 22.

Truth be told, some of my best conversations, over the years, had been with my mother. There were times when we'd talk for, gosh, two or three hours straight on the phone. When we got along like a house on fire. I had been remembering a time when things had been good between us. We were standing in her kitchen, waiting for Philip and Howard to come with a rental truck. Philip had until the following morning to get his things out, so it didn't take a genius to know what kind of mood he'd been in when they got there.

Still, I had resolved that I was going to be on my best behavior that day. I was going to keep my tongue in check. The combination of the three of us—me, Philip, and Mama—were a combustible powder keg, and words were flammable things. One wrong one, one careless comment, one negative-sounding tone—and before you knew it, you had a raging brush fire on your hands. I already knew, given the circumstances, it was probably going to happen anyway, but I was determined this time not to contribute to it. I remember I had been tinkering with an idea for a novel at the time.

"I can't believe you smoked all of it," she said incredulously.

"It wasn't that much really," I replied, defending myself. "Sorry. I didn't know. You didn't say you were counting on some when you got back."

"I did, I did tell you," she shot back, sounding frustrated. "I just didn't know you'd go through it so fast." She tossed the words behind her back as she briefly disappeared into her bedroom. There was resignation in her voice.

My mind came back to the present for a moment. Dusty jumped on the bed, emerging from wherever he'd been hiding from. I'd wondered, if he could talk, what his opinion would be about this place. I don't think I really wanted to know. I'd known this whole ordeal had been hard on him, too, he just didn't have the ability to say so: living in a small cage for a month and a half after you'd been accustomed for two years of having the run of a 1200 square foot townhouse? I felt I had to make it up to him somehow.

I stroked his gray and white fur. It was so warm and soft and comforting that I almost forgot about, or for the moment didn't care about, all the trouble I was going through. But it did seem like my life so far that young year was starting to resemble the lyrics of a song by Danielle and Lizzie's favorite group: *Panic! at the Disco*. All the kids had been into that band. Danielle had even gotten me liking them. I would jam out to the album sometimes after I'd dropped them off at school. I had been largely responsible for what I considered her good taste in music, but it seemed more and more she was turning me on to her music, not the other way around. I didn't mind. Anyway, that's how I knew about this song they had, the last one on the album, called *Impossible Year*. It was by far the saddest song on the album. The lyrics had fit my situation so perfectly I got goose bumps whenever I listened to it.

I'll be honest: there was a part in the tune that referred to troubles "that won't disappear," and it kind of scared me a little. What else was I going to go through this year? I thought. Is it going to get worse? The song felt like a prophecy.

I was taking whatever comfort I could out of the situation, even if that meant I had to sit around and deconstruct the lyrics to maudlin songs. What else was I going to do? I remembered some more of my conversation with Mama.

"You want to watch something else?" I had asked.

"Huh?" she had replied.

"You wanna watch something else?"

The reason I had asked was because the theme from *The Simpsons* was blaring from the TV, and I knew she wasn't a big fan.

"I'm not watchin' anything right now, uhn-mm," she said, putting some plates in an upper cabinet.

(*there was that sigh of resignation again*)

She asked, "Would you dial Philip's number, please, on the landline?"

I had been eager to help her in any way that I could that day. I got up from the dining room table, moving toward the place where they usually kept their landline phone. I asked her, "The landline? Where is it? Is it over here?"

"Wherever you—*no*," she replied, frustration in her voice, "wherever you left it after I called you!"

"What do you mean, 'When I called you?' "

"When...I...called you, you answered the phone."

"I didn't answer the landline," I told her, "I answered my cell phone."

"Oh, ok," she said. "I apologize." I heard her sigh as she put more dishes away.

(*you just hate being wrong, even over the smallest thing, don't you?*)

"No problem," I said.

I could tell things were going to go south, considering the mood she seemed to be in. And Philip? Let's just say the only thing right about him was the astrological sign he'd been born under: Cancer. It seemed he was behind schedule, as per usual, and so I had started helping her put away some of the dishes.

I said to her, "I have a line in my book where it says, um, it's a good time for the main character, and it says, 'We've finally got our piece of the pie.' And then he goes, 'Where's *The Jeffersons*'s theme song when you really need it?' "

She laughed. It was a real laugh. Anything to relieve the stress, I thought.

I asked, "Remember that show?"

"That was the one with the interracial couple, right?"

"Yeah, but in the reverse. In their marriage the husband was white and the wife was black. Did you know the woman who played the wife was Lenny Kravitz's mother in real life?"

"Oh, really?" she replied. "I didn't know that."

"I just know her from that show, though," I said. "I don't know of anything else she was in."

She had her back to me, putting a skillet in one of the lower cabinets, but she was still listening.

"I have a memory of coming in the house one day as a child and you were sitting in the living room watching."

"Right," she said flatly.

The way she'd sounded when she replied made me wonder if I should've even brought that up, even though it hadn't been anything bad. *Man*, I thought, *'memory' is a loaded word, too! I'll have to remember that.*

There was a break in the conversation as she picked up her cell to text Philip. I thought about how conversations were like music, and that the silence was like the space between the notes. That's what makes a song a song, I thought. The space between the notes. She moved to the stainless steel fridge, opened it, and asked me, "Are you hungry now?"

"What are you offering?" I asked, laughing. "It depends, it depends. Not liver. I remember you said something about liver."

I went to the fridge.

"No," Mama said. "Pork chops. I had promised Barbara one." She pulled them out. The aluminum foil crinkled loudly as she lifted it from its shelf.

"How many do you have?"

"There's probably only four in here," she said, picking her cell and looking at it. "It looks like he just called and I didn't answer, cause my phone was down."

"You don't wear your Bluetooth anymore?" I asked. I had to be careful, for that had been another bone of contention, too: she never took the time to learn how to use things, even though she always liked having the latest state-of-the-art technology. In past arguments about money, I had always pointed that kind of thing out, and her Bluetooth wireless, which most people kept on their ears so they wouldn't miss a call, had been Exhibit A. It seemed I was forever walking on eggshells.

She replied, "It's on, but it ain't...I mean, it's on, but, it's been goin' from the car to the..." Her voice trailed off.

(*just face it, you don't have a good reason, do you*)

"Yeah," I said simply.

Then there was a break in the conversation again as she dialed her other son's phone number and then put it on speaker. As his number rang, during the silence between each ring, the voices of *The Simpsons*'s characters could be heard. Don't ask me which episode it was because I don't remember.

Philip had finally picked up and said he was close. *Good,* I thought. Mama was relieved again. I started putting on my shoes. She'd had somewhere she needed to be soon and one thing my brother was not was a respecter of time. Especially other people's.

But still, I had been glad he'd finally picked up and reassured her. He was notorious for not answering his phone most times when you called. She said to me, "I hope y'all can get the big stuff out." She wanted the move to go smoothly. She wasn't going to actually be there herself, and she had been hoping that her two sons could get along for once. She added, "And I hope he gives you enough for you to give me somethin'."

"Oh. I didn't even know he was going to give me anything," I said. "I didn't know—"

"Well..."

(*you're always saying you told me something that you never did*)

"I wasn't expecting anything after what you gave me," I said, honestly confused.

"That was mine," she said. "No, I gave that to you, and then he's 'sposed to give you somethin' and then you recompense me back out of that, I thought."

I never wanted to misunderstand anything. "So," I said slowly, "I'm payin' you back for what you gave me, right?"

"*Yeah,*" she replied, in a tone of voice that sounded like she was talking to a five-year old.

This was new information, but I'd decided I would just ride with it. I mean, I didn't mind giving her some, but I wished I'd known ahead of time, that's all. I asked her, "Five or ten?"

"What did it look like?" She paused while I searched my memory for an answer, but then she said, "Whatever you think it was worth. What you think you can spare."

I should've just given her a definitive answer and left it at that. But as usual sometimes, I had to take pains to make sure I understood the situation. Some of our biggest fights over the years had been over simple misunderstandings. So I said, somewhat sheepishly, "But I just didn't know if it came from him or you..."

"No, that. came. *from. me!*" she yelled, slamming a flat palm on the counter, punctuating each word for emphasis. "I told you that, but you forgot. I said, 'I'm bringing you what I have!' "

Now I'd understood. She had been referring to the little bit of bud she'd given me in the car when she had picked me up. I said meekly, "Okay."

"Y'all don't listen," she said then, the crinkling sound of foil filling the kitchen again.

(*you don't have to make a federal case out of it*)

"That's all right," she said, "we all have feet of clay. Like, they had me runnin' back and forth, like, 'We ain't got yo phone!' "

I didn't know what the hell she was talking about. Or maybe I had known, I'd just forgotten.

She paused for a moment, again trying to keep herself from sweating the small stuff. Then, out of nowhere she exclaimed: "*The Devil is a liar!*"

All of a sudden, my recollections of that day were interrupted by what my eyes saw on the TV. It was tuned to a game show, *Let's Make A Deal*, I think, with that black host who seemed like he would've been a very obedient slave if he'd lived in those days. He was standing next to the contestant in the aisles of the audience. The woman had a nametag on. It said 'Darlene.' Darlene. *Maybe she wasn't such a dingbat after all*, I thought. In a way I was glad the marriage was over. There had been many times during those twelve years that I had wanted to leave myself. But I had stayed. And now, as soon as she got a new (for her, anyway) car, a good new job making good money, she betrays me. And in the most unimaginable way. It hurt so much that not even the sight of Dusty—who was at that moment in one of my favorite poses down at the edge of the bed—was enough to console me. I felt miserable.

Then I recalled something that had happened a few weeks before, at the end of January. Philip had told me he'd found out that Darlene had posted pictures of her black eye on Facebook. At first, when he'd told me, my heart rate increased for a few seconds. I had been staying off Facebook—which I had begun to refer to as 'Fakebook'—at that time. That's another story. But after about a minute, I had calmed down and formulated my response. It didn't take me long to think of what to say. Posting my first status in days, I wrote: "Not all scars are visible to the human eye."

That had been as close to a drop-the-mic moment as I'll probably ever come. *Are you kidding me?* I thought. *You leave me to ROT in my own—whatever!—with no money, no food, no gas— AND you're having an affair on top of that, you all had probably even been doing it by that time—and you don't think that HURTS?!? AND...you were living in luxury the whole time at my own mother's house* (which I had begun to refer to as the Caliphate) *concocting the ultimate scheme to betray me. Okay, post your stupid pic, then. I don't care.* I could imagine Darlene's cherubic, apple-shaped head, as evil as I had begun to believe her to be, performing fellatio on her new flame (I'd found out his name was Edward) during those eight days and nights when I'd been secretly living hand to mouth at our former home. I would've bet you dollars to donuts she'd probably done—*or does*, I thought to myself, anything he wanted, as passive as she was.

(*she wasn't passive anythefuckmore, huh, Tony-boy*)

She had played me, for sure. I wouldn't have argued with you about that. And now, here I was—sitting in this fleabag $39/night hotel, in a small room filled with several dirty and wrinkled articles of clothing stuffed indiscriminately between the bed and the window, along with previously well-kept pieces of art over on the table—alone. And lonely.

I pulled out my iPad. I had a picture of Mount Kilimanjaro as my home and lock screen. It was my wallpaper, too. All of a sudden I thought of that verse from the Psalms:

For every animal of the forest is Mine
And the cattle on a thousand hills

Although the iPad wasn't good for fast typing (I needed my MacBook for that, but I'm sure you can guess where that was), I started putting some ideas I had for a new novel on my device so I wouldn't forget them. Prewriting, basically. I'd learned the hard way over the years to always write my good ideas down and not think I could just contain them in my head forever. I'd forgotten many what I thought had been good ones like that. In fact, the ideas had been coming in faster than my fingers could keep up with them, but I'd gotten a lot of preliminary work done when my thoughts drifted again to that day in Mama's kitchen. I remembered Philip and Howard had come not too long after Philip had called to let her know they were on their way, and when he did, the flammability quotient skyrocketed. Fast.

The front door suddenly swung open violently. Philip charged in hurriedly with a scowl on his face and immediately, without saying a word to Mama, or me, went to the refrigerator, yanking it open.

Mama said, talking to Philip, asked, "Okay. So, everything went smooth?"

Quentin, poor kid, who had also come in, replied, "Yeah."

"I'm talkin' to your father. He's lookin' funny."

When he hadn't seen whatever it was he wanted, he roughly shut the door.

(*and he didn't say a mumblin' worrrd...*)

Mama said slowly, "Don't come in my refrigerator without even saying nothin' to me."

Philip quickly turned around and stormed past Howard and back outside. As he was doing so, my mother called to him uselessly, "Philip, we're tryin' to help you, do you have to give me that *attitude!*"

He was already gone. As the door swung open and closed, their security system said in a robotic female computerized voice, "*Front. Door.*" It was kind of funny.

"What's the matter with him now? What's the matter with 'im?" Mama asked.

Quentin silently shrugged his shoulders. "I don't know," he said.

(*poor kid*)

"He comes in my house, he don't even talk to me? What's the matter now!" She looked at her grandson and asked, "Did y'all have any problems?"

Quentin nodded No. Then, he seemed to remember something. "Well, actually," Quentin said, "Daddy was kinda mad when he came out of the store."

"Why?"

"The man at the rental place kept askin' him, like, questions that, like, he already knew, and he got mad about that."

"*Why he gon' get mad!* This is how the world works!" *Works,* I had thought to myself. *That's funny, too.* Mama went on, saying, "He gon' get mad at the world. This is the way it works, Quentin."

"I know."

(*poor kid*)

"Goodness gracious," Mama said.

"Can I have a piece of that cake right there?" Quentin asked.

"What cake?"

"That one."

"Oh, this? Sure. Get it yourself, I gotta go." It seemed like she was always in a hurry to get somewhere. She added, "If you want to make God laugh, tell 'im your plans. If He ain't in the plan, it ain't gon' go right."

Suddenly, the front door swung open again and Philip again stormed in like bat out of hell, saying to no one in particular, "I thought we was on a schedule!"

(*yes, master*)

Mama didn't say anything. She took a few steps toward Philip, stopped short, and said calmly, "You don't talk to me like th—"

"I'm not talkin' to you! I just—I said, 'Whoever listenin'—"

"No you didn't. You come in here—"

"Oh, *what-ever.* Bye!" He bolted out again.

As he was leaving again, Mama said to him, "Philip, *you the one who needs us!*"

"*Front. Door.*," Ms. Security said, providing an unintentional darkly comic touch.

"Quentin, you need to talk to your father and say, 'Dad, really...' " *Why is it up to him to talk some sense into his father? I re*member thinking. *He's only nine!* Mama continued, "He's the one who needs us! Howard, would you go and talk to that boy! He comes in the house, like, 'I thought was on a schedule!' Well he's the one who keeps walkin' out the house!"

And so it went. That's about all I can remember, to be honest. If you want to know what my childhood was like, there you go. You're welcome. I'm actually glad I didn't remember anymore, tell you the truth. Every time I thought of stuff like that, I'd feel so sad for my nephew. He was a good kid. With a great father. Really.

Anyway, the day was getting on and I was sitting there on the bed after I'd finished the prewriting phase of my idea for a first draft. I was mentally tired. I started checking the Facebook timeline. You couldn't scroll down without seeing Bernie art—Bernie Sanders, the presidential candidate and self-proclaimed socialist—everywhere. People were in love with Bernie, boy. Especially young people.

I hadn't been getting a lot of 'likes' on Fakebook lately. Not even from my closest friends, not since all the trouble had started. It bothered me more than I liked to admit. I was starting to believe that old saying was true:

> *When you laugh the world laughs with you*
> *But when you cry, you cry alone*

Ain't it the truth, I said to myself. I thought about my children. Carrie had been right: they did deserve better. I thought about how they hadn't a stable and permanent residence since the year had begun. I felt that thing in the back of my eyes, you know, that feeling you get when you know you're going to cry but the tears haven't yet emerged. I tried like the dickens to hold them back, but it was useless. All of a sudden I was crying so much I had to get up and wipe my face with a towel from the bathroom.

I went back to the bed. Dusty had gotten up when I did. Sounds funny, but he had always seemed to want to come near me and rub his head against me when I cried. It was like he knew. And this time had been no exception.

I checked the iPad. Someone had just sent me a private Facebook message that I'd missed.

See, several minutes earlier, not thinking anything of it, I'd replied to a post from someone I'd never heard of before. Something, though, about the profile pic she had intrigued me a little. I mean, it wasn't an actual picture of a real person, but of a female cartoon avatar who was wearing these Eartha Kitt 'Catwoman'-type glasses, red hair wrapped in a bun, with a finger over her lips as if it were saying, '*Sshh!*' I don't remember what I'd posted exactly, only that the person was an obvious Bernie supporter, and I'd said something to the effect that I'd become a non-persuadable Hillary person. I remembered thinking at the time, *Man, if I were a boy avatar, I'd take a run at'er.*

Like I said, it'd been a while ago and I'd forgotten about it, tell you the truth. Anyway, the message said: "*So why do you support Hillary?*"

I picked up the iPad and replied, "*Here we go.*"

"*Hey,*" the person—whom I was assuming was a woman, like the avatar—responded, "*you said you look forward to the persuasion. I'm just obliging.*" I checked her profile. It said her first name was Nikki.

"*No, no,*" I said, "*I'll be happy to answer that question, Nikki.*"

"*Tell the truth, Mr. Hillary supporter. Is the only reason you only support Clinton is because she has the word 'Hill' in her first name?*"

"*Next question.*"

"*LOL.*"

"*Call me Tony, by the way...all my real friends call me Tony, and I'm already putting you in that category (if you don't mind).*" I attached a smiley face.

"*I don't mind.*

"*Tony.*"

5

I've met someone. She is already very special to me. Her name is Nikki. Nikki Diane Weaver. She's Caucasian, was born on 1/7 (one day after Danielle's birthday), and she has an interracial child, almost three. She's 28. Her son's name is Phoenix, and they live in a small college town called Social Hill, Alabama.

As I sat in bed yesterday in Rm 116, she video called me via Msgr and we talked for about an hour and a half. It was unexpected, but welcome. She was holding her son in her arms when their faces appeared on my screen for the first time, and they were standing in front of a shower curtain. I told her, "I'm a veteran, you know...You're welcome, by the way." She laughed, a real, genuine laugh that only happens when a person thinks what you said is really funny.

She is very attractive. She's very intelligent. And very political. I like to say she has a revolutionary heart. Also, she's in graduate school in her town. She is a Bernie supporter; I'm for HILLary (but Nikki is "persuading" me to change my vote, and it might be working). I really like her photos with red hair. If I had a woman like her in my corner, there's nothing I couldn't do! She was impressed when I told her

I'm working on a book. Before I even saw what she looked like, I was impressed with her mind first. Although I'm not hatin' the package that mind comes wrapped in, though. I like the structure of her face, the contours of her cheeks, how her hair—currently brown—drapes her face. Maybe she can be my Muse, if nothing else. Every aspiring fiction writer needs one of those. I've been thinking of designing some kind of iconic Bernie campaign poster. I don't know why—ok, yes I do—but that song by Barbara Streisand and Bryan Adams keeps going through my head: "I Found Someone."

My cartographer's map was scanty. I didn't think it was giving me the correct information on how to reach the zenith. I was good on equipment, however. I had my climbing gear, helmet, ropes, harnesses, and more. No GPS, though. The map said the summit was twenty-eight clicks to the east. I didn't think I could make it, though, without my climbing party. I needed them. *Where were they?*

Then I woke up.

A few days had passed. I looked at the nightstand next to me. On top of it was a thin stack of typing paper. My budding manuscript, I then remembered, in its infancy stages. Was Nikki a dream, too? Had she just been a figment of my imagination? No. She had been very real. The evidence was on the iPad next to me.

It had been a whirlwind courtship, if you can call wooing a single mother from 900 miles away a "courtship." I told you I wasn't done making mistakes. And this one was going to be a doozy. It is my hope, however, that one can understand the particularly vulnerable position she had found me in. In matters of the heart, I had never quite enjoyed an embarrassment of riches, to say the least. Not like this one. I'd also never met a chick I didn't lose. Now, I reflected bitterly, you can throw my kids' mom into the mix. That had been the real ultimate joke, the final crusher. Love had employed me, in fits and starts, over the years on a strictly part-time basis, with its infinitely varied cast of horrible bosses, as I'd received one pink slip after another, until the inevitable day I was permanently disenfranchised. And what remained in its wake was just the soul of a single father, fragmented.

This wasn't ancient history. These things had just happened, and while my marriage still hadn't been technically over, I saw nothing wrong in investigating what the situation with Nikki might lead to, especially with you-know-who apparently not giving a damn that we were still man and wife, in the eyes of God and the state of Texas.

she lives on love street lingers long on love street she has a house and garden I would like to see what happens

Nikki and I had that in common, too. We both loved *The Doors*.

Darlene had gotten her groove back. Now it was my turn.

"*After all the shit she's put me through*," I had said to Nikki just a couple days before, when we were just getting to know one another. I'd told her the whole sordid affair already. I'd been sitting up in bed, Dusty purring contentedly at my side, with Nikki's face on my screen as we conversed via video phone. All of our conversations in those first couple of weeks had been like that, since my cell had been only good for texting at the time, and only with Wi-Fi.

"*Do you want to talk about it?*" she asked.

"*What?*"

"Whatever it is," she replied, knocking gently on her head. *"Earth to Tony. Come in, do you read me?"*

I told her I was thinking of my children, how their once stable lives had been suddenly upended, how I'd held the marriage together with duct tape all those years, planning to divorce Darlene after Danielle graduated from high school—if we could've made it that far, I told her—and how I feared now that my kids might grow up now with "issues." A polite way of saying they'd turn out, at best, like the dysfunctional pieces of human excrement on any Jerry Springer show.

"That won't happen," she said. *"Is that what you're worried about?"*

"Suppose it does. Suppose Danielle becomes a regular guest." Nikki leaned forward put Phoenix, who'd been in her arms, on the floor. She sat back.

"I've always felt that children who grow up with two parents under the same roof turn out better. That's all I'm saying."

"You're forgetting one thing," she said.

"What's that?"

"To be a good parent you first have to be a happy one."

I'd never heard it put quite like that before. That night, I transcribed my impressions of the whirlwind:

FR F E B R U A R Y T W E N T Y - S I X T H   8:16pm
Day Five of Tony and Nikki. I think I might be falling in love with her, but I don't want to admit that. Yet. I told myself, after all I've been through, that I would not make my heart vulnerable to another woman ever again. So, I have to laugh, within, at what is happening presently.

I went to sleep relatively early last night. I got another chapter of the first draft under my belt. I'm writing it out longhand right now on a legal pad until I get the MacBook back. I was able to get some good work done because Nikki was busy with her son, Phoenix, and really had no time for what she called a "fluid conversation." Because my nature, as an Aries male, is to want to move things along quickly, I despaired, as I realized that we wouldn't talk or chat anymore that (last) night. It was okay, though. Writing has always been my first love, anyway, even though it's not likely anyone'll ever read my scribbles.

Nikki's giving my trusty pen a run for its money, though. Her reticence to move too fast is helping me exercise self-control in all things, even in my personal habits.

But, yes, I will admit, privately to myself: I think I'm falling in love again in my life. I'm falling in love with Nikki Diane Weaver.

6

"*MY BROTHER IS a horrible person.*"

"*I'm sorry about last night. I fell asleep on the couch with Phoenix watching a movie. You said last night you had something you wanted to tell me.*"

"*It's hard to know where to start.*"

Night. I was sitting in my car in the parking lot of my old school, the Art Institute of San Antonio. The interior lights, removable electronic strips super-glued to the underside of the dashboard on both the driver and passenger side (courtesy of the good folks at Auto Zone), filled the inside of my vehicle with a dark blue luminescence. This had been the first time, in all the weeks I'd been homeless, that I'd gone to my old school to skim their Wi-Fi. It was the only way I could communicate with Nikki. We were talking by video phone again.

I'd wondered why I hadn't thought of it sooner.

I had checked out of the fleabag earlier that day for reasons that should by now be obvious. But I didn't care. It was like that old song, I thought, *When a Man Loves a Woman*. You know, that old 50s song that talks about all the stuff a man would do for the woman he loves, like sleeping out in the rain and all that crap. Sorry, I'm speaking from the perspective I have now, looking back. Far as I knew there wasn't a verse that talked about the guy sleeping in his car for her, but there should have been.

"*Well,*" I said, "*for starters, I really admire your commitment to civil rights.*"

"*That's sweet,*" she said.

We had moved out of the phase in which she had been trying to use her powers of persuasion to change my vote—which were quite formidable, I might add—to the idea of us possibly becoming more than friends. For a while, at least, it appeared that things hadn't been falling apart after all; they were falling into place.

As she spoke, I heard the unmistakable sounds of something country in the background emanating from the speaker of my iPad. *Highway Don't Care,* I think it was, by Tim McGraw. Suddenly it was like I was back in bed with Darlene. Like I had never left. She had loved country music—white soul music, I called it—and she couldn't go to sleep unless the TV in our bedroom was turned to the country all-music channel. I saw myself as if from the ceiling, under the covers, turned to my side in the dark, pillow under my head, hoping Dusty would come join me as Darlene lay next to me, sleeping like a baby. So many nights in our marriage had been spent like that. It wasn't long before I knew the words to her favorite songs better than she did, from artists like *Lady Antebellum,* Jason Aldean, Dierks Bentley, to name a few. From the moment my ears detected that guitar twang common to most country, an instant rage filled me, mingled with dread.

And some unexpected tenderness.

Welcome home, sweetie. Dinner's on the stove. How was work.

Fine. Are you going to kiss me or not?

Nikki continued. "*Phoenix won't sleep without me. He has to play with my hair to go to sleep.*"

She had a Southern accent that I found absolutely charming. I told her I wouldn't mind having a lot more children. Someday.

"*I'm not sure about lots,*" she said. "*My nerves are already shot with just one.*"

"*Not a deal breaker.*"

"*What did you want to tell me?*"

"*Just that,*" I said, "*if, for some reason, things don't work out between us, it won't be the end of my world. I love me. I love me enough for the both of us.*"

That was a lie.

"*I'm still a little gun shy,*" Nikki said. "*I don't exactly have a great track record when it comes to men.*"

"*Same here.*"

"*You don't exactly have a great track record when it comes to men, either?*"

I laughed. When I finally stopped, I told her, "*I've always loved an intelligent woman with a good sense of humor.*"

"*Love?*"

I paused. Then, "*Well, yeah.*"

I had wished the technology existed that would allow me to reach through the screen and touch her elbow or maybe walk through it and go over to her, hug her, kiss the nape of her neck.

"*You already have my friendship,*" she said. "*You are an appealing gentleman. I also find you very attractive.*"

"*I'm listening.*"

"It's just that I have so much stress going on in my life right now. Plus, I'm new to this. It's not every day that someone falls in love with me after just a few days. Especially without meeting me."

It's funny, but as this negotiation of the terms of our affection was going on, while I was earnestly trying not to act too needy, trying to say what was in my heart, and while she was erecting her defenses as an impregnable bulwark against hurt, it was like I was watching all this from backstage or front row center. I had always worn my heart on my sleeve, and I think it must be so with other writers, too. We are observing ourselves as we observe others. This must've been disconcerting for her. As it had been for many women from my past. But I can't ever act completely aloof like a lot of so-called playas claim to because, as I've said, finding an attractive woman who was actually interested in me didn't happen very often.

Nikki continued. *"And you're pretty much everything that I've been asking for. But I'm still afraid that it is not what it appears to be. I'm letting fear hold me back. I'm sorry."*

I thought about saying "Let go and let God," but I'm not Robert Schuller and this wasn't the *Hour of Power.* Instead, I said, *"What are you afraid of? I'm real. I'm here. I'm not a fig Newton of your imagination."*

Now it was her turn to laugh. Then she told me that she knew that already, that she wasn't being catfished, but she was still scared or that it wouldn't be what we were both hoping it would be. That we'd let each other down.

This would've been my chance to run for the hills. Looking back, I kind of wish I had.

"I understand your fears." No I didn't. *"I have that fear as well."* No I hadn't. *"That when we learn each other's tics, our little*

idiosyncrasies, that things might change. I do get it, I do." I guess I sorta *was* a smooth-talking Hillary supporter.

"And I'm trying to work through those," she said. "But I fear that it will take longer to work through them than you can stand."

"Why don't you let me worry about that," I said. I lifted a hand and put part of it on the screen, like she was in prison and I was visiting her, separated by bulletproof glass or something *Orange is the New Black hello piper* She wasn't behind bars, of course. Still, I'd been hoping things between us might progress far enough for me to enjoy the equivalent of a conjugal visit.

"*I'm still figuring myself out. That's where the age difference comes in, I guess.*"

"*Is that your way of saying I'm no spring chicken?*"

"*Not at all. The fact that you have these feelings in spite of us never having met in person, does unnerve me some.*"

I knew that she was right, deep down, and that I should be more patient and take time to really get to know each other before declaring my undying devotion. Love is a plant of slow growth, and yet my love for her was bubbling quickly like a tub full of Calgon. But you know what they say about hindsight and, trust me, in that moment, my impaired vision was not just limited to my physical eyesight.

She continued. "*I remember you mentioning that in the past you had misread signals from women. Does that mean that you had pursued other women while you were married?*"

(*now why'd she have to go and ask me that question*)

"*It does. I'm not proud of it,*" I told her. "*But I only really had one true affair while I was married. It was ten years ago now. We worked together.*"

"*Her name was Tessa.*"

"*Was she white, too?*"

"*Yes.*"

"*You just love you some white women, don't you?*" she asked, smiling.

(*I just want someone to love*)

"Yes," I answered, "*but not exclusively. I love all women. Truly.*"

"*How can I be sure that you wouldn't still be loving* all *women while we're together?*"

"*Well. For one, I didn't have with Darlene what I've found in you. Your mind, Nikki, is what I appreciate about you more than anything else. You love politics, hip hop, soul food—you're a liberal in Alabama, for God's sake. Hell, sometimes I think you're blacker than I am.*

"*It's not Darlene's fault that she couldn't give me that. But I did suffer in silence for many years, thinking it'd always be that way.*" And then I said, "*I'm head over 'hills' in love with you, Nikki. Will you try to trust me?*" Why don't the kids and I come out there in a few weeks. The kids' Spring Break week is coming up.*"

She said, "*I'd love to see you in prison—I mean, person! I meant person, baby.*"

"*Oh good,*" I said. "*You had me worried there for a minute! I don't look good in them county blues.*"

"*They were orange these days, baby,*" she told me. "*You don't watch* Orange Is The New Black?"

She kept talking, but I didn't hear the rest of what she said because all I could think was, I'm all in now. No turning back. All my cards were on the table. If she had bothered to glance at them, she might've seen that I was playing with a bad hand.

A really bad hand.

Nikki, spirited by my words, said, "*I am and will continue to try to trust you.*"

"*That's all I ask. I have faith in you.*"

"*Thank you. And I can say it now.*

"*I love you, Tony Hill.*"

7

MOMARCHFIRST   2:45am

I've never been as happy in my life as I am at this moment. Nikki told me she loved me. Someone really loves me again! God did it! He really did it! He sent someone into my life! She is so special to me!

8

TWO WEEKS HAD PASSED since Nikki had first reciprocated my affection in words, turning things hoped for into substance, things not seen into reality. The word made flesh. And now, as the kids, Dusty and I prepared to drive out to see Nikki (and Phoenix) for the first time, checking out of our third Red Roof Inn in as many weeks and getting on the road for Social Hill, Alabama, I was looking forward to, among other things, another form of reciprocity.

My burgeoning manuscript had become a little thicker, a little heavier, during that time, and one of the things I'd been looking forward to most was writing part of my novel in the state that many called the birthplace of the civil rights movement.

Alabama.

Although I was well-traveled already, it was one of the few states to which I'd never been, and it was not lost on me the fact that I would soon be in a place in which a relationship like this could get me lynched by rednecks. Or worse. A place where the blood of untold number of slaves—my forebears—still cried out from the fertile soil, where families had been ripped apart and their members sold at auction like so much chattel, where George Wallace had first dipped his toe into the fetid cesspool of identity politics and white resentment.

And supremacy.

That what I felt for Nikki Weaver was true love I was thoroughly convinced, and as the kids and I loaded our things into the car, I could almost hear Gutzon Borglum and his team of workers preparing to carve her likeness into the granite batholith as the fourth and final face on the Mount Rushmore of my mind. I had recently begun referring to her as 'Dream Weaver,' after the 1970s hit single by Gary Wright, even going so far as to change her nickname to that on Facebook Messenger. Also not lost on me was the fact that a woman I'd known for only a few weeks was leapfrogging the woman with whom I'd spent the last twelve years.

Go figure.

It was the Thursday before the kids' Spring Break, and we were tying up loose ends as we prepared to get on the road the next day. I'd calculated that the entire trip, with the inevitable stops included, would take about eighteen hours.

"Don't let Dusty get out," I said, as Danielle was about to open the hotel room door again to put Dusty's litter box in the Outlander. My beloved feline and longtime companion had by now, to my great delight, adapted himself to the limited confines of our motoring chariot, and I'd recently taken to calling him a 'car cat.' It was not an epithet, but rather a term of endearment.

"I won't," Danielle said, backing carefully out of the door.

"Jacob, will you put Dusty in the car for me?"

"*Noo*," Jacob replied, as I already knew he would. I liked teasing him sometimes.

"I'm just kidding. I'll do it," I said. "Are you getting excited?"

He responded in the affirmative. Ever since our infamous family vacation the previous year in Chicago, during their Spring Break from school, the kids had become fond of taking long road trips. And this would be the second consecutive year we would do so.

I stood in the center of the room, looking around, and exhaled so sharply my cheeks inflated momentarily with air. I said, to no one in particular, "Well, that looks like everything.

"Let's get some sleep."

That night my sleep was hard won and fitful. Instead of hills and mountains, I dreamed of Nikki's kiss and her body next to mine, woke up thinking she was beside me. I drifted off to sleep again, only to be once more jolted awake by a still small voice in the darkness, and it whispered *I'd love to see you in prison*. Had she really meant it that way, on the DL, as the kids used to say? *Stop it, Tony, you're being silly* I swallowed, sitting up in bed.

I'd love to see you in prison

I flung the covers off, racing to the bathroom sink to splash water on my face. My heart was beating like a jackhammer operated by a Juggernaut. The one from the Marvel Universe. Keep up. Anyway, I grasped the counter of the sink and leaned against it. I lowered my head and muttered a silent prayer. I cast my care. I felt a little better after that. My heart rate had slowed again, finally. I'm good, I said to myself. Yet as

I turned around to return to La La Land, you don't have to be an astrophysicist to know what I heard, whispering in my ear, in the macabre darkness, in spite of my best efforts to forever extinguish it in my Subconscious mind's lake of fire.

I'd love to see you in prison

The trip didn't become real to me until six in the morning when I was going to Walmart—leaving my sleeping kids unattended back in the hotel room—to purchase a cheap engagement ring, a temporary one only meant to be worn until a more suitable (and more expensive) replacement could be afforded.

The beginning of March had seen my debit card newly replenished with dividends from Social Security, my disability benefits, and it was the only reason an excursion like this was even remotely possible. Especially now that I no longer had those pesky things like rent or Dusty's vet bill to worry about. And although what I received every month from Social Security was a pretty decent amount for a single man, I was still on a tight budget because of the cost of the gas required to make the entire round-trip possible. It was only 1800 miles, coming and going.

Piece o' cake.

The trip didn't become real to the children (and Dusty, I presume) until we were actually in the car heading toward I-10 E. *Go east, young man.* That was how it went, right?

We weren't even on the expressway before Danielle had to go to the bathroom. She had already experienced having her first period the previous year. My little girl was growing up too fast for my taste, but it was inevitable. I pulled over at a Shell station and we waited for her to take care of her lady business while the rest of us waited in the car.

Dusty emerged from under the driver's side seat—it mystified me how he somehow was able to fit his fat self down there—and hopped on top of the dashboard above the steering wheel, folding his gray and white paws underneath him and getting into my favorite pose. Sometimes I think he knew it was my favorite pose. He looked like a nature's version of an Autobot whenever he did it. I lifted my hand and stroked his curved back. His head turned in my direction and he blinked his eyes slowly.

Daddy, come here, look.

What?

Just come.

Okay.

Awww!

He's in your favorite pose.

Special lovin' kitty!

"Dusty, you know you can't stay up there. You're good right now, but as soon as Danielle comes back, it's off you go."

Danielle came out. She got back in the car. With Dusty, I put the *ow* in meow. He scampered off. I told the kids to lower their heads. "Heavenly Father, we are so thankful for how you always care for us. As we prepare to take this long trip to a place we've never been—a place that in the past was hostile to people who look like us—please give us transportation mercies, both going and coming back. Deploy an innumerable company of angels to surround us, and frustrate any plans the enemy may devise against us.

"In Your name we pray, amen."

"Amen."

I shifted the car from park to drive. Danielle was in the front seat. Jacob looked out the window. We peeled off in our gleaming gray chariot.

"Can I pick a song?" Danielle asked.

"Sure."

Danielle cheered. Neither the kids' mom, nor mine, had known I was taking them out of the state for a week, of course. I had sworn the kids to secrecy days before. Danielle knew how to operate the Bluetooth technology that allowed me to play my eclectic music playlist on my phone through the car's speakers. The song she picked, *Nine in the Afternoon*—by, you guessed it, *P! @TD*—was another one of the songs she'd turned me onto, so I couldn't complain. It had a cheerful, happy vibe. It matched the mood I was already in.

I sent Nikki a message. "*We're on our way.*" While keeping my eyes on the road, I took a short video of the kids. I told them to say Hi to Nikki and Phoenix. They complied. I was slowly preparing them to think of Nikki as their future stepmom.

After I'd sent the pic, she responded, "*Mi familia.*" Then she added, "*I'm so excited to see you and the kids tomorrow.*"

"*Me too,*" I told her. "*I think it's safe to say we're all excited.*"

"*Leaving for orientation now,*" she said. Although it had been our Spring Break, she hadn't been as lucky; her break from grad school was the following week, and she was counting on us to help out a lot with Phoenix after we got there. "*Love you.*"

"*OK. Love you. Good luck, baby, proud of ya.*"

"*Thank you, baby.*" She sent an emoticon of the little round yellow face with puckered lips, transmitting an electronic kiss, accompanied by a small heart near his mouth.

Oh, I forgot to tell you about that. Those little yellow kissing faces had become a thing between us, and I'd had the good fortune to accidentally stumble upon its exact duplicate—in the form of a small round head pillow—while I'd been out shopping for the ring before sunrise. I bought it, of course. It was going to be a surprise. I couldn't wait to see the look on her beautiful face when I revealed it to her for the first time from behind my back.

I looked at Nikki's avatar. That attractive but nonexistent woman with her finger over her lips, telling me to be quiet. Somehow, I thought, I'd had an intuition that there might be something special behind that make-believe face.

For once, I'd been right.

I believed I had drawn her into my life. It was as if I had broadcast my deepest desires, and Nikki, that fragile Capricorn, felt my frequency somewhere in her Unconscious, and heeded the call. I think they call that telepathy. For better or worse, we attract our friends, our lovers, and sometimes even our enemies.

Some of us broadcast stronger signals. Some of us have more sensitive receivers.

My mind was playing tricks on me. As I cruised the open highway under a bright and blue cloudless sky, my eyes saw what I knew they couldn't have seen. Far off in the distance, I thought I saw a massive but opaque landform stretching itself above the surrounding land, much steeper than a hill. Nonsense, I thought to myself. Ain't no mountains in south Texas on the way to Houston. I stared at it for a long moment, but just at the precise moment I was no longer doubting its reality, there was nothing.

"Daddy, look out!" Danielle screamed.

My eyes focused and I swerved sharply to avoid an oncoming vehicle whose lane I'd drifted into during my brief vision. "Whew!" I said. "That was too close for comfort!" I got another message from Nikki. "*Since I have not completed that online training all the way, my professor may have to reschedule my orientation for next week. I'm hoping that she will go ahead and let me do orientation today if I finish training as soon as possible after the orientation.*"

(*she sure does use the word 'orientation' a lot*)

"*Okay,*" I replied. Texas had recently passed a law banning the use of cell phones while driving, unless you had a hands-free device. And even then you still could get pulled over. Add my pigmentation and location to the equation, and, well, do the math. Thus, I was trying to keep our communication at a minimum while I drove.

Then she sent a still shot of herself behind the wheel of her car. I almost didn't recognize her. Really. She was strapped into her seat belt (*good girl*), wearing a maroon sweater and a navy blue blouse with flowery shapes on it. Her hair was pulled back in a way I'd never seen before. She looked like she we going to a job interview. And she was smiling.

"*I clean up well,*" she wrote.

"*WOW!!!!*" I responded.

"*Thanks.*"

"*You look beautiful!*"

"*Thank you, baby. I don't wear makeup every day. But I turn heads when I do.*"

Then I did something that, for better or worse, would come to be, or at least be related to, the most consequential and contentious part of our visit. As I kept driving, I removed her engagement ring from its box, slipped it on my pinky finger, and sent her a picture of it. The cubic zirconium stone sparkled in the daylight.

"*I love it.*"

The complete freedom with which the citizens of the alabaster cities of America could leave its urban jungles and roam and explore her countryside—far from the madding crowd—her fruited plains, her amber waves of grain, her mountain majesties, felt, in many ways, like a release valve. The cities were much hotter than the rural areas in the dead of summer, for one thing, because of all the asphalt. Hmm, funny word. Asphalt. *Just who is responsible for this mess? Don't look at me. It was my ass fault.* Anyway, I appreciated our liberty to travel across the nation at a moment's notice, and I never took it for granted.

As we plunged over the open road, charging toward Social Hill, I was so happy over my having someone like Nikki love me that I started crying. This time, though, I didn't mind if the kids saw me. I wanted them to know how happy this new woman had made me. Close to both my daughter and long-time companion, in the lavish comfort of the front seat, I felt the awe and surprise of what was happening to me, and how rapidly it had all occurred. I felt, at long last, on an even level with Darlene: she'd found herself a new partner, and now, so had I. But something felt wrong. I couldn't put my finger on it. It was like I was confused about my newfound and improbable triumph, and I couldn't help but wonder what I could've possibly done to deserve it.

Suddenly, I knew what song I wanted to hear.

"It's my turn to pick a song," I told Danielle. I'd been letting her control the song selection for about the first three hundred miles or so.

"What are you going to play?" she asked.

"You'll see," I said with a wink.

It didn't take me long to find it. Called *Tears of Joy* by Rick Ross, the rapper, the song opened up with a forty-five second piece of archived audio of a man speaking to a small but determined audience. They were in Oakland, California. The audience: the now-defunct Black Panther Party, the revolutionary black nationalist organization, formed as a response to the police brutality common to that time (and now, unfortunately, to ours). The speaker: Bobby Seale, one of its two founders. I don't know why to this day why I exposed my children's ears to this song at their ages, but this was the world we lived in; I didn't make it. Besides, they were going to hear the kind of stuff that was said sooner or later anyway, might as well be now.

I pressed Play. There was silence, and then, out of nowhere, Seale's voice and those of his listeners shattered it:

> *Do you know what we are going to do? We are going to defend ourselves! Because Huey P. Newton says that, "Power is the ability to define phenomena and make it act in a desired manner." Power is the ability to define phenomena and make it act in a desired manner!*

The audience cheers. But he's not done.

> *Power! So, if we have the ability to define it, the only next thing to do is get organized. So, when a pig walks*

up to you, or when a pig gets to jiving with the peo-
ple, you be so organized you be learning some tactics,
you be learning some revolutionary principles, you be
having some guns hid out somewhere, you have some
proper tactics! So, when the pig gets to jivin' with you,
the pig is wrong, you whip your guns out on him,
blow him a-way, and then you have made the abil-
ity, in fact, you have made that pig act in a desired
manner.

The audience erupts, and then the music starts, slowly at first, as Cee-Lo Green's soulful vocals begin to harmonize with the tune's slowly-building consonance. Then Ross comes on, simply talking at first, but with authority.

I was enraptured by it. It was the closest I'd ever heard my inner dilemma put into words, but it was the chorus, which came next, that always got me.

Like I said, Danielle enjoyed it. It was kind of impossible not to—as we cruised through the night on the open road—especially if you were a connoisseur of good music, like we were.

The car tires hummed on the pavement and made the children sleepy. Day turned into night. Houston, and all of Texas, was behind us, and heading due east, we approached New Orleans. Gradually, the clear night air receded and gave way to fog. And rain.

In the armrest between the front seats, I had stashed a nickel bag of weed, a small pipe, and a lighter. The 'bad thing.' Since San Antonio, I had driven serenely on until Mr. Sandman paid the kids a visit, because even though Jacob and Danielle by now knew about their father's chemical imbalance, and what he did to rectify it, it was still illegal everywhere except Colorado and the state of Washington, and he had no intention of smoking it in front of them, if he could help it. When they had fallen sound asleep, he reached into the armrest and produced his stash.

On long road trips, I found it near impossible to make the entire journey without my reserve of self-medication. In its extreme form, the addiction I describe—and my need to indulge it across state lines with my offspring present—manifested itself sometimes as questionable risk-taking behavior, not so much a failure of faith as a failure of will.

I inserted a man-sized pinch of the bad thing in the pipe. I put the pipe between my lips, lit the lighter, and left hand on the steering wheel, I took a long drag and exhaled. I shoved it back into the armrest and continued driving.

The Outlander hummed on. Dusty settled in my lap. I saw the reflection of headlights behind me in the rear view mirror, they came nearer, and rain lashed the windshield as the wipers swayed furiously back and forth. Soon siren lights flashed, and the headlights grew brighter. The police.

With the kids asleep, I slowed, pulled over to the shoulder, and stopped. I won't go to jail, I thought. Not with my kids and a cat in the whip. I'm from out of state. Too much paperwork for a simple speeding ticket. Besides, I know how to talk to cops. Just write the damn ticket so we can be on our merry way.

Danielle sat up, startled. "Where are we?"

"In Louisiana. Just outside of New Orleans."

She looked back. "You got pulled over?"

"Yeah. Don't worry, sweetheart. I guess I was driving too fast in the rain."

She gave me a concerned look without saying a word, but I already knew what she was thinking. She knew her father's propensity to drive too fast on the highway, especially when he was listening to his favorite music while under the influence, and she'd designated herself—whenever she was awake—as the unofficial monitor of his velocity. This time, however, her worried look probably had less to do with his speeding and more to do with the smell of marijuana that still inhabited the car's interior.

I told her not to worry, again, that we'd be back on the road in no time.

The officer finally emerged from his vehicle. While he was approaching the driver's side, I heard Jacob waking up in the back seat. I rolled down my window and reluctantly forced Dusty out of my lap.

The cop drew close, stopping just short of my door. I spotted his wide-brimmed hat. This was not a regular policeman; this was a state trooper. And he was black.

(*thank God*)

He put his hand on the door, leaned down, and said, "Do you know why I stopped you?"

"No, sir," I said.

"You were going too fast over the Lake Pontchartrain Causeway Bridge. Did you know you have to slow down over the bridge?"

"No, sir."

"Where are you coming from?"

"San Antonio, Texas, sir," I replied.

"Who do you have in the vehicle with you?" Then, from seemingly out of nowhere, he produced a large flashlight and shined it into the car, damn near blinding me.

I told him who the car's occupants were. I remember thinking that I was glad my daughter was wearing glasses. She looked intelligent, a quality in her preteen features I hoped would elicit sympathy in case—

"Step out of the vehicle, sir," he said.

I obeyed.

"Over here, sir," the state trooper commanded, motioning me to the rear of my own vehicle.

I turned in the direction of his car and walked behind mine. His headlights were glaring, my heart was racing, and my eyes could barely see.

He asked for my license and proof of insurance. The only problem: my license had years ago been suspended, leaving me with its lesser cousin, a Texas state ID; and my insurance had lapsed sometime shortly after the January debacle. Still, I gave him the ID, and then pretended to search for my insurance like a student looking in futility through his backpack at the beginning of class for homework he knew damn well he didn't do. Finally, I gave up the ghost, explained the latter situation, opting to give him an old binder number instead.

"How much do you have in the car?" he asked. "Huh?"

"Don't insult my intelligence, sir," he said, rain forming countless tiny droplets on the brim of his campaign hat. "Weed. Don't play dumb. How much weed do you have in the car, sir?"

Terrific. My efforts to conceal the smell before he had gotten out of his car had been only moderately successful, but not successful enough. I stood there looking stupid for what seemed like an eternity, although it was probably only half a minute. The other half, since the jig was obviously up, was spent trying to come up with an honest answer to his question.

"Not much, officer," I replied. "Only about five dollars' worth. That's the truth."

That's the fact, Jack!

Then all of a sudden the black trooper started lecturing me. You never heard anybody preach as much in your life as that trooper did. I felt like he was old man Cosby and I was some young thug wearing his pants too low or something.

"You're part of the problem, young man. Driving at night, kids in the car, no license, no insurance, across state lines, with weed. Do you understand the seriousness of the situation you're putting your children in, young man?"

(*yezzir*)

"Yes, sir."

"Is this the example you want to set for your children?"

"No, sir."

"Where are y'all headed?"

I gave him an abridged version of the events of the previous two months. It ended with me telling him we were on our way to the Heart of Dixie, the Yellowhammer State, to spend a week with my girlfriend, whom I'd met online, and her young son. I told him it was going to be sort of a dry run, to see if our families, once blended, held any prospects for a longer-term engagement.

I didn't volunteer, of course, that said girlfriend was white, fearing another, even longer verbal epistle. "Give me one good reason why I shouldn't arrest your ass right now."

"Well, for one thing, I'm a veteran of the U.S. armed forces, sir," I told him. I felt like I was on the witness stand and he was Perry Mason or some shit. The only person missing was Della Street. "And I know there are millions of other veterans like me who smoke, not just for the sake of getting high, but for medicinal purposes. I am one of those. You see," I said, "I've been diagnosed with the mental illness known as bipolar disorder."

I had his attention now. I continued, "I'm also an aspiring author and graphic artist. I don't smoke just to get high, I use it as a tool to enhance my creativity."

He listened to all that and looked at me like he'd just put me in checkmate in four moves or something. I don't think I'll ever forgive him for what he made me do next. I don't think Nikki had any connections in Social Hill she could hook me up with. In the first place, like Darlene, she didn't smoke.

"Go get it and throw it over the bridge," he said.

"Yes, sir."

I went to the driver's side, leaned in, and lifted the center armrest. Only, the cop trusted me to do it, not following me. I was glad. I broke off a small piece of herb to save, though knowing myself, it'd be consumed before the trip back. I left a small remnant in the console, took the nickel bag out, and chucked it over the side of the bridge in full view of the trooper under what had now become a light drizzle.

"What would you have done in my place?" he asked. "Tell the truth, young man."

I felt like telling him I'm not exactly a young man compared to him. He didn't look that much older than I was. And that I didn't appreciate being called 'young man' over and over. I was cognizant, however, that I looked much younger than my years, which I chalked up to my clean-shaven face and good genes *by any genes necessary* I bit my lip, though. This was no time to get on my soapbox or high horse or whatever the hell you call it.

The funny thing is, though, I was kind of thinking of something else as we drove away. I put the ticket the cop wrote in the compartment. I was thinking how lucky I am. I mean, I could chew the fat with the cops, the intelligentsia, the Ivy Leaguers, and at the same time feel just at home in a room full of brothas from the hood, or *eses* from the barrio. It's funny: I was both street smart *and* book smart. I knew how to play both sides. It was one of those rare times I appreciated that I wasn't fully one thing or the other.

I was just me.

When we were getting close, I sent her a message. "*Six miles away, baby.*" She responded, "*Ahhhhhh!* " Minutes later, when I told her, "*Five minutes,*" she said, "*Holy shit, I'm gonna vomit.*" She added, "*Because I'm nervous.*"

She wasn't the only one. But one of us had to wear a veneer of composure, at least, so I said, "*You better not. I wanna kiss that mouth.*"

"*It tastes like Marlboro right now.*"

"*This is a nice town,*" I said. And it was the truth. Far from being in an advanced state of senescence, Social Hill was in an excellent state of development: it really was a cozy little college town. Some businessmen from Mobile, she'd told me, had leased the land around it, added buildings, and enlarged the campus a few years back. The investments had paid off: enrollment skyrocketed, the clock tower—the center of town—rang on summer nights with Southern jocundity, and occasionally a shotgun would be discharged, not in lack of the region's famous hospitality but in boundless excitement.

"*I like it,*" Nikki said. "*It has that old downtown feel when you come around the circle.*"

Those were the last words we exchanged before I pulled up in front of her house: a ramshackle on the corner of a quaint little street, in front of a couple of trailer homes, unseen from the street, also in a state of disrepair. I didn't care. *Hell*, I thought as I slowed to turn onto her gravel driveway, *this is the damned Waldorf-Astoria compared to some of the conditions I've lived in so far this year.*

Coffee in hand, she stood with Phoenix on her white porch steps.

"We're here, kids." I stopped the car.

I shut the door softly, went around, and followed her into the house. For the time being, we'd left Dusty and the rest of our belongings in the car.

Then, standing in the middle of her small carpetless living room, she approached me, took me in her arms and embraced me. I, kissing her, drew her to myself, happy, but exhausted.

9

I T WAS ONLY THE MIDDLE of March, but there'd been a blast of early warm temperatures—highs near seventy, the last few days—and students were walking their dogs or jogging or just idling standing on street corners, looking careless and untroubled. I almost felt I was back in college. At the University of Illinois, I'd had one date with a girl in two years, but it had been in the spring, I remember; I'd come a long way since those halcyon days.

Nikki lived in a modest rental house, white, with a large yard and a wide porch. She had fixed up the little house as if she owned it; you could tell even now, things had been even more dilapidated before she and Phoenix had showed up. And last weekend she'd bought four flowerpots and set them on the wooden porch railing, filling them with petunias.

I liked Nikki's living room—the intimacy of it, the good, used furniture handed down from relatives. Her mom (also a writer), most likely. The place had a delightful ambiance. Through the short hallway—if you could call it that—I could see the kitchen, and the entrance to her bedroom. Just off the living room was another small room in which she kept Phoenix's infinitely varied assortment of toys. The house was a one-level, but I was willing to bet it was suitable enough for their needs.

We sat in her tiny living room and watched a DVD on what had to be the world's smallest flat screen television set while Nikki tended to supper in the kitchen. The Crock-Pot near the stove gave off the smell of beef stew. I had promised myself (and Nikki had agreed) that as soon as we got there that I would immediately take a long nap, as bone-weary as I was from our long trek—we'd left at six Friday evening and arrived at three in the afternoon Saturday—but the overwhelming reality of my presence, at long last, in her home clobbered any fatigue I might have felt.

"How was your trip, kids?" Nikki asked, stepping momentarily out of the kitchen, in that Southern drawl that I was starting to find seductive.

"Good!" Jacob and Danielle said in unison, as siblings near the same age often do when adults ask them questions.

Phoenix was wearing a small yellow Polo shirt and navy blue shorts. The bewilderment in his face tickled me; he wasn't used to having company over, much less these miniature adults known as preteens. It was me, though, that he kept looking at.

"Hi," I said to him. I got carried away; I started making funny faces, trying to win him over.

He quickly got up and ran to his mother, wrapping his small arms around her legs and burying his face in her soft, white flesh.

"I didn't mean," I said. "Shoot, now he's scared of me." Which was the exact opposite of the kind of first impression I'd wanted to make: *Don't mind me; I'm your new daddy.*

Dummy.

It shows how utterly uninterested I was in anything but his mother. When Nikki entered the room, this little tyke had been eyeballing me like he was Richard Gere and I was Louis Gossett, Jr. from *An Officer and a Gentleman* or something.

(*Lawd, lift us up where we belong*)

"Look at him!" I said, getting to my feet. "Walking! At his age!"

"He's been walking for months, what are you talking about," Nikki said. "He's two and a half, for heaven's sake."

I thought of the hit show *Two and a Half Men*, and said, in a lame attempt at dulling the embarrassment, "*Mennnnn*," like the end of its famous theme song.

If Nikki had been amused, she certainly didn't show it.

Dummy.

"Phoe-nix," his mother said, turning him in my direction. "Be good. Play with Danielle and Jacob now. Mommy has to finish dinner."

But he was already heading back toward my children, where Jacob had started playing with Phoenix's formidable dinosaur collection. The two of them had that—a love of all things dinosaur—in common. I was hoping, over the course of the week ahead, that they would get along famously.

"Do you mind helping me with something in the kitchen?" Nikki asked me.

"Sure."

Then she gave me a provocative, deliberate smile that turned my kneebones into applesauce, and I followed her past the kitchen into the bathroom.

I kept my gaze fixed levelly on Nikki's back.

In the bathroom, which was right off the kitchen, she closed the door behind us, locking it. We faced each other—surrounded by various toiletries and, um, her lady things—and started kissing. Then she attacked me. No better word exists for what she did. I'd heard of woman-on-man rape before, but never before did I think I would be a victim of it.

I make it sound worse than it was. She undressed me with more than her eyes as I proceeded to return the favor. Once we drew apart when we heard footsteps crossing the kitchen, but it was a false flag and we resumed where we'd left off. I cupped her small breasts—*"Any more than a handful is a waste,"* she'd once told me when I had told her my preference for a more voluptuous bosom—and caressed her milky skin that I could feel after my hands had penetrated the circle-stitched cotton bra beneath her blouse. We lowered ourselves to the floor between the toilet and the shower, fumbling towards ecstasy. When we heard footsteps again—or, rather, when I did—we had to separate and straighten our apparel.

I lost my enthusiasm.

I told Nikki we should continue this after the kids went to sleep—it was impossible, I said, for me to perform under these conditions. Although it had not been for lack of trying. Or lack of desire. I said, "Give me another chance tonight." I didn't push it. I left the bathroom first. I returned to the living room, frustrated. I imagined Nikki slipping back into her clothes, unsatisfied, and scrubbing her face, and brushing her teeth, and perhaps, finishing the job I'd started herself.

After all, if you want something done *right....*

On Monday, and the days that followed, I had a penchant for taking my coffee outside in the early morning, tinkering on my rough draft, when the slowly brightening crimson of the Confederate flags in the distance suggested movement. The vehemence of the Alabama sun was relentless and had a peculiar quality of hope—of triumph. It was both slow and fast, with its unimaginable heat, eternally baptized in its own red flames.

All of a sudden, I thought about Emmitt Till. In the late 1950s, he was the young black boy, barely a teenager, who'd been kidnapped in the deep South shortly after he'd allegedly whistled at a white woman. I thought about how the white men who'd apprehended him had tied barbed wire around his neck, attached it to some kind of heavy fan, and disposed of his lifeless body in the muddy waters of Mississippi. But not without first beating him to a pulp, of course. You had to have that. It hadn't technically happened in Alabama, but who was I kidding, it just as easily could have.

Then I thought about myself. I thought about how I'd been teased and bullied by the black kids at my high school growing up. Dream stealers. I thought about the persistently high rate of black unemployment, which some said was one of the lingering effects of centuries of discrimination. I thought, too, about how—as a teenager—I'd read *The Autobiography of Malcolm X*, and the formative impact it'd had on my life. I thought about how black people today seemed to hate themselves as much, if not more, as the people they claimed were holding them down, how they—or we, actually—divided ourselves by skin pigment and had these litmus tests about who's really black.

Finally, I thought about how I'd always felt like a white man trapped in a black body. A white man who despised the black thugs and the hatred that made them, some of them, go around and assassinate police officers, as payback.

But who also understood it.

Between the day we had arrived and the day I wrote in my journal in Alabama for the first time, about forty-eight hours had passed—long enough for a follow-up to our disrupted lovemaking—but already it seemed to me that my beloved wasn't fully mine anymore. That Saturday night, for instance, Nikki and Phoenix and I slept in the same bed, because hers was the only bed in the house—my kids slept on the living room floor on an air mattress—and, contrary to my expectations, she barely touched me. And the same the next night.

The feeling of passion had been replaced by the feeling of frigidity.

I put off confronting Nikki about it. I decided I'd say something after the weekend was over, so that Phoenix would be out of the house.

On Monday morning—a mild, sunny day, cloudless, the kind of day when it's hard to concentrate on a manuscript, much less anything else—I called Nikki as she was driving her son to his daycare. The kids were outside on the porch, so that I would have privacy. Our whole conversation took place within the span of ten or fifteen minutes—me pacing back and forth in the kitchen several times, stopping to stroke Dusty in this possessive annoyed way that even got on *my* nerves. I was wearing this winter outfit of my favorite sweater, khakis, and K-Swiss tennis shoes minus the socks. I couldn't abide what I saw as three specific incidents that seemed to already indicate, to paraphrase the late B.B. King, that the thrill was gone. She'd lost that lovin' feelin', and I couldn't let it slide. I told her over the phone, "You warned me."

"What are you talking about?"

"You warned me that once we finally met in person things might be different. You also told me that sometimes you have a hard time showing affection."

"Bab—"

"Let me finish. Take yesterday, for example. I couldn't help but notice that you seemed less than enthusiastic about putting on your ring."

Nikki and I had developed a new style of relating to each other now that I was actually there in person. In the flesh. At least that's the vibe I was getting. She was careful never to let our eyes meet, not even by accident, and, in bed, we never quite touched after the bathroom fiasco. With Phoenix between us, in the dark, she would promptly turn her back to me after a perfunctory kiss goodnight and then go to sleep. She stymied my attempts for a repeat performance. Her tone of voice was casual and withdrawn. Like now: "So?" Nikki said. "What are you getting at, baby?"

Maybe I shouldn't have said anything. Brought shit out in the open. How could I put it, exactly? *Hey, um, the loving, sexy, passionate woman you portrayed yourself to be on Fakebook actually really may be a fig Newton of my imagination. Tonight after the kids go to sleep what say you drop your panties and let me have my way with you?*

But I didn't say any of that, and she went on pretending not to have the slightest clue as to what I was talking about. I said, "Like yesterday. You never responded to that text I sent you saying, 'I love you.' The Nikki I knew last week would've been all over that."

"Well, for one thing," she said, "addressing the first thing you brought up, the ring didn't exactly quite fit when I tried putting it on. I told you that."

"Right," I said, "and then I went to the Walmart you guys have down here and got one of those things to make it fit better. And you still didn't seem that eager to put it on."

She didn't say anything.

"You also haven't seemed too jazzed about a follow- up to what happened Saturday. In your bathroom."

"Honestly," she told me as I heard her turn signal clicking in the background, "I didn't know you felt this way. I'm going to try harder to make you feel appreciated. I know I can be distant sometimes. Just be patient with me, OK?"

She was right. I couldn't argue with her logic. I felt like an idiot.

"You're right, sweetheart. I'm sorry. Please forgive me. I love you," I said.

"You're forgiven. I love you, too."

That week was a happy one, for the most part. After the long cold winter, the first warm days had a clean sweet brightness. The produce at the local Walmart was fresh, and over at Social Hill University the rate of enrollment held firm that year. The boys chased butterflies in the yard, winter quilts were hung on the wash lines, and Danielle delighted herself in the generous supply of children's DVDs which Nikki, who could not afford and did not want cable television, had stocked by the TV in no particular order. I, for my part, helped out with the dishes and other chores while Nikki attended classes, looking out the kitchen window above the sink for her late-model car to pull up at the end of a long day, crunching on the rocks, a broom or a smattering of sudsy utensils in my hands, enjoying a brief respite from my abundant harvest of trials.

I have said that Nikki's demeanor toward me had altered somewhat, and that parts of her, as she'd warned me, were closed off emotionally, and that she didn't—or wouldn't—reciprocate affection nearly as often as I would've liked or expected. So much the greater, therefore, were the crocodile tears she shed in my presence after she returned home that Monday after I'd broached the subject of her mercurial tendencies. I think that, while I was staying there, she must've seen me, all of a sudden, not as she had hitherto from Fakebook believed me to be, but as I really was—a hypersensitive, stubborn, insatiable man of forty-four who wished to be loved. But I also think that she must've realized that, given my advancing age, I would never be able to keep up with her in the bedroom, even if I made a pact with the devil. All I could do, in fact, was what I did that Wednesday morning: stand face to face with her in her own bathroom, fully clothed, in front of her naked body (save for the towel wrapped around her head), my hands on her hips, looking into her blue eyes, and tell her, "I told you— I consider this week a dry run, for both of us...I want this week to be for you a taste of what your life will be like with me as your husband."

Those words, combined with my washing of her feet afterward in her living room in front of the kids (and Dusty)—setting an example of servant-leadership and wordlessly showing I had no intention of lording my authority over her (an act, she later told me, her mother had praised)—I'd hoped were just the things she had never succeeded in having in her own life.

That afternoon I'd been sitting out front when she pulled up—proofreading my manuscript and smoking my last. "I would've given you the food stamp card this morning instead of you using cash if I'd known," she said as she came up the porch steps.

I said, "You're welcome," and she said, "Oh. Thanks." While she'd been in class, I had taken the kids to a local museum and, not knowing it wasn't free, dipped into money I'd been saving for the trip home which, in turn, forced me to buy lunch with cash that I could've easily bought with her food stamp card instead.

If I'd been thinking.

Then she plopped down on the sofa and put her feet on the table, exhausted. I held her packet of Marlboros toward her, at one point, but she shook her head. I asked her if she would like a soft drink or something, but she declined.

I told the kids to go play on the porch before the sun went down. They went outside.

When the kids were gone, I ran a dust mop around the tops of the cabinets, then swept the floor. I found a nickel, a green button, and a jagged little pill. The pill didn't look all that interesting, so I set it in a saucer with the nickel and the button. Then we went into the bedroom. Nikki was sitting on the edge of the bed, her face tired and empty. I wanted to ask her how her day had been. But when I cleared my throat, she immediately started talking and I couldn't get a word in.

"I know that you are hurt right now," Nikki was saying. "I know that you are not getting what you need from me. And I'm sorry. I want to try to work on this. But it's starting to feel like you are making up your mind that you don't want to continue. I know that having school and so much else on my plate right now is playing a role in this because I can't give you my complete focus."

"Contretemps," I said. I remembered the word from history class.

"Right," she said, tapping the bottom of her pack of squares. "Bad timing."

I didn't say anything.

"But it's not fair to anyone involved to stay if you aren't getting your needs met. So I understand if you want to leave. That's what it feels like you're pushing towards anyway." She crumpled the empty packet and tossed it in the wastebasket.

"Whatever gave you that idea?" I asked.

"You left your journal out last night. I didn't mean to pry, but it was wide open. I saw where you wrote, 'It's starting to look like I won't be able to give my beautiful children the loving stepmom I had hoped to.' Or something like that."

"Oh." Dammit.

She continued. "And you put in your journal as if I'd been pretending to be someone I'm not. And I feel like our phone conversations and video chats aren't any different than how I am.

"I'm super stressed about everything. And I need your support too. Just like you have to worry about what happens on that eighteen-hour drive and after y'all return to Texas, I have to worry about what happens when you leave and I'm still worrying about stuff right now inside my household, which includes my school work, starting work, raising Phoenix, managing money. I feel like you are abandoning me in support of everything I am trying to do over your pride and feelings toward 'the incident.'

"I don't know what to do."

In the dusk, Nikki was all black-and-white, like a film noir.

"I didn't know you felt that way," I said.

I was talking down into her hair, into the crown of her head. It was damp from perspiration. I started slowly stroking it, for some reason. Maybe she liked it, because she turned her head up to look me in the eyes, and the next thing I knew, we were kissing. Swapping spit. I stood above her, cupped her chin in my hands, and she pulled me close, and I felt her reaching for my belt.

Then I drew back. The kids were just outside the front door, I remembered. The unlocked front door. But she must've been reading my mind, because what she was doing was getting up to go lock it. Then she reentered the room.

"You want to?" I asked her.

"Is the Pope Catholic?" she said. "I'm ready to have you inside me."

No sooner had she said the word 'me' than I was reaching for her once more, as if my body had decided to meet me at the finish line while my conscience brought up the rear. Then she removed my shirt and pulled me onto the bed. The bedsprings made a mournful sound under the weight of our bodies.

I fumbled with her bra clasps. They were the kind you needed both hands to undo, and I had to interrupt our regularly scheduled fornicating to concentrate on what the hell I was doing. I don't think I'd worked one of those since my twenties, but I soon found it was like riding a bike.

"Nikki," I said (whispering, lest the kids hear me), "I'm sorry to say I don't have, um, anything with me," but she said, "You don't need it," and she pulled me on top of her. I climbed on board *holding her hard and mellow* My body was on autopilot, a prisoner of its own reckless behavior.

We lit a fire, and, for a few, irretrievably brief stolen moments, basked in love's fruits as she showed me her room, and I—in turn—exposed the scepter of my Norwegian wood.

Finally, the moment of consummation had arrived. *I would arrive, finally.* I hadn't looked forward to a climax this much since the 'Who Shot JR?' episode of *Dallas.*

At the precise moment of my arrival, in her bed, in between the sheets, I wasn't thinking of black-eyed peas or snow-capped mountain peaks or hills, I wasn't thinking of Carrie or Tessa, or of Masara, I wasn't thinking of Darlene, of Bernie Sanders...or even of Nikki herself.

I was thinking of George Wallace. It was a splendid finish.

10

I 'M STARTING TO THINK we are an animal, which was not meant to be happy. We are an animal, which was meant to procreate. I also am starting to think that life was not built to be enjoyed.

It was built to be endured.

Maybe Christ was on to something when He said that in the latter times due to the abundance of iniquity the love of many would wax cold. Mine certainly has. Wax on, wax off. I used to walk into a room and wonder if the people in it liked me. From the smallest to the tallest. Now, I walk in and wonder if I like them. Bad feelings accumulate like snow. That year (I hadn't known it when the year began), over that midnight dinner of black-eyed peas and corn bread, the forecast had been for a Nor'easter, an *El Nino*, the kind of blizzard where every wounding remark made by your kin is remembered verbatim. I cherished my retorts when I dropped them like Thor's hammer in arguments because of their triumphant accuracy.

Like, the day before the kids and I took the Alabama trip, I had been at Philip's apartment helping him move for the umpteenth time. That's another story. Mama and I still weren't speaking, but Philip was doing his best to act as mediator. Needless to say, he was a poor one. Since I had untethered myself financially from Mama the previous year, standing on my own two and paying my own bills, with the newspaper delivery job that I had worked for over one hundred fifty consecutive nights in my rear view, I had managed to accomplish something my brother had not. As a result, he took Mama's side. She still maintained, more or less, that I'd deserved what they'd done to me, throwing it back in my face, without the slightest compunction, and it was because of how I'd stormed out that third day of the new year, suffused with self-righteousness *I didn't give up my parental space when...*

Most of that job at the paper was in the summer and the kids had tagged along a great number of nights, even on Sundays. Sundays! *When your car is stuffed to the gills with over three hundred papers, each one thicker than a rolled up mattress, and it taking several dozen houses before Danielle—sometimes Jacob, but most often Danielle, because of your special bond with your daughter—could assume a comfortable position in the backseat. Finally coming home at eight after having started at midnight, and now the sun is coming up, and you're exhausted, but happy. The sense of accomplishment is like a drug. Every Sunday would end that way, accompanied by an incredible and indescribable feeling of joy.*

And triumph over complacency.

And what you told Philip when he saw how happy you were while packing boxes and constantly looking at your phone when you were falling in love with Nikki all over Facebook and him saying, "Damn, you grinnin' so much you lookin' like she said she was gon' give you the pussy or somethin,' " and him being jealous because his life was miserable and he wanting everyone to be miserable with him and you have

*to put up with him because you know you're going to at least leave with
some bud which is the only thing you want after all and then what
you said to him after the two of you had gotten into an argument and
he did what he always does and called you a "faggot" and you saying
right back at him sharply "well at least I'm a pussy-gettin' faggot," and
you not knowing where that remark came from deep down and you
remembering that once upon a time you were just like Madison but in
your own way because you were a fundamentalist, too, because you'd
been a Jehovah's Witness as a shorty and were knocking on doors and
shit in some dangerous Chicago neighborhoods in the winter at thirteen trying to earn God's favor by how many hours you spent spread-
ing the good news of Jehovah's kingdom on a street corner*

Hey, holy roller

But still.

It had felt good to come back at him with that retort because, after "Minivan" flew the coop, he never got with anyone
else. Although he claimed to be this legendary "mack."

It was just him and Quentin now. I'm sad to say that I
saw many traits unbecoming of a father while in his son's
presence—everything was *mother effin'* this and *mother effin'*
that, with no qualms about using that kind of language in
Quentin's hearing and at a loud volume—*he was always yelling
even though you were two feet in front of him—(your fundamentalist streak is showing)—being torn, feeling guilty because you just
want cop a dime and be out, but have to instead endure the sound
and the fury of an uneducated misanthrope, tales told by a true idiot, and you wishing he would just talk to your nephew more gently!
and you remembering how it was because of him that you got kicked
out of the Navy*

The last two days of our vacation with Nikki and Phoenix in Social Hill had been spent in relative peace.

Nikki would go to school in the day and, at night, I would sit at the other end of her small couch while she would lay on the other side with her son in her arms *and plop her feet on your lap while the five of you watched anything having to do with dinosaurs to appease the almighty phoenix and spending every night in the dark with her and her son in between the two of you and of course you know or you should've known that it was always going to be this way because he at the end of the day was not your son and you'd gone through this same thing with Masara and her daughter before going into the Navy, but that not being the reason you should have known, you should have foreseen, because of how the first part of the week you and Nikki had struck a discordant tone, getting in the car and saying goodbye, and you having to have her give you fifty dollars because you're dead broke and you know good and damn well that fifty dollars is not enough to make it all the way back to San Antonio but you know that Jehovah will somehow get you and your precious cargo all the way back home safely*

On Friday morning, we stuffed all our belongings in the car, along with Dusty, and as I kissed Nikki goodbye, ending the week on a high note (feeling as I did) I didn't know—waving one last time as she stood on her porch, her skinny legs ascending the small flight of three white wooden steps as our car backed up, and her turning around once more with Phoenix in her arms, that after we got back to San Antonio—something awful was about to happen.

We were off. Another test of my stamina. The lengths I would go to just to get youknowwhat! *Even bringing your kids. And you feeling guilty because you know YHWH would not be pleased with what you did, while your kids were outside, and you stuffing it deep down in the ultimate appeasement to cognitive dissonance.*

Like I said, I should have known. About the something awful about to happen part. But Life often took me by surprise. Darlene had been a surprise. A detour, if you will, on the way to something else. But I wasn't thinking about that now, cruising west toward central Texas, hoping I wouldn't be Mr. Lead Foot again like I had been on the way *to* Social Hill, and get stopped, because like I told you, sometimes I get carried away. That penchant to accelerate when certain songs were pulsating through my Outlander's speakers would also lead to something else unfortunate in the near future, but that hadn't happened yet.

The only time in your life where you knew ahead of time and without a doubt that something awful was in the offing was back in the January between your Christmas liberty from the Navy and the early February when they called you out of A-School (you entered boot camp already an E-4 due to having "some college," something you'd nevertheless been quite proud of)—as the nineties gave way to the 2000s—to come down to the main building because your whiz quiz came back and you'd popped positive because you'd been going to boot camp too close to your old influences

Like your older brother

Great Lakes, Illinois. A one-hour train ride north of Chicago. So close to home. Good job, masters of Fate!

And not only was my Basic in Great Lakes, but I also had the misfortune of attending what they called A-School (I was learning electronics, complicated but fun), also there, after Basic. Looking back, I should have asked to have been shipped out somewhere. Anywhere. Anywhere far away from my crazy family, that urban, all-black version of *August: Osage County*.

What a night! What a bad decision! For so it had always seemed, when I had accomplished my greatest triumph, it was usually followed by some real legends of the fall shit. And so it was. *And then, thought Tony Hill, what a night—standing with his brother on an El platform, shivering, temps below zero, waiting for the train*

And he pulls out a tightly rolled joint

The 'bad thing.' The thing he had panic attacks about sometimes because he could never decide which person he wanted to be—the upstanding father who lived a rigid and disciplined life, or the bohemian—some would say, hedonist—dragging his kids along with him during his Adventures in Acrimony as his still-bitter feud with his mother played out slowly over weeks and months and in chilly silence

He glanced at the joint in Philip's hand. He brought his sleeve up to his mouth to wipe away the snot which was running profusely in a clear stream from his nostrils it was so cold, and then looking away. Then he glanced again. Finally, he snatched it and took a few drags. And then he knew what Eve had felt like—well, Adam, more likely, he didn't think Eve really felt all that guilty, to tell you the truth—when they took that first bite into the forbidden apple. How far he'd fallen from those innocent days in his youth when he passed out Watchtower magazines on Cottage Grove in the dead of winter

In Chicago. Where they call the wind blowing through your bones the "Hawk," like Hawk Harrelson, the announcer for his favorite team in all of sports—the Chicago White Sox. And he remembering how it had been bittersweet when they had won the World Series in 2005 and Fate had just so seen to have transplanted him down to central Texas when it happened. And it had been something he'd wanted to happen for so long...

In those stay-at-home dad years, during the summer months, he'd spend countless hours subjecting the rest of the family to either watching a Sox game, an epic three-and-a-half-hour affair, on the big TV in the living room, or subjecting them to his smothering aloofness as he buried his head in his laptop, watching the game online

And he couldn't go to any games when they'd won the Fall Classic. Playing a Texas team of all things. The Houston Astros. And they'd swept those boys. That team, that year, had been so dominant, they set some records that still stand

Yes, he had known for the first time in his life that something awful, something really bad, and humiliating, was about to happen. Not on the way back to San Antonio, as they were presently returning to, but after returning to Great Lakes, after that night with Philip on the El platform, waiting for the train

Looking back, the metaphor of waiting for a train seems quite apropos. And there was nothing he could do about it but, as they used to say, 'Hurry up and wait.' And wait he did, for four agonizingly long weeks as he sweated out every possible scenario and wondering how the hell he'd ever break the news to everyone because he already knew the Navy's policy was zero tolerance

Dummy.

What are you talking about? It led to you having your two beautiful children. But, in that January of waiting, there was nothing to do except pace the barracks room you shared with two other young white guys— (one of them named Storm, you remember, because you just remember a name like that), walking back and forth, rubbing your hand through your increasingly receding hairline.

He had been voted, months earlier in that summer of 1999, the Most Valuable Recruit of Division 317. All-male division. They had coed divisions, too, but he didn't think he could handle that. During those three months of basic training, getting up every morning at five, at morning chow, girls you would never look twice at on the street suddenly became the sexiest creatures in the world, and they all had asses fatter than a ten thousand dollar hamburger, as they put giant scoopfuls of hash browns and whatnot on your tray, as you prepared for another long day in Uncle Sam's Navy, in a long room filled with metal bunk beds, ten years older than most of your eighty-nine peers, who were just out of high school. And in that time, Tony Hill had established for himself a reputation as somewhat of a peacemaker. He broke up a lot of fights in the laundry room by trying to talk sense into both sides. He thought about maybe getting a job as a hostage negotiator when the government didn't own his ass any longer. And so, in the middle of boot camp, Tony Hill's eighty-nine peers had voted him the unofficial chaplain of the division, and each night, at lights out, he would walk up and down the room, in the dark, as everyone was quiet

And they would listen to him pray

The reason was simple: they liked his prayers. All his life, people had been amazed with his prayers. So, he'd walk up and down the barracks—all his shipmates dead quiet—and he would lift his voice for about five minutes, and let them listen in on a small talk he had with the Great Power within, as Tony reposed his hope in the promise of mercy and the moderation of age at the Final Judgment. When the last scrolls were opened

And now those same shipmates, because of my stupidity, were soon going to find out—the same ones that had voted me Most Valuable Recruit at the end of those three months of Basic, from July to September (the proudest moment in my life, to this day), that I had an addiction more powerful than my desire to be a good sailor. *And they would watch you die a slow death as the powers that be took a month to process you out, walking around the Navy base with the military equivalent of a Scarlet Letter—you're not kidding—there really had been something yellow affixed to your long black jacket, having the same conversation over and over again with your fellow recruits who'd known you as the upstanding citizen, the MOR. It gets freezing cold in Great Lakes, too, which shouldn't be much of a surprise. You remember getting up early mornings, the feeling of jogging to the cadence of your commander, singing military songs as the sun rose orange and cold on the glistening Lake Michigan to your left, just one in a column of thirty or so jogging shipmates, and feeling like you had finally managed to escape from your crazy family and your mother's control and attain whatchamacallit.*

Discipline.

(well that worked out real well didn't it!)

But Claire! Claire Baez, the girl from Ecuador. She had been one bright spot for me during my brief career as a sailor. My best friend and daughter of parents who'd emigrated from South America—I've known her for twenty years now. But at that time I was in the Navy I'd only known her for three. Claire, who'd stood by my side during and after my fall from grace. Claire, who I still know today.

The reason I thought of her all of a sudden, while the stripes of crossbeam shadows passed over us through the windshield as the kids and I raced toward San Antonio, was because she had driven me back to the Naval Base one Sunday after I'd spent the weekend with her and her rather large family of seven brothers and sisters. Having my best friend, my rock in many ways, near—I collected female best friends like some people collect souvenir coins—was the one thing I did like about still being close to Chicago during boot camp.

Claire and I had known each other for about three years, like I said, around the time I signed up. I'd met her at one of those good jobs I'd had in my spotty work history—United Air Lines. Bill Clinton is President. *Seinfeld* has the nation in stitches.

As the Goodyear tires pulsated on the concrete, speeding toward Alamo City, my thoughts went around and round and it occurred to me that if I really ever did finish that novel I'd been pecking away at, it might be a "stream of consciousness type," and deal with nineteen hours in the life of a man, and his kids, in a car on the way back to his chaotic life at wherever home is. Pick a city.

Gil Scott-Heron had it right. They used to say home is where the heart is.

No. Home is where the *hate* is.

So, the discharge from the Navy, characterized (at the time) as Other Than Honorable—have you ever heard a more passive-aggressive title in your life—had been a real blow. For the whole family. They had questioned my decision to enter the military at first, at age twenty-eight, but afterward it'd become a reality, they'd all been on board.

(*all aboard! this El train is leavin' the station folks and make sure you stub that joint out before you get on da train boy yeah I see it that's all you got on it freezin' out hurrr*)

They'd been so proud of me at my graduation, standing in a place of honor, in front of the nation's highest-ranking admirals in full military regalia.

Triumphant.

And now I was going back to Chicago. In disgrace. Darlene had come into my life shortly after that.

We approached New Orleans. I was operating on pure adrenaline. I had been having one of those manic surges again, feeling unstoppable after having accomplished, albeit belatedly, one of the purposes of my trip. And pushing back any second thoughts.

Thanks, Philip Another crab at the bottom pulling me down. But hey, no one'd had a gun to my head when I took that drag. At the end of the day, it had been my decision. And yet, the detour had led to my relocating to San Antonio, where my mother and Howard had already been living for six years, to rejuvenate my ever-narrowing prospects for self-sufficiency. The prevailing consensus was the Tex-Mex and the air coming in from what they called the Hill Country might do me some good. Invigorate my bloodstream *you know what there's a new thing called ambition, get some*

And because of that detour, I had created two beautiful human beings that I loved more than anything in this world. And that I would do anything to protect. And keep. Their mother had gone off the reservation. I hadn't heard from her in a while. No matter. As long as the kids were with me, I felt they were in good hands.

Sometimes I had nightmares that they were taken away from me. The specter of just such an outcome haunted me.

Again, our car walloped the pavement as we entered Houston, passing Minute Maid Park where the Astros play—the closest, I thought—as we were passing the giant stadium to Jacob's astonishment at a cruising speed on my left of seventy miles an hour, light pole after light pole going by in rapid succession as I flowed with the traffic—I would ever again come to where my beloved White Sox had played in the World Series ten years ago.

That had also been around the time I met Paula. Paula Bradshaw. One of the angels I'd worked with at that Fortune 500 bank I told you about. Around the time Danielle had been born. In those days, in the parking lot on my one-hour lunch breaks under a stifling hot sun, I would sit in my car and write—longhand—a full-length novel that ultimately never got published. Called *The Speaker*, it centered around the idea of a first black Speaker of the House, and what would happen if the offices of the Prez and Veep were—essentially—decapitated, vaulting said Speaker to become the first black President of the United States. First black president, *by accident.* I had been in love with my idea. It had cache. I wrote it like my hair was on fire, like I was beating someone else somewhere in the world with the same idea to the punch. Typewritten, it had come out to about 300 pages. As George Costanza would have said, my idea had cache all right, *it had cache out the ying-yang!* But then, you know what happened, right? Obama got elected in 2008, and said idea lost all said cache. What had once seemed impossible suddenly became a reality. Not that I was mad...

I just wished someone'd warned me before I spent hundreds of hours writing the damn thing in a hot-ass car for hours on end. Still, it had been good practice.

Paula had been around when I'd first been diagnosed with a mental illness, too.

She was a Caucasian woman with four children. Married to a man named Ken. We'd worked in the collections litigation department of that large banking concern, collectors in the last bucket of six for former cardholders on their way to bankruptcy. Their last chance to get it right. Some days working from seven in the morning to seven in the evening. What they called Power Days. Huh! Can you believe that? It'd be dark when we'd arrived in the morning—every last Thursday of the month—and dark when we left. I was very anti-social back then. I think that's really why I spent those countless lunch breaks in the hot sun writing that novel for months—because I would've rather done that than be around people.

Even a good friend like Paula.

Like I said, she was my best friend in San Antonio at that time, and her whole family were Mormons. We'd debated many times on religious topics, but we had never let it devolve into acrimony, and I never held the fact that blacks were only admitted into leadership positions in the Church of Latter Days Saints in the late 70s against her.

For once, I had a female friend I wasn't always trying to screw. Well, I'd had Claire, too, but she was still back in Chicago anyway.

With Paula, I was content to remain in the friend zone. I really liked her. She had a good sense of humor, the kind I like. Intelligent.

Anyway, I may have already told you that we'd lost touch in the intervening years after my diagnosis. Up until the year of this story. My road to Damascus year. Paul had always been, along with King David, one of my favorite persons from the Bible anyway. And I had always loved that line where he'd written "To live is Christ, to die is gain." I'd always thought it had been a good use of the verb *is*. I'm crazy. Most people didn't even know that *is* was a verb. When the man on the street thinks of verbs he thinks of words like *clobbered* or *destroyed*.

Home wasn't far now. Of course, my stamina flagged on the way under the weight of its own vehemence. Somewhere near Houston I pulled over at a designated Rest Area before dawn and reclined my driver's side seat in the dark as the kids remained asleep in the back. I took about a four-hour nap. Man, that feeling when you wake up, and it's daylight, and you realize you still have a long fuckin' drive ahead of you before you get home, and you're probably, no, *definitely* going to have to beg for a few dollars from people along the way, at Shell stations and stuff—well, let's just say it's not the best feeling in the world.

Yeah. *Is*. We really have to fix our education system!

11

S OMETHING AWFUL DID HAPPEN.
Not long after the kids and I got back to San Antonio—
it doesn't take a rocket scientist to figure out what happened, and my guess is you may have already figured it out by now—Nikki Diane Weaver dropped me like a bad habit. And what I had previously called my abundant harvest of trials was about to yield a bumper crop.

Nikki. Last of the Red Hot Lovers, space on Mount Rushmore confirmed and ready for chiseling.

The three of us, and Dusty, had left Social Hill on Friday of that Spring Break week, arriving back in San Antonio Saturday, at dusk, the weekend before the kids had to go back to school. We'd just had the vacation of our lives, at least from their point of view—I'd comforted myself in the knowledge that I'd at least given them one happy memory in the midst of our unceasing drumbeat of trouble, which had only scarcely begun.

I have to jump back to something for a minute. Because of the stunt my mother and wife had pulled two months prior, the plan for Darlene and I to file our last joint tax return together as husband and wife—which, I had estimated, would net us a minor windfall just north of seven large in early February (if we filed early)—had never gotten filed! The plan was completely derailed as a result of, I'll say it again—the *shenanigans* of hostile actors. In other words, what my mother and Darlene had done to me set off an unintended domino effect that neither of them had cared enough to foresee. It wiped out, in one fell swoop, my plan to reunite my family under one roof, as well as damaged us financially for the long-term *thank you Mama is this your revenge*

I felt innocent.

Spinning character assassination dressed up as self-justification, bragging about that which one should have been ashamed of—interfering in an important financial matter between your son and his wife *how could you*—my mother had recast her betrayal, not as something for which she should offer her son an immediate and profuse apology, but as a profile in courage. A moment of uncommon valor! *while I sat bolted to that seat and her saying see I told you to stop runnin', now you done hurt yourself in the car that night with no gas and no food and no money as they both sat and pulled the strings from a distance—the Barzini family meeting, that confederacy of traitors—as I played the unwitting minstrel in their Sideshow of Horrors in front of the curtain are you not entertained the unwitting victim in their ministry of diabolical complicity*

Two days before I met Nikki online, February 20, had been one of the worst days of my entire life. I had hit rock bottom. I called it quits on YHWH. I was furious with Him.

It had been shortly after the Carrie Armstrong debacle, as well as the incident outside my mother's house with the two policemen. Anyway, I'd had to return the children to her house once again, having run out of funds—*again*—and it was just me and Dusty, on a Saturday night, in a filthy lived-in car, skimming free Wi-Fi from the Jack in the Crack, watching the cars go by in the lowering sunlight near the Loop 410.

Alone.

Well, there was Dusty.

That rock-bottom day, his companionship had buoyed my spirits, vanquishing the cloak of isolation and rejection which had begun to envelop me like a garment of iron *invigorate me by Your Word and use Your decrees to put iron in my soul*

The day you shook your fist at the heavens. Cruel fate! How could it have come to this? Your idyllic family has been decimated. By evil. They had acted wickedly, and one day, by your lights, they would suffer the recompense for their whatchamacallit

Treachery.

Darlene had taken an ax to the family trunk, but first my mother had thoughtfully and sanely sharpened and wiped the blade, dipped it in oxblood, and handed it to my wife for swinging, tearing the foundation up root and branch.

"You didn't keep Your promise!" Tony shouted at His Heavenly Father that night, two days before his greatest blessing—Nikki—close to Dusty in the awful confinement of the front seat, listening to the same sports radio station for hours on end. Now, whether the God he claimed to revere was real or imagined, he couldn't prove, of course, and had gotten into many verbal skirmishes with the keyboard cowboys of Fakebook over the question. Still, Tony was firmly convinced in his own mind that Jehovah was real, and that He had been communicating with him through his thoughts and feelings via those one hundred

seventy-six verses of Psalm 119, which he had carefully and diligently, over a period of several months, inculcated within his mental framework as a bulwark of defense against negative emotions. The twenty third and fourth verses spoke of rulers plotting together against His servant—the role Tony had cast himself in—saying, And those who think they know so much, ignoring everything You tell them, let them have it! Don't let them mock and humiliate me I've been careful to do just what You said *Tony read those words, and others like them, and he felt like God had made a covenant with him to always stick by him through thick and thin. That He would always discomfit Tony's enemies and arm him with weapons of righteousness on the right and on the left, to prevail in any situation, no matter how bleak. That no weapon formed against him would prosper*

But, at my lowest point, it was Paula, whom I had not seen in a decade, (and her husband, Ken) who came to my rescue that lonely night. When I felt truly forgotten. They had seen the pity parties on my timeline. You never saw someone as pathetic online as I was being in those days.

I had become a real laughingstock, an online spectacle, standing in the center of the virtual Coliseum that is the Internet, where one man in the center of the arena desperately needs rest, and the bloodthirsty onlookers in the stands desperately need exercise.

(*are you not entertained!*)

And yet, I was operating under the decades-old premise of Zora Neale Hurston: "*If you are silent about your pain, they'll kill you and say you enjoyed it.*"

Looking back, I'm kind of embarrassed by how I carried on. And yet, it was Paula Bradshaw, the Mormon, with whom—although we disagreed about many things—I had in common a rather apocalyptic view of the end of the world, my long lost friend from the days of Danielle's birth, who came to my rescue.

I still remember her as if it were yesterday, as she and her husband came cruising slowly to my spot in the abandoned parking lot near the Jack in the Crack shortly after the sun dipped below the horizon, her late-model car rumbling from its old muffler; a full-boned, heavy set woman of around my age; her long blonde hair falling over her ruddy features, prominent cheekbones suitable for such an intelligent wit; her fingers thick, with good nails; and her mustached husband, the head of their conservative but compassionate family. They filled my empty tank with gas and gave me a $50 gift card to Target.

I wept.

If I hadn't been so eager to rush into a relationship on the rebound from a place of extreme vulnerability, I might have seen that what Nikki and I had wasn't exactly made of the kind of stuff that would outlast Gibraltar.

In the car, back in the present, the radio announcer pontificated on the primary campaigns and candidates—there had been several important primaries in different states the Tuesday of our week in Social Hill—and their interpretations of the U.S. Constitution. "Today we will be discussing," the announcer said, "which candidates are strict constructionists and which believe the Constitution is a living document." It had reminded me of one of my favorite memories of Nikki.

As a result of our growing familiarity in the weeks after our online introduction, I had made it a point to be frank in matters of intestinal fortitude.

Bowel movements.

"You are the woman of my dreams," I'd told her once during one of our several online chats in the weeks leading up to my visit.

"I love you," she replied. *"I'm home. Going to finish up this outline and get some good rest—hopefully—so I can do well on this test in the morning. It's eighth grade level reading, math and English stuff. I'm not too worried,"* Nikki said, *"but still."*

She sent a picture of Phoenix playing with his dinosaurs.

"Awww!" I exclaimed. *"He's such a good-looking boy."*

"He really is," Nikki concurred. *"That's one thing I'm not humble about. My kid is good-looking, smart, sweet, et cetera. He's perfect."*

"I feel the exact same way about my daughter," I told her. *"Can you take us to Selma when we get there, please? I think the atmosphere there might help me get inspired as I finish this novel."*

"Oh, bring it! I can't promise we'll go to Selma, however. It's in the lower part of the state and I'm up in the northeast. That's a long ass drive. I can't wait to read your first novel."

"Slow your roll," I said. *"There's no way it'll be finished before the end of our visit. But you can take a look at what I've already done, if you want."*

"I love you," she said. *"I'm heading to turn in this paper and get Phoenix."*

"And if I haven't said it before," I wrote, *"let me state for the record that I will not deliberately impregnate you, until the day you say you are ready, whenever that day may be."*

"That is my word to you."

"I know, baby. I just know you're excited to do it."

"It's that obvious now, is it?"

"Oh yeah, it's obvious. But I know you would not intentionally do something that would hurt me," Nikki said.

"*Thank you,*" I said.

"*Whale cum,*" she replied. I erupted in laughter, which no one heard but me, and then she said, "*You better be STD-free. Lol.*"

I told her, "*I am, babe. I guess I knew all those years not to be too wild because there was someone waiting for me.*"

"*Who?*"

"*Duh.*"

"*Oh,*" she said.

"*No worries,*" I said.

"*Do you and the kids have a place to stay tonight?*"

"*I wished you hadn't asked that,*" I had replied. "*I've been struggling with telling you this for the last few hours. But, I didn't earn as much today as I'd hoped or needed from my plasma donation. And we don't have a place to stay tonight, other than the car. And I don't want you to worry because you have enough to deal with.*"

Money, even in the best of relationships, is always a point of tension. I didn't like discussing it, especially since my poor handling of it put me in a bad light with someone I had heretofore been bending over backward trying to impress. She responded, "*I'm confused about the money situation. I didn't know you were that close to running out.*"

"*Well,*" I said, "*I haven't provided a daily tally of what is costs for me to keep doing what I've been doing. But it adds up pretty quick. Needless to say. And when you figure that I have to always keep refilling the tank with gas and I'm the only one providing for the children because, at least for the time being, their mother is out of the picture.*"

"*I'm not asking you for anything. Simply telling you the truth.*"

Oh, how it hurt me to say that!

"*I know,*" she said. "*And don't ever try to hide anything from me, or lie.*"

"*I'll know.*"

We both didn't say anything for a while. Then she sent the following text: "*Find the cheapest but safest place with an opening for tonight, and give me the phone number so I can book it.*"

Oh, the unsung virtues of passive aggression! They go grossly underreported and largely undocumented. Still, the kids and I would have a nice clean place to stay that night, my dignity still intact.

Sort of.

And yet, I had been glad I'd been honest with her about our dire straits that day. I didn't want to start our relationship like some people do, equating mind reading with love, hoping she would somehow miraculously divine from the macabre tone in my voice that we had to sleep in our car another night and ride to my rescue without me having to say anything outright, instead of doing the manly thing, the courageous thing.

And be forthright. I had learned over the years, the hard way, that when you ego trip, you just lose your luggage. She followed through on her word, too. She booked us a room at a Red Roof Inn on the outskirts of town that night. When the kids and I (and Dusty—it was one of the few hotels in the city that accepted pets) had arrived, the reservation had already been booked and confirmed. All we had to do was check-in and get the room key.

Later on, when I had thanked her, I told her, "*I know you're strong.*"

She said, "*I am. I have my breaking points. But I'm resilient as fuck.*"

Okay.

And that's when our private joke, the one about bowel movements, had started. I texted her that I'd be right back, that I had to take care of "my morning constitution." Except I talked about it the same way Jerry, George, Kramer and Elaine had talked about masturbation—indirectly—with euphemisms, in the style of that famous *Seinfeld* episode known as "The Contest." So I said, in the same vein, "*I think I'm about to become the Founding Fathers again. Lol.*"

"*I agree with you,*" she said, simply. "*Go write your constitution, babe.*"

And, moments later, when I'd returned to the car, I informed her, "*The constitution has been signed and sent off for ratification.*"

"*I'm sure your stool was full of patriots,*" she replied.

"*Okay, that's enough.*"

"*Yeah, you're probably right.*"

Anyway, that Saturday of our return home, having begged total strangers for gas during the last several miles of our trip, I had started to get mad. At Nikki. Looking at the ring in the center console that she had never accepted, a root of bitterness grew in me, thinking the price of that ring was now the difference between joy and a decent meal for my children.

Privately, I began to resent the fact that I'd spent the few dollars it had cost at all, and began to attribute our poverty and my inability to feed my children that first night back in town, with the fact that she'd basically misled me about her desire for engagement *I love it* and the kids and me outside of Walmart on the outskirts of town *and leaving the kids in the car to see if you could return it even though you hadn't bought it here and the look on your face when the clerks told you they couldn't accept it because you knew those few dollars would help you feed your kids* I love it *who hadn't had a decent meal since before leaving Social Hill the day before on the way back getting chips and cheap snacks for them to munch on dipping into your gas money stupid stupid stupid get it together you have to be more disciplined with money you don't and you getting madder and madder at her* I love it *because the subject of the ring was an unspoken source of tension the whole trip and now you were being pulled by the emotional undertow. The riptide*

I love it

I returned to the car. I put the ring back in the center console. Stupid Walmart! I didn't know what to say to the kids this time. None of us would be eating that night. The kids read my face.

The glimmer of hope held in their features upon my return to the car collapsed into knowing silence.

Don't talk to Daddy right now.

Fuck, I thought. We had just enjoyed a wonderful vacation, a respite from reality, and now, no sooner had we returned to San Antonio than the memory of it, even though it had just occurred, it was marred by my increasingly bitter thoughts. Those happy days in Alabama were now eternally frozen in carbonite, like Hans Solo, never again to be recaptured or relived, as irretrievable as the sand that has fallen down to the bottom of the hourglass, as you stare straight ahead with your kids in the back seat as the sun goes down and you have nothing to feed them and you have no one to blame but yourself.

Stranded.

That's when I did the thing that led to the end of my relationship with Nikki. Mind you, up to this point we had still been on good terms. She knew we had made it back successfully and without incident, and she had been glad, but now my growing resentment toward her rebuff of the ring had become like a festering scab.

I just had to pick at it.

My illness, and proclivity for self-sabotage, again, rearing.

Self-improvement through self-flagellation.

You should try it.

The radio was on, playing a song by Chris Brown that Danielle and I had really liked. The smell of exhaust fumes from the main street nearby entered our lungs like a spur. Outside, the world continued to hustle and bustle, as countless automobiles passed back and forth in front of our vision as we idled for hours in that Walmart parking lot, indifferent to our plight *Hey y'all we just got back from Alabama can you spare a few dollars for a veteran and his children*

Yet, the radio was always a welcome distraction from our troubles. And it certainly was that night. Still, it has to go down as one of my worst nights—and one of my most humiliating—as a father.

Sometimes we would hear a police siren in the distance, but not often. Mostly, it was just the low hum of uncongested but steady traffic. We got so into it sometimes—the radio—that we were momentarily transported from the sense of shame and embarrassment, and we didn't feel the hunger pangs that roiled our belly from the lack of sustenance. Bereft of a plan, stuck on the edge of town, and increasingly bitter over what I began to interpret as rejection, I texted Nikki: "*Right now I'm at a Walmart trying to get a refund for the ring you didn't want, but it looks like they're not going to take it.*"

Petty, I know. You don't have to tell me.

I continued, "*I'm not mad at you, baby, but I kind of wish you had told me when I'd sent you a picture of the ring before you put it on.*

Because we have absolutely no gas now and we are stuck on the side of town that is far away from everything, so I don't know what I'm going to do except sit in my car for the next few hours until someone comes to our rescue."

I said a lot of other self-defeating crap after that, and then at the end I had the nerve to put, *"I love you."*

"Please do not bring that up again," she replied. *"I'm sorry that everything has turned out like this. If you want to be mad at me, you can. It's like you want to be, but you don't want to admit it."*

(who are you, Sigmund Freud)

"But the honest truth," she said, *"is that you knew you would need that money for you and the kids, but you spent it anyway off an emotional impulse. I'm sorry if that makes you mad."*

"I realize that," I said. *"I shouldn't have brought it up. This is my fault and I have to deal with it. That simple."*

"I forgive you," she said. *"But I just can't be with you anymore."*

(what)

"All of this is a recurring pattern. Three red flags in such a short period of time. Setting up situations to place blame if they don't work out. I know that you don't intentionally do it. And you are quick to apologize. But I can't live like that.

"You're not a bad person. I don't hate you. I just don't love you anymore. I hope you understand."

And that was that. Some other words were exchanged. The dismantling of emotional infrastructure takes place in words, after all.

And words are the currency of the heart, the medium of exchange used by lovers to convey the wealth of their devotion, or lack thereof, fumbling from mouths that, once locked in kisses, now spit bullets in the form of verbal invectives, insinuations and spiteful comments and, as Nikki so astutely observed, *guilt trips*. Needless to say, I was devastated. So much so, I made a fool of myself again online, posting my heartbreak for all the world to see, live and in pathetic Technicolor. I'm loath to admit it, but I guess Nikki, and others, had been right about me.

I *was* sort of a drama king, with more issues than a magazine stand.

Looking back, as I said, I'm really quite embarrassed by how I carried on; I really wore my heart on my chest, so that everyone else could see it, too. It had felt like it was going to burst. Alone at a table for two, and I just wanted to be served.

Life really was a trip, a journey, *and* a vacation. All in one.

Goodbye, Nikki. See you in the funny papers.

On Monday after Spring Break, while I was taking the kids to school the first day back, driving over deceptively-dry drizzle-slicked roads too fast, bawling to Steve Perry's *Foolish Heart* under a fittingly weepy and dour sky, kids looking on somewhat blank-faced in the back, I came around a curve doing forty with brakes that weren't doing the job.

Accident.

Kids take a cab to school. You and Dusty hitch a ride with tow-truck driver to dealership. Car disabled. No insurance. Labor and parts, you're lookin' at five grand. You tell the head mechanic it's going to take you a couple of months to come up with that unless you can get your stupid wife to cooperate and file this last damn tax return well I hope you don't mind walkin' places buddy boy cause that's what you're gonna be doin' for a while hahehehaha

He didn't know how right he was. About the walking part.

Anyway, after the events of that Saturday, the one before the Monday I met Nikki, after I had looked heavenward and told Jehovah I was giving up on Him, Who (I'd then felt) sent an angel of mercy, Paula, to feed me like the ravens had fed Elijah under the juniper tree, and then what happened just two days later, on the 22nd—meeting Nikki—maybe you can see now why I thought she was the answer to my prayers. And disillusioned when I suffered the death of a vision.

But, alas, I'd been wrong. Again. And now, with Nikki gone, a new, darker chapter in my life was just about to begin. A thousand times worse.

And more tragic.

12

O NE OF MY FONDEST memories, and also one of the scariest—at least to me—were my days working at the Physical Plant in the middle of the night during my ill-fated and short-lived days as an undergrad at the University of Illinois.

What risk! What danger! For so it seems to me now, looking back, riding my bike in the wee hours from my dorm room in the heart of the campus to these far-flung buildings, remote and isolated in the complete dark, and separated from the mass of buildings in the center of the 36,000 student, Big Ten school. I'd enrolled there the year *after* that famous Fighting Illini basketball team made it to the Final Four, the one with Kendall Gill and Kenny Battle—undoubtedly the most talented squad ever assembled in the history of U of I. That year's team was so physically gifted they could run and alley-oop baskets above the rim using even players off the bench, and the record number of 100+ point games prove it.

Just my rotten luck that I would start there, after four miserable years of high school, the year *after* they'd been to the

Big Dance, with all the pandemonium and girls in a good mood, since the team pretty much sucked every year after that season.

They haven't sniffed the Final Four since.

Still, to make ends meet in my brief stint there, I held what I think I even realized *then* was a somewhat dangerous job. Then why do I like thinking about it so much? Leaving the security of my dorm room, which I shared happily with my best friend from high school, Richard Smith, near midnight, in the freezing cold, *punch in with a bunch of older white men into one of those old-fashioned machines that made a loud noise when you stuck your time card in to get punched. And then, after you'd been given your assigned building, somewhere on campus, or off in many cases, you get the keys for your building that night—or morning, since it was really after midnight—which is closed and empty, and clean all the rooms. You'd go to the place that held the mops and brooms and cleaning agents, and it was so spooky. Often you saw big cockroaches scurry by at lightning speed across the dull floors in the middle of the night in these non-refurbished non-updated old classrooms. Imagine having to deal with that every night. Or sometimes the buildings you'd be sent to would be further out, in the middle of nowhere, and you would ride your Schwinn in silent terror, listening to Pat Metheny's haunting* Daulton Lee *instrumental in your Sony Walkman—only serving to make you more terrified, since you kind of got a rush out of the fear you were feeling anyway—until you got there, entering into brightly-lit interiors with white linoleum floors and getting to work, hoping that on the way some crazy white boy wasn't lurking in the darkness to smother your black life out of existence with no one to hear you scream*

Not even showing up on a statistics report. The death of a bachelor. A glorified teenage janitor barely out of high school whose job was the only way he found something at night to screw in college. Your whole life condensed into a one-hour Cold Case episode with that blonde chick whose hair looked like a rat's nest. Still hot, though

And now, I look back on those nights, *thought Tony Hill, what a risk, the night air chill and sharp and yet (for a boy of nineteen as he was then) solemn, petrified as he was, pedaling like a madman—all five senses taut, nothing but empty corn fields around him in the blackness, tall stalks covered with winter frost, his breaths exhaled in sharp white puffs out of his mouth, thinking about Madison, his college sweetheart six hundred miles to the east at Howard—to make it to his destination in one piece, clean it, and get the fuck back to his dorm room on the eighth floor and the warmth of his bottom bunk by, say, five in the morning, while his two roommates snuggled obliviously in the beds because they'd both had two parent families, unlike him, who'd been able to support them financially, unlike his, the Osage County Gang who couldn't shoot straight starring Carol Clark as the conniving mother who conspires with her daughter-in-law to betray her son and send him on a journey that would be fraught with pain but you weren't thinking about that were you just had to teach him a lesson didn't you because you didn't like the way he asserted his authority about the way he disciplined his own child he's not a little boy anymore*

But hey, it was a job. Yet, unlike his days at the soul food restaurant, Tony Hill *emerged from those cold, scary nights more than merely unscathed.*

He emerged victorious.

13

Brrrrrrriiiiiiiiiiiiiiiiiiinng!

The alarm clock clanged through Tony's Bluetooth ear buds in the dark and silent bathroom. The floor was hard. A vacuum whined somewhere in the distance.

"I better get out of here," he whispered to himself, willing his body to rise from the bathroom floor of his old art school in the wee hours by force of the true grit that had gotten him this far, unscathed *more than unscathed*

Then he was stone-still; the vacuum slid by just outside the door and was so loud that whoever operated it couldn't hear Tony's alarm, which he'd accidentally played out loud for a second before quickly silencing it.

He hated himself at that moment. Why was he acting and feeling this way? He wanted to wave his hand and blot out the person who was making him feel all this.

Darlene.

She had taken the kids back—for a few days, anyway, was the understanding—since the car accident. Dusty, too. Darlene and her beau, Edward, had been staying at an In

Town Suites in a section of the city called Leon Valley. That really killed him, having to let his kids live in a small hotel room with their mother and in the company of a man who wasn't their father. *That position has been filled, thank you very much*, Tony thought to himself. But he'd had no choice. He'd taken that car for granted, not realizing it was the last—and bottom—rung on the ladder between shelter and true homelessness. And now all the belated appreciation in the world wasn't going to get him from A to B any faster than his own two legs would carry him.

It was April now. Two days after his birthday. The fourth.

Around two in the afternoon, in the school library, several hours after he had successfully navigated his emergence from the men's room to the break room undetected, Tony was working on his novel. His old art school was full of activity now. And he was privately celebrating, having just passed the seventy-thousand-word mark, something personally important to him as an aspiring author. He'd always been told that a good novel was around eighty thousand words, and so he'd felt like he could, at long last, pump the breaks a little and bring the B-52 that was his rough draft in for a soft landing.

His phone vibrated. A message. Text message. It was from Darlene.

Tony paused before picking it up. He swallowed, a lump going down his throat, wondering what it could be. He could count on one hand the number of times she had texted him since the end of January, and now that she had been in custody of his children since the end of March, since the accident, he couldn't help but for a split second imagine the worst scenario for a parent in such a situation. He took a swig from his Thermos, still warm, lightened with hazelnut. He was still wearing his favorite sweater even though the winter coolness had long since given way to San Antonio's notoriously early summer.

He picked up the phone. He read the message. Darlene wrote: "*I'm sorry. But Dusty got away when we were opening the door. He's gone.*"

He completely forgot about his novel in that moment. *Who cares,* he thought. *No one's ever going to want to read it anyway. I'm a leper.* The only thing he cared about in that moment was Dusty.

He had loved that animal, with the exception of his children, more than anything in the world.

He got up, exiting the library's glass doors. This was a phone call he definitely didn't trust himself to conduct quietly within the hallowed confines of one of America's most cherished dying institutions—a library. Hatred and anger and sadness converged to a nexus. Tony was confused as he walked to a secluded area at the end of the red-carpeted hallway, past the school's giant logo affixed near the elevators, the smell of even more coffee from the break room filling the air, and dialed Darlene's number.

She didn't answer. He tried again. No response.

This little bitch! was all Tony could think to himself. *She probably let him get away on purpose!* She wasn't answering, so finally he sent her a text asking her to pick him up from his location, about a fifteen-minute car ride. Tony was already pacing, chomping at the bit to have her scoop him and bring him to the last place ol' Dusty had been seen. He had a bag of hard cat food he could bring. He could shake it to lure him out. Tony wanted to, immediately, conduct a hard-target search of every gas station, residence, warehouse, farmhouse, hen-house, outhouse and doghouse within a thirty-mile radius.

No, a hundred.

Darlene

This was typical of his scatterbrained wife, Tony thought to himself. Something had arrested her development, not just in matters of a secular education, but also on a much deep-er, decision-making level. He wondered how she could leave a message like that and then not even have the decency to have a brief conversation with him as to what exactly had hap-pened. And how.

He hoofed it back inside the library, shoved his manu-script back into his school bag, and raced outside into the humid afternoon sunlight from the building's rear entrance on the lower level.

As he exited the back door, he took a short video of the door closing. He sent it to Darlene, with the message, "*I'm on my way. To where you are. I've calculated how long it will take me to walk there by foot. Two hours. Please pick me up somewhere between now and there. Because if I step foot on the property of that hotel having walked the whole way, where you are living with your boyfriend and my children, where you let my cat go on purpose prob-ably, I'm afraid when I get there I may not find you as I want you to be.*"

Then Tony added, without a trace of humor, "*And you may not find me as you want me to be.*"

Outside, on the streets, heat simmered in waves up from the pavement. The streets were unending paths pointing through an urban jungle, not quite as dense as the one Tony had known as a youth in his hometown of Chicago, but all cit-ies were alike in some way at the end of the day.

He was confident. During the last few days and nights, he had either slept secretly in the school's bathroom or under the stars. He was alone, truly. On his birthday, he had slept behind the school building. The moment when he had confronted Darlene on his mother's lawn in the middle of the night so many months ago, when it was a temperature he'd give anything to feel now for just—as he was hoofing it with breakneck pace down Wurzbach Street—ten seconds, had entered his flesh and blood. Now everything was getting out of control. His mother had betrayed him. His wife had betrayed him. He had lost his children. He had lost the money he and his wife were going to get from the filing of the previous year's taxes. His brother was useless. And, now, not Dusty. No.

Not Dusty.

As Tony advanced, he felt that he had destiny in his grasp. He was more alive than he could ever remember having been; his faculties and acumen were razor sharp, focused toward a goal. For the first time in his life he moved consciously between two sharply defined opposites: he was moving away from the law of Death, from those deathlike black eyed peas that brought him nothing but misery and anguish and tightness and hotness in his chest; and he was moving toward the law of the Spirit of life in Christ—only this wasn't the Jeffery Hunter *King of Kings* version, Who suffered children and lepers gladly, but rather that other (some might even go as far as say, manic depressive) incarnation—the one that caused Him to violently drive the moneylenders and thieves out of the Temple, overturning tables as pigeons and turtledoves fly everywhere, and purging and scourging them at the business end of the whip, and just in general goin' off on motherfuckers.

Backed by the full faith and credit of Jehovah Himself.
It must be a terrible thing, Tony had always thought, to fall
into the hands of the living God. Sort of like Daddy Dearest.
That's probably how Darlene is thinking about me right about now,
he mused to himself.

At least, he thought, *she better be.*

The hate and wrath he felt for her drove him. It drove
him forward, even as he despised the stench coming from
his own un-deodorized pits in temps north of one hundred
degrees.

It was unseasonably hot. The sun, again, baptized in its
own red flames. Except, this time it was not hopeful, and it
was not triumphant.

It was vengeful.

He hightailed it off the sidewalk and walked up the In Town
Suites parking lot, barged into the front office and checked
with the hired hand to see if a Darlene Hill was staying
there.

The manager says he can't give out that kind of information.

Tony flashed a tight-lipped smile. He knew this was one
of two In Town Suites within a five-block radius and he had
never been quite sure which one she and her lover had been
living in sin at. The manager asked Tony why he needed the
information. Tony quickly rubbed the area below his nose, not
a scratch, just a barely perceptible movement, and said he was
a patron at a restaurant she'd been dining at and she'd left
her cell phone behind.

And he was looking for her bad. *Real bad.*

Tony shot out, journeyed for another half hour in the baking temperatures, to the other In Town. Same thing. They can't give out that information, *sir.*

Tony stepped away from the front and set out, stroking and rubbing the nape of his neck. He exited the office door.

He shot Darlene a text. He didn't think he'd been threatening in his message, not enough for her to continue driving around with the kids in the car—they'd been out of school for a few hours now and Tony had not seen their mother's car in either hotel's parking lot—as she was obviously doing. He promised if they returned—he had, at long last, deduced which one they were calling a temporary home—he would not do anything violent. He would not hit her *what you think I wanna make my kids into orphans come on don't be serious* His main focus, he told her, was finding Dusty, and now it was going to be dark soon. Tony's walk from the confines of his school's library to his betrayer's lair had been, all told, about three hours. His favorite sweater clung to him; his perspiration was acting as an adhesive.

"*You promise?* " It was Danielle. She was doing the texting for Mommy, who was driving.

Tony stopped and, before answering, felt an acute sensation of excitement flood through him. He was leaning against an iron guard rail at the entrance to the correct hotel, watching for his wife's return, exhausted, but propelled forward by an inamorata of a kind similar to the one that had been with him when he'd left his parents behind in Chicago. Only a thousand times hotter. He figured maybe it was just his fate to clash with the two most important women in his life. He, in a million years, could never imagine having such a relationship with his adult daughter.

And he, for the life of him, couldn't understand why everyone seemed to have it in for him. In his mind, he had been good to Darlene. He had tried to be a good son. He was a good man.

In his *mind.*

Darlene's car came crawling at a slow pace through the entrance, speeding up slightly as it entered the property, proceeding to the back. Tony quickly followed, not wanting to lose sight of them. Or worse, have his wife get the kids in the room and lock him out. In more ways than one.

So, he sprinted to the back. He made it. He was standing in front of the car's hood as she turned off the engine.

He flushed hot with anger when he saw her face through the windshield as she parked. What the fuck! Was she laughing at him? Was she making fun of him? He felt conspicuous standing in front of them like that, his unshaven face roughened by stubble and sweat, looking mean. What would people looking out their windows think? He was very conscious of his black skin and there was in him a certain conviction that Darlene and women like her made it so that in the end he would be captive of that black skin. But he wasn't going to let her make a fool of him. No way. No way.

"Come on, kids," she said as her driver's side door opened. Tony looked behind him. It was one of those properties where the rooms are accessible from the street, and they had pulled up in front of room 110. Was this it? Was this the room?

"Hi, Daddy," Danielle said, getting out.

"Hello," Tony whispered. He was aware of the effort to breathe; he swallowed and fumbled nervously with his White Sox cap, which was soaking wet.

"Where's your room?" he asked his wife.

Tony felt trapped. Oh, goddamn! He saw in an instant that she could have made all of this very easy if she had simply acted like an adult from the beginning and picked him up hours ago from school. She always had to make things harder than they needed to be! He recalled, for a moment, a lesson he'd taught his daughter along a similar vein months prior. He had remembered telling her, basically, that sometimes the person who drives the fastest doesn't always get to their destination before the slower guy. Except, with Darlene, she was backwards: all her schemes only served to *delay* the inevitable. They were going to *eventually* have to file that tax return anyway. He was *eventually* going to find out which hotel she'd been staying at. He would eventually find his family.

And he did.

He made no pretense of being in a good mood. Once he had observed that she was out of the car, free and clear, he grabbed her arm tightly and forced her to show him which room they were in. It was 110, as he had figured.

She slipped the card key in its slot. The green light flashed. He muscled her in. The kids loped behind.

Tony wiped his mouth with the back of his hand and closed the door behind them. He heard Darlene whisper something to the children; then he saw them both nod. He looked at their mother. The sight of her face repulsed him. He thought of the cruel contradiction that loving his children and hating their mother presented him. Maybe it was an oxymoron. Maybe *he* was an oxymoron.

But that meant he was still a moron.

He was still looking intently at her face, standing in the middle of the small efficiency, thinking about what he wanted to do to that face's false sense of security. He could only think of one word.

Fracture.

The first thing he did was, confiscate his wife's phone and call her boyfriend, with whom she had been living in that very room for weeks now. He quickly found his number in her Contacts under the words "my honey." The sight of those words only served to make him angrier. After several rings, her new honey picked up. Tony was short and to the point. "Do you know who this is?"

After a pause, the voice on the other end said haltingly, "I...I th-think so."

"Good. Because this little honeymoon you two have been on—it's over. You hear me? I am still the head of my family until the day I am not! And another thing: *I'll* be staying in this room now. Starting tonight. And good luck finding someone to pick your ass up from work, because Darlene sure as hell won't be."

With that, Tony ended the call. For the first time, though, he suddenly longed for the days before cell phones, when—during those times when you hung up on somebody in a rage—you could hang up on they ass hard as hell and really get that bang for your buck. Nowadays you just softly tapped End on a glass screen with your index finger. *How the hell could they know how angry you were just by doing that?*

The realness of the room fell away; in its place was the vast city of white people that sprawled outside. He was going to punish her, he knew, a second time. He had to get her phone away from her. She took it out of her bra. When she handed it to him, the recorder was going. She had been recording him, his tirade. But, had she? No! Yes! Maybe she had gone for help? No. If she had they would have been here by now. Because he had been spending the last several hours pacing the room back and forth, his family of three serving—as they had so often during those twelve years—as his silent and fearful audience, and yelling a summation of all the injustices—as he saw them—of the last four months.

And beating her. With his belt.

He had taken off his belt, even more incensed by the discovery of her latest deception, and—in between twenty minute diatribes in which he paced and yelled some more—made Darlene remove her pants, and, in front of their kids, applied several sharp lashes to the back of her panties with full force.

And with extreme prejudice.

Only this wasn't the kind of prejudice

Whap!

that barred blacks from lunch counters and water fountains

Whap!

that forced Negroes to sit in the back of the bus

Whap!

not the kind of prejudice that bore strange fruit from the poplar trees in Alabama and the South

Whap!

that saw their women violated by the seed of white men who sold enslaved and murdered and raped and abused and lynched

Whap!

that saw the Scottsboro Boys railroaded and executed for a crime they didn't commit or the Central Park Five forced to spend most of their adult lives in jail for the same injustice while Donald Trump called for their execution

Whap!

No, this extreme prejudice was in the strict, clinical meaning of the term. Having briefly served in the Navy, Tony Hill knew that in military and other covert operations, *terminate with extreme prejudice* was a euphemism for aggressive execution. In the context of military intelligence, it was generally understood as an order to do one thing.

Assassinate. Like in *Apocalypse Now.* Tony felt like he had a license to kill, but it hadn't come from M.

What was that! A knock at the door? No! *knock knock* Yes! There was a knock! Shit! Had he been too loud? he thought to himself. He motioned Darlene into the bathroom. She fumbled with her clothes and shambled in, out of sight. The kids looked on. Their eyes were wet, watching.

"Who is it?" Tony asked, approaching the door.

"We got a call from room 110 about a disturbance in this location."

"That can't be right. No one called from here."

"This is the San Antonio police, sir. Do you mind opening up the door?"

Shit. Five-O. Tony turned the handle. The door opened.

"Place your hands behind your back, boy. And say *adios* to your jungle bunnies.

"You're going to jail tonight."

BOOK III

Requiem

1

SCHOOL IS THE WORD. You can't stop hearing it when you're inside. "You all right, school?" "You fuckin' with me, school?" "I got two soups for your dessert, school." "Fuck you, school." "Shi', school." "Sheet, school." "Shit, school." It doesn't mean a thing. Everyone's nickname is *school*, it doesn't matter who you are. Amazing, Tony thought to himself, as he crossed from the toilet to his bunk bed in his orange jail jump suit and flip flops, that the incarcerated were suddenly fascinated with a word which represented something for which they apparently held no interest on the outside.

And all this time he'd thought *grease* is the word.

Sixteen days is a long time to be in jail for someone like Tony, but it's five minutes for a lot of the guys he finds himself locked up with. There's nothing to do but play chess with career criminals who just happen to be America's unheralded and unsung Bobby Fischer's, and find another pastime to embarrass you. You've got to find ways of making time go faster. Jungle—during his third year they started calling him Jungle, but his real name was Calvin Edwards—Jungle took up weightlifting. That made time go faster, but not fast enough. What Tony really needed was a time machine. A way to erase the actions that had led to him being locked up in this hellhole.

For Tony, already anti-social by nature, a lot of his time, at least in those first few days, had been spent for hours on end in his own private cell. He had liked having his own cell all to himself, as he did those first few days, if he had to be here. But then, in his typical hotheadedness, he had gotten into it with the head officer, and he'd sent Tony here.

Tony wrote, too. He'd been lucky; by some stroke of luck, they had let him bring his almost-three-hundred-page rough draft with him into his quarters after he'd been processed and booked. That night had been the last time he had seen his children. He still couldn't, all these weeks later, figure out for the life of him how Darlene had managed to get a call off to the police while he'd been punishing her. Not that it mattered anymore, anyway. It was just that he remembered apprehending her phone almost as soon as he'd gotten there, and the police didn't come until about three hours later. Surely, they would've come sooner if she had called before then.

what really happened

But he wanted out, all right, so bad that he was forced to use the few opportunities for a phone call he received to call his mother. The purpose, initially, had been only to get Darlene's number, which Tony had not committed to memory. Eventually his mother visited—occasionally—talking to him on a phone across from bulletproof glass. *You look like you've lost weight* and him saying *that's what eating scraps three times a day without getting seconds will do for you* His mother, Carol, acted as an unofficial third-party between her son and Darlene, who refused to visit or pony up money for his bail. Neither did—as far as the bail money—for that matter, did Carol Clark.

He thought his mother had suddenly given up her faith in the power of positive thinking.

As for Tony, although he firmly believed in the power of tears to cleanse the soul of grief, he had not had the time—or privacy—since that fateful day, and night, of his arrest to sufficiently process the loss of his beloved companion, Dusty. Sometimes, lying in his top bunk as the lights turned out, in the cacophony of sixty other guys—mostly hardened criminals—coming face to face with the reality that they had to call it a night much earlier than young men their age normally would if they'd enjoyed their freedom, he would allow a few salty tears to reach the surface while he looked upward under the covers.

Then he would quickly sniffle, suck it up, snuff them out, and go to sleep.

"Asshole. Hey. I'm talkin' to you. Asshole."

Tony opened his eyes. Standing over him was an inmate Tony had seen before but, as with most of the dudes in this godforsaken place, paid little attention to. He was big. Tony wasn't big. When he'd come in, two days after his birthday, or sixteen days weeks prior, he'd been five nine and weighed about a buck fifty. Since then he'd lost fourteen pounds, mostly muscle, what little he had, but he wasn't big, not compared to the man calling him asshole. This man must have weighed as much as Denver Bronco linebacker Von Miller; not *swole*, but not small either. He had a jaunt, angular face, long black greasy hair, a long salt and pepper beard, and lonely teeth, what few of them there were, and a half-healed hole in his lower lip where a ring must have fit—jewelry was off limits. It was like having a nightmare while being wide awake. He had just placed his lunch tray on the stainless steel table and finished saying a blessing over his food. Tony closed his eyes again. It wasn't the first time.

"Hey. Asshole." Tony felt a kick on the ankle of his left foot. A hard kick. That was going to leave a mark. He opened his eyes.

"I'm talkin' to you. Only Mexicans sit at this table, *homes.*"

"Guess again," Tony said, conscious as he spoke of Jungle's gaze.

"Huh?" the big man said. He paused a moment, lips parted. Tony noticed that the big man was sporting jewelry after all—a silver stud stuck in the fleshy tip of his tongue. Mexicans. They loved silver, Tony thought. He gave Tony another kick to the ankle.

"You're new," Tony said.

The big man's forehead reminded Tony of his brother's. Permanently deformed. "I'm new *up in here, homes!* I'm not new to the scene, like you, you nerd-ass lookin' motherfucker! I did three fuckin' years in fuckin' Q, man. So get yo' five dolla ass up before I make change, fool. Every joint got a table where only the Mexicans sit, and *this* is that table."

"We sup*posed to be brothers!*" I shouted suddenly, seemingly out of nowhere.

"Huh?"

"Before your time, don't worry about it," Tony replied. Then he whispered to the young whippersnapper, leaning toward him, "*I'm old enough to be your father.*" They hated when you told them shit like that. Then Tony said, "*So you understand why I can't let you punk me in front of the brothas sittin' over there, right?*"

But he kicked Tony again, this time with a windup like a punter. Tony winced; he couldn't help himself.

"You don't say," Tony said. "You said you were Mexican, is that right? I could've sworn you were Jamaican."

"How's that, faggot?"

"Cause," Tony replied calmly, "Jamaican me mad."

Tony rose. The big man, a foot taller, took him by the shoulder and gave him a shove to facilitate his departure. Tony let himself be shoved, but at the same time he pivoted and stuck his hand into the middle of that jaunt face, stuck it right into the fleshy wet pie hole, sliding his middle finger through that tongue ring. The defender of Mexican pride's hands went up then, but he was much too slow. Tony had curled his finger around the tongue ring; now he gave it a firm yank.

First there was a sound of tearing flesh and spurting blood as the ring came free in Tony's hand. Then the big man gurgled blood out of his, as the Donald would have said, his *whatever*. The agony hadn't quite made it from his tongue to the nerve receptors in his cerebral cortex when Tony caught one of his massive wrists in both hands, spun behind the broad back and jerked the wrist up as high as it would go. Something snapped. No louder than a breaking twig in the backyard on Thanksgiving Day. The big man bellyached and fell forward on the table, not far from Jungle. Did Jungle move away at all, or simply sit there? That was the kind of detail Tony couldn't remember later.

The big man was still bellyaching and wracking in pain when C.O.s came bursting in. Tony was back in his top bunk.

"What the hell?" said one of the C.O.s.

"Muh'fuckas don't believe fat meat is greasy," Tony explained.

"What the fuck are you talking about?"

Jungle spoke. "The *ese* bit his tongue," he said. "You know how that…what is the gringo word? Smarts? That doesn't sound right."

The C.O. opened his mouth, like he was about to say something. Then he closed it. They took Pancho Villa away. He left a pool of blood on the stainless steel table. Jungle noticed that it had spread to one corner of those hundreds of pieces of typing paper Tony constantly carried around. He pushed the pages away in distaste while Tony wasn't looking.

A few minutes later, after things had settled down, Tony said to Jungle, "Thanks."

"No problem, school." Jungle contemplated something in his palm: the tongue ring. Tony couldn't remember how he'd gotten it. Jungle—a dark-skinned black guy, physically imposing in his own right—slipped it into his jump suit shirt pocket and looked at Tony. He had soulless eyes, like the space between galaxy clusters. "*Muh'fuckers don't believe fat meat is greasy?*" he said, chuckling.

Tony shrugged. "It's something I used to hear nonstop growing up in the soul food restaurant I worked in as a teenager. It means sometimes niggas insist on having to learn the hard way."

"Is that how you got in here, huh? Your ol' lady didn't believe fat meat was greasy?"

"I guess you could say that."

"And…lemme guess. You got beef with ya moms, right? What's wrong—she wouldn't letcha nuts hang?"

Tony winced, nodding uncomfortably. "Something like that," he said.

Jungle smiled at him. He had the whitest smile Tony had ever seen on a juvenile delinquent, marred by a missing molar. "Chess?" he said, as though they were sitting in smoking jackets at a country club somewhere.

"I'm trying to quit. Haven't you seen me get my ass handed to me since I've been here?" Tony said. "I never knew there were so many good-ass chess players on the inside." Giving up anything wasn't easy inside, where Norman Vincent Peale and Tony Robbins's *Personal Power* held no sway.

Tony wanted to go off in a corner and just cry more often than he was able to let on in this place of unregenerate thugs. He felt he was a lamb among wolves.

"What you in for, school?" asked Jungle. That's what everyone had wanted to know when they saw someone like him enter the cellblock. The difference between now, however, and his high school days, had been something so obvious that he would never have guessed it—his glasses. His Ray Bans. If Tony had a nickel for every time a fellow inmate had asked if he could put them on for a quick second and look at himself in the mirror, he would've had enough to post his own damn bail. As it was, he was depending on his mother to soften her heart and trust him to pay her back in a few weeks when he got his Social Security benefits. He'd been so glad that he'd taken affirmative action back so many years ago to secure those benefits for himself, which were still paying out every thirty days all these years later without a hiccup. He was especially glad now, when he needed some form of income most—when his life was in shambles and he needed to build something resembling one out of the wreckage when he got out.

Then, across the cellblock, he saw his friend.

David.

How he met David: when the first C.O. had tried to "punish" Tony, moving him from his solitary cell to a pod housing sixty other inmates—where he'd have to sleep out in the open in a large room full of metal bunk beds—he had noticed about two or three guys who got up early each morning, sat at a far off table, and had a small Bible study. The leader of the study, a man with the same name as Tony's nephew—Quentin—a Hispanic man about his own age and of jovial manner, was being released and now the small study had no one who knew enough about the Word of life to lead it.

Tony remembered the scene like it was yesterday: David and the other guy, the first morning without their former leader, Quentin, staring aimlessly into their opened *Daily Bread* pamphlets, looking like sheep without a shepherd.

Tony stepped in.

Over the course of two weeks, he opened up the Word to them—David, in particular—like no one ever had for them before. David was another Hispanic young man. Tony had once remarked to him, in a rare moment of levity behind bars, that he looked like the movie star Colin Farrell. He was Irish, but still. The resemblance, from the dark eyes and heavy eyebrows to the facial stubble, was uncanny. At one point, when Tony had been breaking down a passage on the Gospel of John that dealt with God's love, David had begun to cry. Tony placed a hand on his shoulder. Tony didn't cry; this was David's moment. His chance to grieve the unwise choices that left him in here, separated from his girlfriend and their newborn son, Xavier. His chance to express contrition over the feeling of disappointment his mother justifiably felt in him because of what she saw as his lost potential, and Tony explaining to him, imploring him, to never let anyone—*anyone*–in your life put a Period where God put something else.

A Comma.

Tony looked at Jungle and replied, "Married, domestic violence. It was classified as a misdemeanor."

"Shit, you was lucky," Jungle said. "Normally they be givin' out felonies for that shit."

"Am I?"

"What?"

"Lucky."

"Oh, shit!" Jungle said, laughing. "Luck is what you make it, school. Shit, I see you carryin' those papers around. You walk around here like you on a mission. Like you gon' do somethin' important when you get out. That was some sick shit how you dealt with homeboy a few minutes ago. I wouldn't have seen no shit like that comin' from someone like you."

time to make a change ch-ch-changes

"Six months ago," Tony told him, "I would've agreed with you."

Jungle laughed his cawing laugh. "You done gone through some shit, huh?" he said. "You a peaceful, intelligent dude. I can tell. But you don't take no shit off nobody, either. I like that." He held out his hand. Tony took it, felt the black, slightly damp fingers wrap around the back of his own. Those fingers reminded him of something in his novel, but he couldn't think what.

"Look like you been hurt, too," said Jungle. "But those fly-ass shades hide it real well."

"*Hill!*" one of the C.O.s called out loudly, having entered the room unawares.

"Right here," Tony said.

"Pack your shit," Jungle said, holding out his hand a second time. "You're getting out."

2

I HAVE ALWAYS LOVED two things: my children, and things that are bittersweet. Especially music.

On nights when Jacob and Danielle would accompany me on my delivery route, tossing papers in the wee hours at subscribers' homes until the sun came up, I would often play—frequently at Danielle's request—a song called *Heartburn Waltz* by Vince Guaraldi, the famous pianist behind those old 60s *Charlie Brown* holiday movies. Anyway, talk about bittersweet! It's an instrumental; no words. But none are needed. There was something about the way he played that electric piano, the way it quickly rose in a note that is hopeful, forward-looking, if something without words can sound hopeful and forward-looking—and then just as soon falls mournfully, still retaining a sense of hope, yet now marred by some unnamed quality in the second chord by a knowingness of how life really is.

After sixteen days in Bexar County Detention Center, Mama had bonded me out. It took so long from the time I had been informed of my pending release and my actual *freedom*, that I'd wished they'd left me blissfully ignorant and started the process without me, only telling me at the precise moment I could exit those doors and feel the warm air on San Antonio's last night of its annual downtown Spring Fiesta celebration.

We reconciled, amazingly. I think one of the main factors in the thawing of our cold war was her slow realization, and regret, of the role she had played in all of the bad things that had happened to me since the start of the year. She never quite acknowledged what, in my mind, had *started* everything. However, she did express regret over having let Darlene use her to do what she did. She told me she felt manipulated. I was grateful for that small concession.

The day after she had secured my release, I accompanied her to my bail bondsman's office. We paid them. We talked. And talked. And talked some more. I stayed at her house for a few days. I remember walking into the Caliph—I mean, into Mom's house—for the first time in so many months. It was hard not to reflect, in spite of myself, of how different things had been the last time I had been there: all of us, sitting around the table, eating those damn black eyed peas.

Then, all of a sudden, I remembered something Paula and Ken, the Mormons, had revealed to me about that New Year's custom that I had not known before. They told me the day that they'd come and helped me with gas and food, two days before meeting Nikki.

It was new information.

Contrary to what I had previously believed, the custom of eating black eyed peas was *more* than just about eating like a rich man every day of the year thereafter. In fact, Ken had told me, it wasn't even really *about* that. It was about something else entirely, he had said.

It was about blessings in disguise.

It was about, he said, angels of mercy coming to your rescue when you need them most. It was about people who come into your life for seasons and then depart, having fulfilled the goal for which the Universe sent them your way. *It was about,* I had thought to myself standing next to Ken with a gas pump in my hand, filling my tank, *the lights coming on all of a sudden and the heat too when you don't have two nickels to rub together and you're just trying to help your kids get through a cold night even though you don't have a place to live*

The reconciliation, more a fragile truce, was agreed upon under two conditions, one from each of us. For Mom's part, she had wanted me to check in to the VA Hospital post-haste and get an emergency prescription of my anti-depressant and mood stabilizer pills, medications I had been unwisely without for more than a year. I agreed. In fact, I was chomping at the bit for her to drive me there. I was looking forward to getting back on my meds. I had a lot of plans. It felt like I was getting a new beginning. And that was the condition of the reconciliation that I brought to the table: I made her promise, if I got back on my meds in exchange for her letting me stay with her for a couple of days—until I could find some kind of veterans' shelter or something—that she would *not bring up anything from the past.* Nothing. No past hurts. Under no circumstances would she bring up my past mistakes, and I would not bring up hers. I don't know what she had to go through to make that happen, but as for me, I made a covenant with my mouth, not to rehearse her, or anyone's, past transgressions.

Sixteen days in jail had given me a lot of time to think. I can't say I didn't grieve Dusty in jail, among other things, now that I look back. During those first few days in my private cell,

I do recall bawling quite a bit in the solitude afforded within those dull, gray concrete walls, atop a wafer-thin mattress that will cause you to have a deep pain in your upper arm muscles as a result of its lack of support.

I wanted to move forward.

And, more than anything else, I wanted to get my kids back.

At 9:58 in the morning five days later, Mom was next to me gripping the steering wheel, gazing straight ahead. We had been having a good conversation. We even laughed at points. She was driving me to the County Courthouse on official business; Darlene had taken a protective order out against me, barring me temporarily from seeing her. *Good,* I thought. *The feeling's mutual.* Still, I had to go downtown to sign some stuff about it, anyway, and Mom, as she had been so often since my release, was my ride. We were also in good spirits because I had secured for myself a temporary residence in a transitional housing unit—a halfway house for veterans and ex-cons in a building, formerly a nuns' rectory, built all the back in 1928. It was a relief, for we had both, I think, tacitly agreed that the less time we spent under the same roof, the better. And I was enjoying my brief time so far there, even though I was very lonely.

She said, "You hung up on me, Tony. When I visited you in jail that last time."

"I apologize," I said. "I didn't mean that. Of course not."

"If I believed that were possible, after all my suffering."

"Of course it's not," I said. "I didn't mean it."

"I hope that at least is spared me," she said.

"Sure it is," I said. "I'm moving forward. As soon as I get the kids back. They should be there, right? In the courtroom, or whatever?"

"I don't know," my mother said. "Darlene didn't even tell me if she'd be there. All I know is I have to rearrange my day to take you."

"I appreciate it."

"If you went back to jail because you missed this court date, I couldn't bear it."

"Then quit thinking about it," I said. "Let's be positive. I'm in a good situation now, right? No rent to pay, able to save money, about to get the kids back, and you and Howard can focus on your projects with all of us out of your hair, for once." I laughed, a little. "But I do appreciate you, um, rearranging your day for me."

"I'm just a poor old woman. I was raised to believe that people should deny themselves for their own flesh and blood. That's what I'm doing. You were right to reproach me."

"Nonsense," I said. "Why are we talking about this? Make a left here. No, not this block, the next one."

We were almost at the courthouse.

She said, "And I worry about you at the shelter. I know you're not allowed to smoke there. But I also know you be sneaking some of the product in with you. I just worry, that's all..."

"You're the one who gave it to me."

"I know!" Mama said. "I'm just—"

"If it makes you feel any better, I'll tell you what happened the other day. Every few weeks they bring these dogs in, right? These canines to sniff the rooms for any contraband. So, my room is the last one at the end of the hall. Now granted, I didn't have any stuff in my room. Maybe some residue at the most, but no bud. Anyway, the dog comes in, sniffs around, turns around, and leads his trainer out and to the next victim. And she says to the dog, 'Good boy!' And they were gone. See? Nothing to worry about."

"What! Are you serious? You could've been…what would've happened if…don't you know that if you…this is just like when you got kicked out of the Navy!" she said.

"Oh my God, seriously? You're doing it *again?*" I said. "You promised you wouldn't bring up the past!" I lost my composure. Just blocks from the courthouse, where—if I was going to see my kids, as I expected—I wanted to be self-controlled, I lost my composure.

I said, "You just can't help yourself, can you! Look, Ma, *I am so sorry I've hurt you with all the mistakes I've made in my life! You warned me not to get with Darlene, and I didn't listen! I'm sorry about that; I'm sorry about everything!* You know what, let me out here—"

"What?" she said, stunned. "I'm in the middle of traffic. I'm sorry, Tony."

"It's too late for sorry. I'm so tired of this shit," I said, clenching my teeth, shaking my head, and looking out the window until she slowed to a stop at the curve. When she did, without saying another word, I clutched my school bag—the one with my manuscript in it—and began to exit the car.

Just as I was getting out, my mother called, "Wait!" I turned around. Her eyes were filled with tears.

I halted.

Mama said to me, in between sobs, voice quivering, "I'm so sorry, son. I w-wish I knew where I failed you. I tried to be a g-good m-mother to you—"

Before she could finish, I quickly got back in and rushed to embrace her, and we both fell on each other's shoulders, sobbing violently. My right hand was on the back of her head.

For two minutes, no words were exchanged.

Then I said, "We all have feet of clay. I have to go."

"I know, son."

I opened the car door. I began to get out. I looked back at my mother. "Thank you for giving me life," I said to her. "I do love you, Ma. Please remember that."

Carol Clark smiled through her tears. "I love you too, son." She drove away.

"I can't remember," the District County attorney was saying to me, "did someone discuss the agreed order with you before today? Or did you let the bailiff know you didn't get an attorney and that you didn't plan on contesting the order?" I was sitting across from a group of lawyers, about five or six of them—all women—at the other end of a large oak round table in a conference room just off the main courtroom. The doors were closed, but I could still hear the low murmur of voices. Other parents, other plaintiffs, other defendants—all caught up in our own domestic dramas.

"Um," I replied, "the latter, I think. Initially, I was going to get one, but I have a separate criminal case going and it would complicate that if I fought my wife on this temporary protective order. So I told your people to go ahead. Where are my kids? I thought they'd be here."

"All right," the woman said. "Well, the agreed upon order is beneficial in your case for a couple of reasons. In the first place, there's no affirmative finding of family violence in an agreed order. There are certain provisions under the law for which the state can get a protective order for people. Some of the provisions require a finding of family violence or sexual assault or something like that."

"Okay," I said. "Where are my children?"

She continued. "In an agreed order, we go forward under a provision of the law that just allows for the applicant and the respondent to enter into an agreement for the protective order with no affirmative finding of guilt of violence against your wife or the children. So that's beneficial to you for that reason. Additionally—"

"Wait," I said. I sat up in the chair. "This protective order just applies to Darlene, right? I mean, it doesn't apply to my kids, right? I can still see them. Right?"

At this point, the main lady—an attractive, light-skinned African-American woman with glasses—paused, holding her papers, and looked at me with great empathy. I didn't like that look. I didn't like it at all. "Oh, I'm sorry, Mr. Hill. I thought you had been informed already."

"Informed already about what?"

"The protective order applies, not just to your wife, but to your children also. *You are not allowed, under penalty of further incarceration, to see or talk to your wife—or your children—for a period of twenty-four months. Two years.* Starting today."

I think I whispered the word *what*, but I can't remember honestly. All I do know is the waterworks starting coming on again. Big time. *Two years!* One of the attorneys handed me a Kleenex, but I pushed it away and fled from the room. In a further embarrassment, I had to reenter after a few steps, remembering I'd left my school bag back on the table. They were all looking at me when I came back in with the sorriest looks on their faces, having to endure the awkwardness of watching a grown man cry.

My eyes were so blinded by tears I couldn't see what I was doing or where I was going. Somehow, I made it outside. To the street. Mama was long gone. Eyes still compromised by pain, no sooner had I stepped onto the downtown sidewalk than I bumped into a man. My school bag, which had been unzipped at the top, released its contents all over the concrete as I tripped and fell, wiping the tears from my eyes.

As I collected the scattered pages of my draft off the ground, I felt something in me rise before I did.

I was no longer *Bedlam Boy.*

I was Phoenix. The last child.

I stood, straightened my back amidst the slanting rays of daylight, gripped my manuscript firmly in my hands, feeling its thickness, and looked upward, wearing the emperor's new clothes. My intellect was suddenly illumined by an interior light.

And then, all at once, I saw it again.

Canaan.

Now, I had arrived in uncharted territory, and my sketchy map wasn't of any use to me anymore. I was at a crosspoint. My sherpas, my guides, my climbing party had all diverged, each having gone their separate ways at some point during the ascent. Seventeen steps remained. The zenith of the mountain rose before me, and then I knew, instinctively, that every answered prayer is a process of crucifixion.

I was all alone. My only comfort, as I looked upward, was the recollection that nobody ever reached the summit—in the end—unless he went by himself.

THE END

43574549R00166

Made in the USA
San Bernardino, CA
21 December 2016